A Well-Read Woman

A Well-Read Woman

THE LIFE, LOVES, AND LEGACY
OF RUTH RAPPAPORT

Kate Stewart

Little
a

Published by Little A, New York

www.apub.com

Amazon, the Amazon logo, and Little A are trademarks of Amazon.com, Inc., or its affiliates.

ISBN-13: 9781503904156 (hardcover)
ISBN-10: 1503904156 (hardcover)
ISBN-13: 9781503904149 (paperback)
ISBN-10: 1503904148 (paperback)

Cover design by Kimberly Glyder
Cover photography courtesy of Guy Rosner

Printed in the United States of America
First edition

For the librarians,

including
Jack, my grandfather
Silvia, my aunt
Alice, my mother
and Peter, my friend

Contents

AUTHOR'S NOTE

Research into Ruth Rappaport's life led me to a seemingly endless array of sources in many archives and in multiple languages. I started with her oral history and tried to verify the stories she told. As it turned out, some of them were impossible to track down in other sources, and I've tried my best to reconcile the sources I could track down with Ruth's own words. While some historians don't trust oral histories, I'm a firm believer that even though stories can change over time and memories can become fuzzy, interviews can reveal how a person sees their own life and how they want to be remembered. The translators who worked on Ruth's diary, which was written in German, agreed that she had an unusual writing style that was either uniquely her own or reflective of a teenage trend at the time. They and I have tried to keep Ruth's writing style while also altering it for readability.

Prologue

I was working at the American Folklife Center reference desk at the Library of Congress, or LC, as we librarians often call it, when my coworker Peter Bartis stopped by to invite me to an estate sale. He told me that a friend of his, Ruth Rappaport, had died six months earlier, and she had chosen him to be the executor of her estate. She had been a longtime employee of the Library of Congress and retired in 1993, long before I began working there. Her row house, just a block behind the Supreme Court building, was filled with papers, books, and objects she had acquired over her eighty-seven years. Peter told me about Ruth's life: she had escaped from Nazi Germany as a teenager, lived in Israel during the 1948 war, and worked as a librarian for the US military in Japan and Vietnam during the 1960s. While I wasn't very interested in acquiring any more clutter for my own home, I was certainly curious about this woman and her long, eventful life.

The estate sale was on a beautiful April day when cherry blossom petals littered the sidewalks of Capitol Hill. Despite my feeble resistance, my boyfriend, Greg, and I bought several of Ruth's belongings, including a fondue pot, a wooden sugar bowl, an old knitting machine, two obscenely large brass candlesticks, a few silk scarves, two Asian prints, and a Jewish cookbook. At home, and surrounded by her things, I searched for Ruth's obituary online and found a tribute written by neighbor and *Washington Post* columnist Petula Dvorak.[1]

Dvorak described Ruth's adventurous life, her sharp wit, her penchant for regaling others with captivating stories from the stage of her front porch, and her refusal to move out of her home as she aged. Everyone in the neighborhood knew Ruth, and she had friends all over the world.

Ruth continued to hover in the back of my mind for the next few months. Every time I looked at her things in my house, I thought about her and wanted to know more about her life. When I hosted parties, I pointed out to my friends that the ridiculous candlesticks standing at both ends of the couch had belonged to a globe-trotting librarian named Ruth Rappaport. I would tell them, thirdhand, what I knew about her—in, I later realized, my own game of telephone, where I had jumbled the original facts.

A year and a half after the estate sale, I went to the American Library Association's (ALA) midwinter conference in Seattle and stayed at a hotel across the street from the new Seattle Public Library. My family—my mom and stepfather, my two brothers, their wives, and my three nieces—came up on the train together from Portland to spend the weekend with me. In a family with four librarians spread across three generations, is there any better place for a family reunion than the ALA conference? ("You guys are like a medieval guild," Greg likes to say.) Like kids in a candy store, we rushed straight to the exhibit hall, where publishers distributed free advance copies of books. Late at night, alone in my hotel room, I thought about all the ALA conferences that Ruth must have attended and wondered whether she had ever run into my grandfather at any of them (or more likely, at a nearby bar). I remembered from Dvorak's column that Ruth had lived in Seattle when she first came to the United States as a teenager. I imagined her in the 1940s climbing those steep hills, probably in heels, on her way to the stately old public library.

I searched online again for that article in the *Post*. I found it, but this time I browsed through the other search results. I couldn't believe what I discovered: a link to Ruth's oral history at the United States Holocaust

Memorial Museum (USHMM) in DC.[2] Was this really her? *My* Ruth Rappaport? The interview had been recorded just a few weeks before she died of lung cancer. I stayed up well beyond midnight listening to it. I was delighted by her German-accented, rough voice, peppered as it was with Hebrew phrases, curse words, and her hacking cough. I felt as though I were finally meeting her, as if she were speaking from beyond the grave and through my computer to me. Even on the first listen, I could tell she was bullshitting somewhat, exaggerating her connections to famous people, and brushing off her interviewer's attempts to extract some testimony about the trauma that she undoubtedly experienced as a teenager and young adult. But what I latched on to, more than anything, was this fellow librarian's memories of reading and her love of books. When asked which authors were her favorites as a teenager, she replied: "Everybody who was forbidden: Lion Feuchtwanger, Max Brod, Leon Trotsky . . . and what we did was we passed around the paperbacks. We read them, and as we finished reading, we tore up the pages and destroyed them so we wouldn't get caught."

Back in DC, I couldn't wait to talk to Peter about the interview.

"You know I donated her papers there, right?" he said.

I felt so stupid that I hadn't asked him before. I just assumed that because she had such a turbulent young life, she wouldn't have been able to save anything from that time.

Peter walked me to his desk and handed me a file of photocopies of Ruth's ID cards, a job application, and letters she had written from Israel in 1948 while the war for a new Jewish homeland raged around her. The collection comprised only a small sample of the diaries, letters, documents, and photographs he had found in an old metal suitcase in the basement of her house. Most of the items are now at the Holocaust museum's archive.

That night I read through what he gave me and realized that here was another story, the one Ruth couldn't or wouldn't fully tell when she had been interviewed. This was a heartbreaking narrative of a confused, angry young woman, bitter about the lot she had been dealt in life and upset with her futile attempts to find a home, a family, and a career that would satisfy her ambitions after so much loss and upheaval. But somehow she still had that singularly Jewish sense of humor, making screwball wisecracks and laughing at herself, despite her deep melancholy.

In the memorable episode of *Seinfeld* titled "The Library," Lieutenant Bookman of the New York Public Library shows up at Jerry's apartment to investigate his decades-long overdue library book from 1971. The next scene cuts to Kramer and the librarian, appropriately named Marion, shouting "Helloooo!" in the cavernous Fifth Avenue library after hours. Lieutenant Bookman startles them, then strolls up to Marion and tells her, "I remember when the librarian was a much older woman. Kindly, discreet, unattractive. We didn't know anything about her private life. We didn't *want* to know anything about her private life. She didn't *have* a private life."[3] The audience roars with laughter: Who *would* want to know anything about an older librarian's private life?

Ruth knew that her own life was worth documenting and that her experiences were, as she put it, like something from a novel. While in Israel, she kept a detailed diary with the aim of one day writing a book about her experiences there. For whatever reason, she gave up on that goal, although she continued to sarcastically tell friends in letters "I should write a book" when describing any number of her classic stories.

I repeatedly came across glimpses of Ruth's reading life in the extensive paper trail she left behind, not only in her papers at the Holocaust museum, but also in other archives and personal collections around the world: a mention of an author here, a title recommendation there, her work as a research assistant for a few authors, an extensive bibliography on German Jews she had written as a library science student, lists of books she ordered for soldiers in Vietnam while chain-smoking late at night. In her application to Berkeley's School of Librarianship, she wrote that watching book burnings and reading banned books had inspired her to become a librarian. On LC's internal staff website, I found Ruth's cataloger code on a list of former employees, searched the catalog for it, and pulled up a list of the many thousands of books she had cataloged or corrected over her twenty-two years there. Mesmerized by the never-ending flood of books that had floated across her desk, I saved the list as a spreadsheet. These were all her books, and she had wanted to share them with the world. Books were the one constant in a life full of trauma and turmoil, and she always turned to them for reassurance, renewal, and solace when she had no one and nothing else. Librarianship was not just a job for her, but her *tikkun olam*, the Hebrew phrase for "repairing the world."

Above all, this book is a tribute to a teenage girl who understood the power of forbidden books: that by reading them she would find a way to liberate herself. She devoted the rest of her long life to liberating them for the readers of the world. That includes you.

Part I:

Everybody Who Was Forbidden

Leipzig, 1923–1938

Chapter 1

When Ruth Rappaport left Germany at the age of fifteen, she was a completely different person than who she had been just a few years earlier. She remembered herself as a shy young girl, and a photograph reveals that she was cute, with dark, curly hair and a mischievous smile. But by the time she was a teenager, her circumstances had changed dramatically. She had also developed the physical characteristics—frizzy hair, a larger nose—that instantly marked her as a conspicuous foreigner, a Jew, which, to the Nazis, also meant a radical. Shyness, in other words, was no longer an option.

By this age Ruth had grown into a diligent, intense, bespectacled bookworm who questioned everyone and everything. She had also developed an interest in photography and fashion, and dressed to make an impression. She would have rarely left the house without a camera or a book in hand. Or without a particular thought on her mind: after what she had seen and heard in Leipzig over the past five years, she knew she had to get out of Germany. And when she saw an opening to escape, she took it. When she left, she carried a suitcase with her worldly possessions, including clothing for every season and documents that proved her identity and accomplishments. She saved those papers for the rest of her life and guarded that suitcase and its contents with a fierceness known only to the stateless and the orphaned.

Ruth came into the world at a most unfortunate time and place for someone who happened to be Jewish. Her parents were part of a wave of émigrés from eastern Europe who had come to Leipzig, Germany, to take advantage of its international trade fairs and growing business opportunities for Jews. Although Ruth was born in Germany, she was not considered a German citizen. Born to immigrants, she was immediately marked as an outsider and classified as an immigrant. She remained classified that way—by one government or another—until she died.

Her father, Mendel, was born in 1877 in Roztoky, a small town in the Bukovina region in the Austro-Hungarian Empire.[1] His family owned forested land and worked in the lumber business.[2] Mendel moved to a larger town nearby, Vyzhnytsya, and married a woman named Rachel Kamil. She died in childbirth with their first baby, Clara, who was raised by Rachel's parents. Mendel moved to Leipzig in 1911 with his second wife, Frima Feiger, and younger daughter, Mirjam (also spelled Miriam). He joined the booming furrier business there.[3]

Leipzig had long served as an important trade center not just for Germany, but internationally too. Since the Middle Ages, each year the city has hosted two fairs, which remain the oldest continuously operated industrial fairs in the world. Leipzig was also a cultural center with a world-renowned publishing industry and was the home of composers Johann Sebastian Bach, Felix Mendelssohn, and Richard Wagner. Bach was the cantor of Saint Thomas Church, a monastery that sponsors a boys' choir that, founded in 1212, remains one of Europe's oldest and most famous.

Since the 1300s Jews had been permitted to participate in the fairs with various restrictions, but they were largely banned from living in the city until the nineteenth century. The first large, permanent synagogue was built in 1855, and twenty years later the Jewish population was about seventeen hundred. By 1914 the fur industry in Leipzig consisted of nearly four hundred businesses, nearly half of them Jewish owned. Most of the businesses were located on or near the Brühl, a Jewish neighborhood and market street in the center of the city.

When Germany entered World War I in 1914, every family in the country was affected. Mendel Rappaport was drafted into military service in 1917 and served with the Austro-Hungarian military in forestry service.[4] He was discharged and returned to Leipzig on November 12, 1918, the day after the armistice agreement was signed. Just six weeks later, his wife, Frima, died of tuberculosis in Leipzig, leaving yet another motherless daughter. Having been widowed twice in such a short time was undoubtedly traumatic for Mendel, although not unusual for the time. The horrific violence of World War I and rapidly spreading contagious diseases, including influenza, had ravaged families all over Europe. Mendel was just one of many widowed in Leipzig. Mirjam was sent to live in Vienna with her mother's sister for a time.[5]

Ruth's mother, Chaja (also Chaya or Helena) Rubinstein, was born in Mielec, Poland, in 1885. Her parents were Markus and Reizel Perlsheim Rubinstein.[6] One of Chaja's cousins (or second cousins), also named Chaja (later Helena) Rubinstein, would immigrate to Australia and the United States and start a successful makeup business. Two of Ruth's uncles on her mother's side, Carl and Abraham, immigrated to the United States in 1900. Carl had been so desperate to leave Poland that he stole money from his father to fund his trip.[7] Another one of Ruth's maternal uncles, Leo, and his growing family moved first to Hanover and then Leipzig, where he started a metals and rag trading business. When Ruth's mother moved to Leipzig is unclear, but she was living with Leo and his family when she married Mendel on October 4, 1922.[8] Ruth was born the following May.

By 1925, two years after Ruth was born, the Jewish population in Leipzig had reached its height of 13,030, or 2 percent of the total population, largely through immigration from eastern European countries, especially Poland and Russia.[9] This influx, nearly 70 percent foreign-born, created a division within the Jewish community between more-assimilated German Jews and the Orthodox Jews from eastern Europe, known as the *Ostjuden*.[10]

Rabbi Ephraim Carlebach arrived in Leipzig in 1900 to start a new Orthodox synagogue, Etz Chaim. A popular rabbi who was German-born but served the immigrant Orthodox community, he was an important mediator among the different factions of the Jewish community.[11] Ruth's family attended his services at his synagogue, an ornate building newly constructed in 1922—the year before Ruth was born.[12] Ruth's parents were Modern Orthodox. When her uncle Carl later asked her if her father was Orthodox, she was unsure how to answer. On further reflection, she questioned, "Did I tell the truth? I think so, but actually I don't think Papa himself knows what he wants and what he is."[13]

Many of Ruth's memories of her parents' Judaism focused on their traditions, including food:

> My mother lit the candles and you know we always had challah, and gefilte fish or regular fish, or matzo ball soup, or noodle soup… My mother kept kosher for my father. So, we had a kosher kitchen. But, when we traveled, she and I ate treif and actually with my father's blessing. He just said he was raised Orthodox, he couldn't get himself to change. But he was really, he was sort of an accepting, liberal kind of guy. And, like if I was sick in bed and needed a treat, he'd come home and bring me a package of ham. For sandwiches. So, you know it was a tradition, not religion.[14]

If Ruth attended synagogue regularly with her family, the services would have been sex segregated and led by men. Ruth never learned Hebrew or had a Bat Mitzvah, which was the norm for girls at the time, but she attended the Hebrew school at the synagogue and her teachers gave her good marks on behavior in her report cards. Although she probably learned stories from the Torah and Jewish culture at the school, she was not participating fully in Jewish life in Leipzig. She revealed later that she had stopped believing in God when she was about eight years old, although she did not explain what in particular had led her to atheism.[15] Perhaps she came across the concept in her extensive childhood reading, or maybe something traumatic led her to question the existence of God. In her seventies, when she joined the Hill Havurah, a Jewish group on Capitol Hill, Ruth warned the group to not let any one person become too powerful and to guard against Judaism's traditional sexism.[16] The roots of this sentiment were laid when, as a girl in Leipzig, she questioned long-held practices of silencing women from religious expression.

Ruth's family lived in a mixed neighborhood in Leipzig at 18 Salomonstrasse, just a few blocks east of the center of the city in the Graphisches Viertel (Graphics Quarter), famed for its many publishing houses and bookbinderies. The apartment building at 18 Salomonstrasse was large, with three wings separated by courtyards. The Rappaports lived on the second floor of the middle wing, B. In addition to apartments, several businesses were housed in the building, including a restaurant and sausage company. Ruth's apartment was just a few blocks from the train station, the University of Leipzig, the symphony hall, and the Brühl, the street where her father probably worked. She played with non-Jewish friends and attended a public elementary school (*Volksschule*), a mixed school with both Christian and Jewish children, although the records for this school do not survive.[17] She described herself at this age as "a snot-nosed kid," but, she added, "I was bright."[18] She may have been quiet, but the books she rapidly consumed started to introduce her to new ideas and instilled in her a sense of skepticism.

When asked what kinds of activities she participated in, she explained, "Mostly reading. I wasn't too much into sports, because I was really nearsighted as a kid. And in those days, we didn't have plastic glasses. So, you know, I couldn't go in for sports. A tennis ball and pair of eyeglasses can be fatal. So, I was a little bit removed from sports and tended towards books."[19] A photograph of her around age five reveals that she didn't wear glasses yet, but some time in elementary school, Ruth developed eyesight problems—including a lazy eye, likely inherited from her father, who also had the same ailment—and her nearsightedness was no doubt caused by intense reading. Even though she claimed she did not participate in sports, among her papers from her childhood is a certificate showing that she passed swimming lessons; it would remain her favorite form of exercise throughout her life. She also belonged to Bar Kochba, a Jewish sports club in Leipzig for children, and a photograph reveals that she played basketball with a group of other children when she was thirteen.[20]

To Ruth, the most important group she belonged to was the Brith Habonim, a Zionist youth organization. Her small group, or the Bund, as she called it, was known as the *Arbeiterbund* or labor union. She recalled that she was one of only two in the group that were considered middle class, while everyone else was classified as the Jewish working poor.[21] Leipzig's Zionist movement grew throughout the 1920s and '30s as it became increasingly clear that Jews were not welcome in many areas of public life. There were several organizations for adults, including the Zionistische Vereinigung für Deutschland, a mainstream group, and Poale Zion, a group for the working class. Ruth's father considered himself a Zionist, and her sister Mirjam probably joined an organization as well. Ruth remembered attending a Zionist meeting at age six, where she questioned the reverence of a Zionist hero:

> It was sort of a commemoration of somebody who was a hero, Joseph Trumpeldor, who died, ta-da, ta-da, and here's this little six-year-old and she says, "What's so great about dying for your country? Isn't it more important to *live* for it?" I thought that was a pretty astute comment from a six-year-old.[22]

Although Ruth would remain involved in Zionism for the next twenty years of her life, this story illustrates how from the beginning she was wary of the movement's ideology. She would later mull over in her diary her feelings about it, her arguments with other Zionists, and whether establishing a Jewish homeland was truly a solution to the "Jewish question." More than anything, this commemoration that she remembered more than eighty years later is reflective of Ruth's inclination to question everything.

Reading was central to Ruth's childhood. Her parents encouraged their children to read, as Ruth remembered that her sister Mirjam was also a bookworm. But like most parents of children who read voraciously, they also had their frustrations when their daughters would read so much they avoided other activities. Later in life Ruth wrote, "I remember when I was a young child, sometimes father or mother would scold Mirjam because she would read a book rather than do a chore . . . She did a lot of living through books."[23] Like Ruth, Mirjam remained a lifelong reader.

The Rappaports took advantage of living in a city that revered books. Since the seventeenth century, Leipzig had hosted an annual international book fair. By 1930, Leipzig had 436 publishing houses, 277 printers, and 69 bookstores, and one in ten residents worked in the book industry.[24] Growing up in this publishing neighborhood influenced Ruth's interest in books and intellectual pursuits. She remembered:

> There used to be a very famous German encyclopedia called *Brockhaus*... and the Brockhaus family lived across the street from us. Leipzig, of course, was a publishing city, and very few people know that, but not pocketbooks, but paperbacks, quality paperbacks, were published in Leipzig long before the names were coined, because we had these publishing houses in Leipzig. And boy, I had a whole collection of English novels by the time I was ten years old.[25]

During the 1930s, there were thirty-nine publishers or other businesses in the book industry located within three blocks of Ruth's childhood home. In her apartment building alone, there were seven: Johann Ambrosius Barth, a medical publishing company in existence from 1780 to 1999; Curt Kabitzch, another medical publishing company; Alfred Mesiter, a printer; Quandt & Händel, a science publishing company; Leopold Voß, a publishing company started as a bookstore in 1791 and noted for its specialty in science and philosophy, including the works of Kant; G. Fr. Wanner, a book binder; and Wilhelm Wobersin, a travel bookstore.[26]

Leipzig had another advantage for young people interested in foreign languages. A special school for translators trained and hired them to work at the industrial fairs, which attracted merchants from across Europe. This program was also open to local children. Ruth had already begun studying English in school when she was eleven years old, probably because her mother wanted to immigrate to the United States to be near her brothers. But this program (probably a summer class) seemed to have been very effective for her:

> It was a three-month course… I didn't have to live at the school, because I was from Leipzig, but most students lived there. And it was immersion study. You had breakfast with your teachers. You went for a walk. You couldn't use anything but English. If you couldn't say it in English, you couldn't say it. It was agony while it lasted; however, when I came to the States as an immigrant, I didn't have to take a single required English college course.[27]

Chapter 2

What had been a typical childhood for a Jewish girl in Leipzig suddenly changed when Ruth turned ten, soon after the Nazi Party came to power. Even at such a young age, she understood the seriousness of this new political regime. She heard about it for the first time on the radio around her tenth birthday in May 1933 and sensed the fear that was in the air. At some point later, Ruth was crossing a street in Leipzig when a motorcade passed by; she knew instantly it was Hitler. He was sitting up straight in his open vehicle with his arm raised in the air. *"Sig heil!"* he yelled. Others in the crowd around her repeated the salute. But Ruth refused to, and in hindsight she doubted that anyone would have noticed the defiance of a short Jewish girl, just one of many in the crowd.[1]

In April 1933 Ruth was accepted to the höhere dreistufige Mädchenschule der Stadt, Leipzig's college preparatory public high school for girls, based on her test scores.[2] In 1935, a law was passed banning Jewish children from public schools.[3] She had to return to her public elementary school for a time before transferring to the local Jewish high school, the Höhere Israelitische Schule, also known as the Carlebach School, which was founded by Ephraim Carlebach in 1912.[4] It is unclear why Ruth and her parents did not opt for Jewish schools to begin with. Perhaps attending public schools was a sign of belonging to the bourgeoisie. But Ruth remembered one advantage of attending this Jewish private school that had had its origins in anti-Semitism: almost all of her teachers were Jewish professors from Heidelberg University who had been fired in the sweeping bans of Jews from many professions.[5]

Hillel Shechter, who grew up in Leipzig and also attended the Carlebach School, remembered that some teachers belonged to the Nazi Party, including a biology teacher who wore his Hitler Youth uniform to class and others who made it clear that they had anti-Semitic leanings.[6] The Carlebach School was overwhelmed with new students and asked the Leipzig School Board for funds for a new building. The request was denied because most of its students were designated as foreigners, like Ruth, even though a majority of them had been born in Leipzig.[7] It is clear that she struggled for the first few years at the Carlebach School. Her teachers' comments on her report cards at this time included, "Ruth is immature, she has no concept of order . . . She is very impertinent . . . Her work is barely acceptable . . . Ruth is not industrious or diligent and does not participate in classroom activities." The subjects she struggled with were religion, English, and math.[8]

The year 1933 was significant in Ruth's life, and not just because of the obvious political changes in Germany. Ruth's mother, Chaja, became the manager of the österreichisches Vaterlandsheim (or ÖVLH), a local club and restaurant for Austrians in Leipzig, specifically Jewish immigrants. She may have worked there before becoming the manager, but regardless, it appears to have been a demanding job, and she was not at home most evenings. Ruth remembered this as a time when she had to step up at home and become more self-reliant.[9] She may have also assisted her mother at the restaurant and claimed in her diary, "Through the Ö.V.L.H. I had a certain amount of life experience."[10] She described the members as "pompous con men— with debts—but, worldly and bon vivant, [who] look down on people, and bamboozle others." It appears that it was also a sort of second home for the Rappaports; she remembered that on Yom Kippur in 1938, the last one she would spend in Leipzig, her family ate dinner together at the restaurant.

Her mother may have started working because Mendel's business may have been failing, likely because of Jewish boycotts and the worsening economic conditions of the Depression. When asked about this, Ruth answered, "I don't think he was closed, shut down, or anything like that. It was just the Depression. Actually, I think it's kind of funny looking back." She joked, "I don't know if there was a middle-class Jewish trade or not, but you know Jews were never poor—they just had cash flow problems."[11] One of Ruth's uncles (probably Leo Rubinstein) had done very well financially in Leipzig; Ruth remembered that he owned a Rolls-Royce that her family borrowed occasionally. Ruth's parents also continued to employ a maid named Else, who Ruth took a photograph of washing dishes at the sink at home in the summer of 1936. Else wore an apron and a scarf on her head and faced away from the camera as she diligently worked, but she seemed to be suppressing a smile, as if knowing that Ruth was trying to artistically capture her.

Since 1927 Ruth's sister Mirjam had worked as a clerk for the film company Globus AG in Berlin. The company closed in 1930, and she had trouble finding work.[12] In 1933 Mirjam decided to go to Palestine and left the day after Ruth's tenth birthday.[13] She probably went with her friend Hadassah Schneider, who moved with her family to Palestine in the 1930s. Mirjam later married Hadassah's brother, Max, in 1940 in Jerusalem.[14] Between 1933 and 1935, eight hundred Jews from Leipzig immigrated to Palestine.[15] Mirjam came back to Leipzig in 1937 for a visit, looking tanned in a photograph with Chaja in front of their apartment building.

One of Ruth's most vivid memories was a book burning in Leipzig in 1933. Across Germany in April and May, university students burned or destroyed "un-German" books and literature, in what became known as the Action Against the Un-German Spirit. Initially the plan was to burn writings by Jewish authors, but it quickly expanded into a sweep of all literature considered pornographic, Communist, modernist, or any other "ist" deemed a threat by the Nazi Party. A librarian, Wolfgang Herrmann, created a list of books to purge from Berlin libraries. He had Nazi leanings, although the book burnings themselves were not ordered by the Nazi Party or the Ministry of Public Enlightenment and Propaganda. In Berlin the bonfire of books at the opera house on May 10 was accompanied by a speech by Joseph Goebbels and broadcast nationally.[16] During the month of April, Leipzig's public libraries and the private libraries of Communists were searched and forbidden books were taken away.[17]

On May 2 the library at the *Volkshaus*, a community center for trade unions and Communists in Leipzig, was ransacked. Books by Karl Marx, Heinrich Heine, Kurt Tucholsky, Erich Kästner, Sigmund Freud, and eighty-nine other authors were torched by University of Leipzig students.[18] The building was south of downtown Leipzig, and Ruth, just ten years old at the time, heard that it was happening. She set out to see it for herself and described the heaps of books set on fire in the road. She was stunned to see this happening in her hometown, the world-famous city of books, and did everything in her might to not cry as she passed by and watched.[19]

This book burning, however, was one of just two that occurred in Leipzig. On May 14, 1933, the Association of German Booksellers met in Leipzig. Joseph Goebbels spoke about Leipzig's importance in the international book trade and tried to calm the outraged booksellers, who were concerned about Leipzig's reputation. He promised that their businesses would not be damaged and encouraged publishers to stop printing un-German literature and focus on printing new Fascist books. Although there were no more book burnings in the city, many publishers in Leipzig left Germany altogether.[20] Members of the Brockhaus family, who owned the publishing company across the street from Ruth's home, were deemed half-Jewish or one-quarter Jewish, but they petitioned Hitler directly for permission to be included in the new Chamber of Literature (approved publishers), probably because of the prestige of the company and the fact that they published two well-known pro-Nazi writers, Sven Hedin and Colin Ross.[21]

Since 1930 certain magazines and journals had been banned in Germany, but in February 1933 President von Hindenburg issued the "Decree for the Protection of the German People," which allowed local police to confiscate books that were "apt to endanger public security or order."[22] Other regulations expanded the types of materials used and the power of the federal authorities to intervene if the locals in charge were not obeying the new censorship regulations. In 1941 Jews were banned from public libraries (they had earlier been banned from many other public places, such as movie theaters and concerts). The banned books list created by Herrmann, as well as other lists, such as one crafted by librarian Ernst Drahn, were managed by Goebbels and the staff of the Chamber of Literature.[23] But these lists did not prevent Germans from seeking the forbidden books, if they didn't already own them. Ruth and other members of the Habonim had access to at least some of them. They gave each other books by Jewish authors and those considered radicals and destroyed them when they were finished. Ruth reported, "By 13, I had already read Trotsky, Maxim Gorky, Traven, Remarque, Sholem Asch. At 12 and 13, I was very knowledgeable and involved with socialism and communism. I questioned if there is a God and thought about the effects of industrialization."[24] These authors deeply influenced Ruth. Besides shaping her views on Socialism, Zionism, and Jewish identity, authors like Erich Maria Remarque, whose antiwar book *All Quiet on the Western Front* was banned in Germany, would affect Ruth's views on war and violence.

In a city with such a thriving publishing industry, it was not too difficult for Leipzig's teenagers to acquire these banned books that had yet to be destroyed or confiscated. But what level of risk were they taking if caught? Would they be imprisoned, fined, beaten? In this frightening new era, friends, family, and passing acquaintances fled the country or disappeared. To Ruth, breaking the laws regarding what she was allowed to read was worth the risk, whatever the consequences might be.

Chapter 3

The Brith Habonim had a large influence on its young members, and it was in some ways a more significant influence in Ruth's life than her parents. She noted that Zionist youth groups were "a double-edged sword" for the parents.[1] The older generations, particularly those who were native Germans, were not so supportive of Zionism, because it implied that Jews could not fully assimilate into German society. They worried that it gave Germans a pass on their responsibility to be a fully democratic, inclusive nation. Many German Jews, and even a Zionist immigrant like Ruth's father, viewed Nazism as a temporary aberration in Germany's history that would soon blow over. Ruth remembered her father feeling this way even though he was an immigrant and probably experienced anti-Semitism on a regular basis: "My father was totally unrealistic. 'Hitler's going to last six months, and the Germans will know when to bargain.' God almighty! I mean, never mind. When I remember, I still get angry. Because there was no excuse for being that much of an ostrich!"[2]

Was Ruth's father oblivious to the dangers lurking ahead? This is how she remembered it, but the records indicate that he indeed tried to get his whole family out of Germany. In the spring of 1938, he corresponded with Jakob Gross, who was living in Nairobi, Kenya. Gross described what steps the Rappaports needed to take to immigrate to Kenya and the business opportunities for Jews available there.[3] Ruth's family also wanted to immigrate to the United States, either to Seattle to be near Chaja's brothers or to New York, where Mendel's brother, Irving, lived. Mendel was especially focused on getting Ruth out of Germany. Her name was placed on a waiting list in August 1938 at the American consulate in Berlin.[4] In 1937 or 1938 Ruth's sister Clara moved to Paris to marry her boyfriend, Salomon Rosner, also an immigrant from Vyzhnytsya, who had first tried his luck in Berlin.[5] The letters and other documents that described her father's efforts were all in Ruth's papers that Peter, my Library of Congress colleague, found in her house, so none of these efforts to immigrate were concealed from her. But she still angrily remembered her father as oblivious to what was to come.

If most Jewish parents in Leipzig tried to protect their children from unnecessary worry, teenagers in the Habonim and other youth Zionist groups received a very different message from their group leaders: get out now. Ruth explained that the leaders of the group were urgently encouraging their members to go to Palestine as soon as possible if they could. In hindsight, the group's efforts to teach its members agricultural skills seemed like a waste of time to her considering what was looming, but as she later said, "At the time it was a solution to a problem."[6]

Ruth was conflicted about "making a decision": choosing whether to move to Palestine and live on a kibbutz or leave Zionism behind and assimilate into Leipzig's (or possibly America's) bourgeois culture. She agonized about it, weighed each option, and examined her own personality and flaws. Was she physically and mentally tough enough to work on a kibbutz and forsake most physical and intellectual comforts? Would a bourgeois middle-class life as a housewife be too empty?[7] If there was one thing she knew she wanted, it was to work hard and to become a professional. What exactly that profession might be, especially since there were so few open to women, remained unclear to her.

On Ruth's thirteenth birthday in 1936, her parents sent her alone on a trip to Romania to visit Mendel's family. She remembered:

For my birthday, I received a suitcase and money for traveling at the Pentecost vacation. I was very into the Chaluzisch movement.[8] When I then traveled to Romania, I totally felt like a traveling lady, totally independent, which I actually was... Most of all, I was also in a good humor and I made my vacation with the yucky relatives very nice.[9]

Ruth might not have ever been to Romania or met her father's family before. She obtained her Romanian passport for the trip and took photos in her father's hometown. Traveling on her own might have been a marker that she was mature enough to go to Palestine alone if she wished. She also described the trip with sadness and revealed her propensity to act tougher than she really was:

In Romania, the relatives were so different from me, and at times we even butted heads, and everyone admired me because I refused to let it get to me; they thought that I didn't care and I'm going my own way, a different child would not be happy anymore, would have cried, and the vacation would have been ruined, but nobody knew that I was desperately unhappy in the evening in bed by myself.[10]

It may have been the first time she did not connect well with her extended family, especially without the benefit of her parents to bridge the distance, but it wouldn't be the last.

On New Year's Eve in 1936, Ruth started a diary. She reported that her uncle Leo (her mother's brother), aunt Dora, and cousin David had just left for the United States, yet another Leipzig Jewish family making a break for it while they could. David was the youngest of four children; the oldest daughter, Deborah, lived in Hanover in a mental hospital, and Meier and Rosel, his middle children, had already left for Palestine.[11] Ruth acknowledged that she had not made an effort to see her relatives recently and did not get along with them, but now that they had left, she missed them. It felt like everyone was leaving, and Ruth feared that she would be one of the last people stuck on an obviously sinking ship.

Despite the fact that their world was beginning to crumble, Jewish girls in Leipzig sustained intense friendships with one another. Most of Ruth's friendships grew out of the Habonim. She revealed, as only a thirteen-year-old girl could, the reason why she had started her diary in the first place:

> With Esther things are very different on the outside, but basically we play act. We talk about many different things, but we don't talk about anything really personal. I get along better with her than Miriam, for sure, but it is not a friendship, because she will not let me read her diary and I won't let her read mine, which I just started to write today.[12]

A few days after she'd begun the diary, Ruth wrote about her conflicted feelings concerning the Habonim, and, in particular, her disagreements with Ury Rotschild, the leader of the group. She explained that he had recently left Leipzig on a trip and that since his departure everyone had formed their own cliques, despite their frequent criticism of them. Ruth wanted to leave the Bund. She couldn't stand their judgments about wearing flashy bourgeois clothes, when clearly these working-class kids coveted them.

Ruth abandoned her diary for the next two and half years. But when she started writing again later at age sixteen in Switzerland, she picked right back up with reflections on why she decided to quit the Habonim in Leipzig in 1937 or thereabouts. Her parents had been pushing her to act more like a middle-class girl, which she had resisted while in the Bund. But the group had distracted her from school, and to her embarrassment, she failed and had to repeat a year.[13] Although she got along with the other girls in the Habonim, she developed tensions with the boys, Ury in particular. After going to a Zionist summer camp with the group, likely in the summer of 1937, she had had a big fight with him and finally quit.[14] He had accused her of being a conceited bourgeois girl concerned only with clothes and makeup. Ruth knew this flatly wasn't true; she was an intellectual who cared deeply about class issues, Palestine, and the fate of Jews in Europe. But she couldn't blindly adhere to any one ideology; her deep independent streak forced her to acknowledge that she would likely be unhappy on a kibbutz. Ruth revealed, "We were brainwashed in the sense that the way of the Bund is the only one, this is the way you have to go or you are losers."[15]

She explained the sense of liberation she felt when she quit the Bund and how she could finally go out and do the things she wanted to do without risking criticism from Ury and the others in the group. Her grades and her teachers' comments on her report cards dramatically improved in 1937. Even though she feared she was drifting into shallowness, she longed for a normal teenage life:

> I didn't have any real girlfriends, because I was already so influenced by the Brith that the typical young girls who only knew about fancy dress, silly movies and books were way too childish for me. But given a little time, I almost turned into the same kind of person. I wore clothing that was more stylish, a bit sporty, not like before in the common dress, but with a degree of elegance and for Leipzig, I stood out. I was an equal with all of the rich girls in my class. What I didn't yet do was dancing, use makeup or powder. I often went out to a coffee house with my parents, and I was able to have amusing conversations with the young men. In any case, everybody thought I was 17 or 18 years old.[16]

She looked back at this period with some sense of regret, however: "I was, by the way, until January of 1939, very much on my way to being a superficial, vain, dumb, which means good middle-class society girl, just like Ury Rotschild had predicted."[17]

In 1936 Ruth started using a camera and kept a photograph log with captions and dates for every shot she took. The initial captions from 1936 reveal outings with the Bund and names of members in each photo. The captions from later in 1937 and 1938 are only of Ruth, her family, and friends Edith and Esther, often in parks or in the squares of Leipzig. There are a few of Ruth alone, posing like a fashion model in a park, trying on her new liberated identity. Meanwhile, letters of complaint flooded into the Leipzig parks office demanding that Jews should be banned from parks or, at the very least, from sitting on park benches. Leipzigers were especially concerned about Jews in the large Rosental Park, where Ruth had taken many photos.[18]

As Ruth became a teenager, she grew into a very independent, outspoken person who clashed with her parents at times. She remembered, "I was much closer to my mother. We had a good relationship. I think my dad was a little bit of a control freak, but I think most parents were in those days."[19] After she left Leipzig, she reflected on some prescient advice that her mother had given her but she did not want to hear: "Your two best friends, your two least jealous friends, are your parents, but you will learn that too late." Ruth lamented, "How rightly she had it! I know today that, when I didn't speak to her, she also understood me better than anyone."[20]

By the time Ruth was fifteen, she saw herself largely as an adult, free to come and go as she pleased on her own, even at night. Later, when she moved to Seattle to live with her aunt and uncle, she would long for these times in Leipzig when, she claimed, she "did what [she] wanted and went where [she] wanted."[21] The streets of Leipzig were becoming increasingly dangerous for Jews, but Ruth desired to go out and watch what was unfolding, which she described as akin to being a reporter.

She said, "In a peculiar way . . . I'm not sure I can explain it, but I guess I always kind of went along feeling it's better to see than not to. I felt more in control being able to watch. I wasn't so puzzled. I could see what was going on. But I just sort of hoofed it around."[22] Her Romanian passport didn't say she was Jewish, which meant she didn't have to follow the curfews for Jews. She revealed that the police in fact suspected she was Jewish, but when they confronted her, they couldn't prove it.[23] Ruth defiantly roamed the streets on her own, half flaneur and half spy.

Chapter 4

The events of fall 1938 were the most vivid of Ruth's memories of her childhood in Germany. Nazi authorities announced that Polish Jews would be expelled from Germany in October. Since Ruth's mother had married a Romanian, she was not included in this group. Leipzig had a very large population of Polish Jews, who, on October 28, congregated at the Polish consul's villa to seek passports that would allow them to stay in Germany or flee to other countries.[1] Those who were denied passports were sent to the Leipzig railway station to wait for trains that would send them to Poland, where they would be turned back from the border, stuck in limbo there.

Her home just two blocks from the train station, Ruth walked over to see for herself what was happening. She saw people arriving in night-gowns, having suddenly been forced from their homes. An idea popped into her head: these people needed toothbrushes. She looked up a man who owned a sundry store and knocked on his door. He gave her the toothbrushes, and she went back to the train station to distribute them. She considered it her first act of volunteering but also acknowledged, "Of all the crazy—well, I guess it was appropriate as anything else, wasn't it? Kind of weird in retrospect."[2]

Just two weeks later, the tensions came to a head during an event known as Kristallnacht, the "night of broken glass." The murder of a German attaché in Paris by a seventeen-year-old immigrant Polish

Jew sparked a "spontaneous" nationwide pogrom on the night of November 9. The Nazi Party ordered its members and sympathizers to destroy synagogues and Jewish businesses while wearing plain clothes instead of uniforms. A neighbor, who Ruth later thought may have been a Communist, warned the Rappaports not to go out that night. But Ruth defiantly went out despite the danger. She would never forget what she saw.

Orthodox Jews had been ordered to line up against a wall near a river, probably the Karl-Heine-Kanal. Ruth watched as they were ordered to face it and Nazis fired guns into the air. She said, "It didn't kill them. They just pretended to kill them all. And in some ways that was worse, because you heard the shots, opened your eyes, and they were still standing."[3]

Wandering through the city, Ruth also saw her own school, synagogue, and the reform temple, just two blocks away from one another, on fire.[4] She couldn't remember many details about what was happening around her—if anyone tried to put out the fire, if people seemed to be horrified or gleeful. But she never forgot how she felt watching the destruction of these buildings that symbolized her community, her family, and herself: "Shocked. Disillusioned. Sad . . . [but] I don't think I was *afraid*. I think what saved me was not being afraid. I think that's what helped me get through it. I was just sort of leading with my chin up front. Maybe I'm too stupid to be afraid."[5]

The next day it was announced that the Höhere Israelitische Schule was closed. Her parents, no doubt panicked and wondering what to do next, had to figure out what to do with Ruth. They must have talked late into the night, considering what they could do, where their family could go. When asked what she did to fill her time after her school was closed, Ruth simply responded, "Reading . . . did a ferocious amount of reading."[6]

~

I took a trip to Leipzig to try to find out more about Ruth's family. My dad and my stepmother came along with me, and they visited historic sites while I spent several days in the state and city archives with a translator I hired named Elke. We skimmed through microfilm and files of documents for the names Rappaport and Rubinstein and celebrated when we found crucial information. My parents and I walked and drove through the cold, wet streets, stopping by landmarks that Ruth had known so well: the train station, the symphony hall, and the Volkshaus worker's hall that had been the site of Leipzig's major book burning. We went to a concert in the old Saint Thomas Church, where Bach directed the choir for many years, and rested our feet in the Saint Nicholas Church, which had led the revolution against German Communism in the 1980s.

A new, modern apartment building is now at the corner of Salomonstrasse and Kreuzstrasse. The address number on one side of this building was 18, but I deduced from old maps that Ruth's apartment building probably would have been located in the vacant lot next door. At night, in the drizzle, we found the site of her former synagogue on Otto-Schill-Strasse. Just around the corner was the memorial to the victims of the Holocaust: 140 empty chairs arranged in a grid, on the site of Leipzig's other major synagogue that had been burned to the ground. The 140 chairs represent the 14,000 Jews who once lived in this city.

~

Part II:

A Whole World of Ideas

Chapter 5

The last photograph Ruth took in Leipzig was a self-portrait in the courtyard of her family's apartment building while hanging laundry on a clothesline, a strikingly ordinary and peaceful scene captured on November 8, 1938, the day before Kristallnacht. On November 23, she took a photo of her mother standing in the snow in Saint Moritz. Sometime during those fifteen days, she had boarded a train in Leipzig with her mother. In the 1950s, Ruth wrote a narrative, titled "Curriculum Vita," as part of her application to the United Restitution Organization. She explained in it why she had gone to Switzerland:

> My mother, on doctor's orders, was planning a trip to Switzerland and all arrangements for this trip were completed during the early part of November. Since the Höhere Israelitische Schule was closed at the time of the pogroms, it was considered best that I accompany my mother for a few weeks to Switzerland, and accordingly about the middle of the month of November we arrived in Switzerland.[1]

They went to Saint Moritz, a well-known spa and resort area in southeastern Switzerland where Chaja could receive medical treatments. On November 18 Ruth and her mother met Roger Garfunkel, a distant relative of the Rubinsteins', who lived in Zurich but was visiting

Saint Moritz, probably on a ski trip. Roger was born in France, and his parents were Polish immigrants from the same area where Chaja had grown up.[2] He was twenty-five years old and a leader of the Zurich branch of the Hashomer Hatzair, another Zionist youth group.[3] Ruth later wrote in her diary that his mother had died four years previously and his father was wealthy. Roger's father supported him financially while he worked to convince Jewish children and teenagers they should move to Palestine.[4] She explained that she had first thought he might be a "true chaver," a friend or mentor with whom she could discuss Zionism in depth, develop her own beliefs, and find the path she would take in the future. Roger told her to get in touch with him in Zurich, and Ruth looked forward to getting to know him better. Sometime in late November or early December, Chaja and Ruth took the train from Saint Moritz to Zurich, where they stayed in nice hotels and visited the Garfunkels again. Chaja planned to go back to Leipzig with Ruth after visiting Zurich.

What happened next was a turning point in Ruth's life. She and her mother boarded the train in Zurich, but as it began to leave the station, Ruth grabbed her suitcase and jumped off. She just could not force herself to go back to the hell of Germany. As she put it, "No ten horses could get me back there." When asked if her mother knew what she had been planning, she explained, "Well, yes and no, because when we packed for the trip, she went through my luggage and she said, 'You don't need'—some of whatever season of clothes I'd packed was the wrong season. So, she knew what I was planning. But there wasn't much she could do. And when I jumped off the train and the train moved on, that was it."[5]

Did Ruth really jump from the train and run away from her mother? She told this story often to her friends and neighbors on Capitol Hill, and who wouldn't love it? She framed it as a crucial moment in her life, when she grabbed the reins of fate and started to forge her own path. But she never referred to this incident directly in her letters or diaries from the time. Perhaps Ruth remembered herself as a daring, rebellious teenager who would jump from a train to escape being dragged back to the horrors of what was to come in Germany; perhaps her parents wanted her to stay in Switzerland because they knew it would be safer. But a few months later, Ruth obliquely referred to what had happened the previous winter with a simple phrase, "When I made the decision to stay in Switzerland," indicating that the decision was hers alone, not her parents'.[6] She wrote that she had stayed briefly at a Salvation Army women's home. She didn't explain how she ended up there. She might have gone to the Garfunkels first, but clearly they had no interest in allowing her to stay in their home. She disparaged them later as relatives who were "for the birds." She wrote:

> Yes, when my Mother left, and I didn't have anything, I simply slept at the Salvation Army. All the people thought that it didn't bother me at all, you can't get her down. Yes, it did not harm me, but especially the contrast, first living in a hotel, to eat in a first-class restaurant, always together with Mother, then suddenly to be totally alone in an ice-cold room without love, so truly in poverty, with immigrants, where everything is disgusting. While I, in the past, even though I never mentioned it, had a loathing for poverty, looked at the poor with disdain, I am now deeply convinced that poverty is not shameful...[7]

Reading this diary entry convinced me that Ruth was indeed the girl who jumped. At the very least, there is no doubt that Ruth ran away from her mother in Zurich and refused to return to Leipzig.

An annual report from 1938 explained the mission of the Salvation Army home for women in Zurich. Many of the women there were immigrants; some had sad stories of alcoholism, abusive husbands, or abandonment. The goal of the organization was to train poor women to work as maids in Zurich. Every weekday, residents took classes in sewing, ironing, cleaning, and cooking until they passed tests and earned a certificate. Some residents were extremely difficult to work with, but it was always considered a triumph when these downtrodden individuals succumbed to the good influence of these progressive women of Zurich, accepted their lot in life, and became obedient maids for the wealthy.[8] Ruth stayed only for a few weeks, but she probably had some training in how to perform the housework she would later be expected to do as a foster child.

On November 22 Richard Röschard wrote to the Schweizer Hilfswerk für Emigrantenkinder (the Swiss Aid Society for Emigrant Children, commonly known as SHEK), offering to house an orphan or immigrant child who would be treated as a member of the family.[9] SHEK had been founded in 1933 by Dr. Nettie Sutro, a woman who had earned her PhD at the University of Bern. Living in Zurich as a Jewish immigrant from Germany, Sutro was moved by the plight of the starving children of Russian émigrés in France. She founded the organization to bring these children for just a few weeks to Switzerland, where they could eat heartily and regain their strength before they were sent back to France.[10]

Sutro enlisted the help of women across Switzerland and opened offices in several cities where local families were recruited to host children. This program continued until November 1938, when Kristallnacht changed everything. Sutro decided that German Jewish children would now be the top priority. She wrote up a list of German children who wanted to enter the country, titled "300 Kinder Aktion," and submitted it to immigration authorities in Switzerland for approval. She organized the Frankfurt–Switzerland line of the famous *Kindertransport* train. Dr. Ruth Westheimer, known then as Karola Siegel, was one of these children. She spent the war in an orphanage in Switzerland before learning that her entire family had been killed in concentration camps. Westheimer was then sent to Palestine with other orphans. While Ruth

Rappaport was staying at the Salvation Army in Zurich, someone who worked there probably contacted SHEK on her behalf. Even though she was already living in Zurich, her name was also placed on the "300 Kinder Aktion" list for approval. Making the list was what ultimately allowed Ruth to stay in Switzerland for almost a year.[11]

Dr. Bertha Keller, a SHEK employee who had a law degree and a PhD in economics, was assigned to Ruth's case and replied to Mr. Röschard on December 7. She explained, "At the moment we have a 15-year-old girl from Leipzig. Her name is Ruth Rappaport . . . She is very intelligent and very independent for her age. Please let us know soon."[12] Dr. Keller, an intelligent and independent woman herself, immediately recognized a self-reliant, if somewhat defiant, free spirit inside this bookish and bespectacled teenage girl.

Chapter 6

On April 20, 1939, Ruth started a new diary. She might have bought it earlier that day at a stationery store in Zurich, or maybe her mother had mailed it to her from Leipzig. Ruth had just returned the day before from a weekend Zionist camp at a castle in Elgg, where she and other Jewish teenagers had dug potatoes, sung songs, and prepared for life in Israel. On the first page, she wrote her full name and the word *"Tagebuch"* (diary). She must have been thinking about the importance of friendship when she wrote out the Golden Rule above her name. Under her name she wrote the word "Zurich" twice, once in pen and once in pencil, underlining both with dashes. She may have hesitated before turning the page to begin her first entry, where she would start to diligently document her new life in this city over the German border and at the foot of the Alps. At the bottom of this first page with her pencil, she wrote, "I wonder who will find this diary."

As Jewish children and teenagers began their exodus out of Germany in the 1930s, they were unaware of the new roles they were expected to assume in these new countries. Too distracted by planning logistics and not wishing to worry their children, most parents did not explain much to them about their impending new lives or were unaware of exactly where they would end up. Grateful that their children would be the lucky ones, they bid them goodbye, told them to "be good," and sent them on to the Swiss foster parents who had been generous enough to open their homes. Most probably told their children they would be together again soon, whether they truly believed that or not.

Many of these children later wrote as adults about their confusion, guilt, loss, or complete ignorance about what was happening in Germany. Their titles alone are telling: *A Boy in Your Situation*, *A Child Alone*, *A Lesser Child*, *A Transported Life*, *Against All Odds*, *Girl in Movement*, *My Heart in a Suitcase*, *Shedding Skins*, and one of the most well known, Lore Segal's *Other People's Houses*. Segal was placed on the *Kindertransport* from Vienna to England and was politely shuffled among many different families. Even when her parents were later able to come to England themselves, she was not allowed to live with them initially. As former business owners who had lost their wealth, they were now expected to assume deferential roles of housemaid and gardener and to be grateful for such opportunities.[1] Ruth was no different from any of these children forced to live with strangers due to the tragic circumstances of German Jews, whose lives and families were ripped apart in the 1930s. She used her diary as an outlet to describe in detail how she felt about being a foster child, how she missed her parents and friends, her opinions on Zionism, and her concern about what would happen to her in the future.

In Zurich, Mr. Röschard agreed to take Ruth. Just three weeks after Dr. Keller had written to him to ask if he could take her, he wrote a confidential letter to SHEK:

> As you know, a short time ago we offered to provide a home and a family for an emigrant child. We thought to take in a poor person for whom we could replace what their homeland had taken, to be their father and mother, to give them something and to be someone for them.
>
> You then sent us Miss Ruth Rappaport, daughter of rich Jews, spoiled and self-important, with a personality that

just doesn't fit in with our plain-thinking family. I don't want to criticize Miss Rappaport at all, as she is just a product of her upbringing and surroundings, but it is nevertheless difficult for us to bring about any type of assimilation, which very much goes against her specific personality.

In short, it is <u>far from</u> what we expected and hoped for, and we ask you to organize an exchange. If you do not have a sweet-natured, poor girl, either from Sudetenland or Germany, we would rather pass on a German addition to the family and open our home to a Swiss girl . . . You can quietly and calmly change the situation. Miss Ruth does not know anything about this letter and we will also not allow her to find out.[2]

Dr. Keller wrote back to him a few days later, apologetically explaining her own feelings about Ruth:

We are very sorry you were so disappointed with Ruth Rappaport and had so much frustration. We thank you for trying so hard. We can understand your frustrations as we also found her very arrogant and stuck-up. In the last interview we felt this, but she talks very nice about you. We hope to find a place for her soon. We only have Jewish children so cannot supply you with another girl. All of the Christian children have been placed.[3]

But Mr. Röschard felt guilty about Ruth and didn't want to appear so eager to cast her aside. He decided to give it more time and notified Dr. Keller, "She is too grown-up for her age. We will try it once more and see if we can work things out."[4]

Ruth had been under the impression that her relationship with the Röschards would be more like that of an employer and employee. She wanted to retain her independence and come and go as she pleased. Immigrants in Switzerland were forbidden from working for pay, so Ruth imagined she would help with household chores in exchange for room and board. It appears that Ruth was not able to attend a free public school in Zurich.[5] She explained to her American uncle Carl Rubinstein in a letter written in her awkward English, "I am not allowed to earn money in Switzerland, and my parents are forbidden to send me any . . . Every day I spend in Switzerland is lost time for me . . . If there were not the new law that also parents, whose children are abroad and want to go to school, are forbidden to send money out from Germany, I would go to school here. So I have no opportunity."[6]

She had to fill her days with something. Ruth went out frequently to socialize with other teenage and young adult members of the Hashomer Hatzair, a Zionist youth group that she had recently joined. Months later, she revealed that, in her opinion, she had worked hard for the Röschards and they had been generous to her. She had no complaints about the family or living with them.[7] If she realized that Mr. Röschard found her behavior to be intolerable, she never indicated it in her diary. While living with the Röschards, Ruth inquired to several organizations in Germany and England about the possibility of joining one of the *Kindertransport* trains to England, but she was ineligible for various reasons. Near the end of January 1939, she was sent to a new family in Zurich, the Herzogs.

Kurt and Doris Herzog had two children, including a toddler daughter named Ursi.[8] Ruth was responsible for caring for them to some extent, and she took photos of herself and Ursi out on walks around Zurich. After living with them for about three months, she compared them to the Röschards, angrily writing in her diary that although they were comfortably middle class, the Herzogs were stingy.[9] She explained her difficulty playing the role expected of her:

On the other hand, supposedly the Herzogs wanted to have someone for whom they could do good, who would completely belong to the family, talk about everything with them, and who feels at home with them. And I didn't want that. 1. Nobody owes me anything here, 2. If I really was the way they are accusing me that I am not, then surely they would have said that I am demanding, 3. They never were very warm towards me, and I have always tried to avoid being any bother to them, 4. I did not know that they wanted to have a relationship with me, like for instance, a child with her parents, or with an uncle and aunt, 5. We are so different in our views and with everything, that surely would not have worked, 6. I always thought they were not that interested in me. [10]

Ruth also wrote about the feelings welling deep inside that she could never express to anyone:

It may be my mistake that I come across so cold. As much as I can talk about meaningless stuff with all people in a superficial way, when it comes to my own affairs, I am totally closed up. Even if I speak about those things with someone else, I always have such a cold and superficial tone, as though I am not even speaking about myself. It is not meant for me that I, with warmth, would repeat the things I feel, neither with my parents nor with anybody else. And it is not even theatrics what I feel say or do. Whereas people see me on the outside as hard-working, strong, etc., and they think that I know no sadness, at times I feel bitterly miserable. [11]

At the end of April, Ruth's father came to Zurich, and shortly after, her mother visited for a few days. They stayed with Ruth at the Herzogs', and she worried how this would play out. Had she given everyone in Zurich the wrong impression of her parents? She was particularly embarrassed by her mother's brazenness in asking other families to financially support Ruth. She noted, "My parents really don't have very much anymore. I actually feel sorry for them. They have worked very hard their whole lives and now they have nothing to show for it."[12] But she was thrilled to see her father again: "Papa is here now, and I am so happy, and if it wasn't the fact that it is Germany, I would have for sure have gone back home, but . . ."[13] She trailed off, not needing to explain the obvious.

Even though Ruth had expressed that it wasn't allowed, Mendel had been sending her money periodically. She also received small sums from Dr. Keller and a hundred francs a month from her uncle Carl Rubinstein in Seattle. When Kurt Herzog discovered that Ruth was receiving money, he informed her that since she "didn't have the need anymore," she couldn't stay with them any longer. She had already concluded, "The longer I am with the Herzogs, the more obvious it becomes how totally different we are . . . It already bothers me enough that I must be a burden to strangers, and needless to say when I am told about it constantly. I know that I owe the Herzogs many thanks, but the way they behave now is really not very nice. They are petty people."[14]

Ruth was not an easy person to live with. Although she tried to be considerate, something in her personality turned off both the Röschards and the Herzogs. By this point in her life, she was strong-willed and spoke her mind. She explained what her ideal living situation would be in Zurich: "In any case, I just want to go where I can work and be with people who don't just want to do something good, but where I have a real business relationship, working ½ day and the rest of the time I am free. The nicest thing would be if I could take a room somewhere and study something, but that is just not possible."[15] Ultimately, she just wanted to be treated as an adult.

Soon she would be living with a Jewish family, the Langers, who had a daughter near Ruth's age, Rose, whom she met through the Hashomer Hatzair. By July, she would be shuffled to the Jakobowitch family, who had two daughters with whom Ruth would attend a Zionist camp. Ruth's father wrote to her in July explaining that he was looking into moving her to Lugano, Italy. She wearily wrote in her diary that she had packed her bags eleven times since she came to Zurich and was loath to move to a new place again. She stayed with the Jakobowitch family until she left for the United States in October, complaining in her diary only occasionally about the antics of their daughter Gerda. Like other Jewish refugee children, Ruth had eventually learned to act as grateful toward her foster parents as she could, despite her growing bitterness.

Chapter 7

Out of school for a full year, Ruth had more free time than she knew what to do with while she waited for her visa to the United States. She helped out with housework daily for her foster families and occasionally studied English. She was annoyed with herself for wasting time that she should have spent preparing for her move, but she had trouble focusing. As she would for the rest of her life, Ruth wavered between her dual desires to, on the one hand, go out, socialize, and be frivolous, and, on the other, to focus on her solitary intellectual pursuits. She could now read openly all the books that she had to be careful to hide in Leipzig. Regardless of where she read them, openly or in secret, Ruth knew that reading risqué or radical books was a marker of her own sophistication.[1] She also seems to have started smoking, another habit she surely thought was sophisticated. In a letter to her cousin Rose, Carl's daughter in Seattle, she alluded to this, explaining a photograph she had sent: "The last one, with the cigarette, was only a joke, because I was imitating a lady, and in truth I am an 'ANTI SMOKER.'"[2]

Now she finally had the chance to openly pursue any topic that interested her, no matter how controversial. But she was disgusted with the fact that she was just not motivated and wasted time during the day taking photographs with her friend Teddie. She chastised herself in her diary but also partially blamed the political circumstances she was mired in:

Because of my surroundings in the last two years and because of the situation in Germany, I have become what I have never wanted to become, a person without an inner life, which means I don't engage in anything intellectual, and I have no interest in the world, movies, etc. Like I already said, I am totally blah. That will definitely need to change completely now.[3]

An omnivorous reader, Ruth read whatever she could get her hands on: books owned by her foster families, books borrowed from her new friends, books she might have bought in Zurich's plentiful bookstores, and books available at libraries, including the Zurich Central Library or possibly a synagogue library. Although she claimed at the time she didn't do "anything intellectual," decades later, when applying to library school, Ruth thought about this time in her life differently. She wrote, "I can truthfully say that the most memorable point of my stay in Switzerland was access to libraries and books which opened for me a whole world of new ideas that had been strictly taboo in Germany."[4]

While the Zurich Central Library would have had a wide selection of books, newspapers, and magazines, it was not what we think of as a typical public library today, especially when it comes to children. First, there was no children's or young adult department. Children younger than eighteen were not allowed to check out books. Only citizens had borrowing privileges, so Ruth would not have been able to check books out even if she were older than eighteen, although her foster parents or the parents of friends could have done so for her. Anyone was allowed to visit the library and read whatever he or she wished.[5] It was located in the Rathaus Quarter, the oldest part of Zurich. Due to the narrow cobblestone streets dating to the Middle Ages, it is still largely cut off from car traffic. Built in 1914 after a merger of several small libraries, the sturdy stone building now serves as both the city's public library and the main library of the University of Zurich.

Ruth wandered the streets of Zurich during the day, waiting to meet up with friends after they got out of school. She could have passed the time in bookstores, shops, and cafés, but only at the public library was she not obligated to buy anything. She could browse for hours, read German newspapers—including, probably, her hometown Leipzig newspaper—write in her diary, or write letters to her friends and parents. In hindsight, it didn't matter what exactly she read at that library. What mattered was the feeling it gave her: a sense of peace and safety and the opportunity to read, or not read, whatever she wanted to without judgment or regulation. Ruth was just one of many exiles who found refuge at Zurich's public library. Many Communists and radicals from around Europe came to Zurich during times of crisis in their own countries. Vladimir Lenin lived just a few blocks from the library in 1917 and spent most of every weekday reading and working there.[6]

When her father visited, she felt guilty for spending time with him in a carefree way:

> I spent my time in the exact manner that is frowned upon in the Bund, had invitations for dinner with Papi, gossiped and played cards. As a newcomer to the group, I can even openly talk about this but deep inside I am ashamed of myself. I have become so completely without any care and energy, that it is a total shame. I was disgustingly bored, but in the Bund, if we don't have Sichot [discussions] about books or problems, then I am just as bored. This shows quite definitely that I stand for nothing, not in society nor in the Bund.[7]

Like the Habonim in Leipzig, the Hashomer Hatzair would provide Ruth a social circle to discuss her intellectual, religious, and class questions. And like the Habonim, the Hashomer Hatzair would not live up to Ruth's expectations of finding "true chaverim." She was continually let down by this group of young Jews, who appeared to her more and more superficial and self-absorbed over the year she lived there. Most of all, she was disappointed with the group's leader, Roger Garfunkel. It wasn't just that he had rebuffed her after meeting him in Saint Moritz and that she was nursing an unrequited crush. She came to understand that he was a hypocrite, a comfortably middle-class person who encouraged others to practice hard physical labor in preparation for a new life in Palestine but didn't seem to have any desire to do this work or move there himself.[8]

Ruth remembered the activities of the Hashomer Hatzair in her oral history and described the group's trip to the castle at Elgg in April 1939:

> I dug potatoes. I *harvested* potatoes. And one of the other strange things in all this mishmash was, there was some really large Swiss corporations. And they owned acreage in which they grew stuff. And when I went to Switzerland I volunteered to dig up potatoes for the Swiss chemical companies. These chemical companies owned farmland and they actually cultivated them, and we volunteered to dig up potatoes for them, in exchange for which we got to live in a Swiss castle.[9]

Ruth compared herself to other girls in the group, jealous when they appeared more popular, condescending when they seemed naively enthusiastic about Zionism or kibbutz life. One girl, Ruth Zucker, who was also an immigrant, particularly annoyed her. Rappaport judged that Zucker's standing was above her own because Roger had asked her to join the Hashomer, while Rappaport was left to explain to others in the group why if she was related to the Garfunkels they didn't seem to help her out in any way. As she would her entire life, Ruth used humor to make fun of herself and convince others she didn't care: "When I am asked how I can be here then I always tell a lighthearted and superficial story, but how I truly feel about it inside I don't show that, I feel shameful about my situation."[10] Whether she fit in was a primary concern, but on the other hand, she knew she would not stay in Zurich much longer, so why bother to try?

She became increasingly frustrated when the group did not discuss Zionism seriously. She observed a difference between the Habonim in Leipzig, a working-class group in which escaping Germany was imperative, and the Hashomer in Zurich, where Zionism was a theoretical abstraction that very few had to seriously consider.[11] She reflected on how the last few years in Germany had hardened her: "I believe strongly, that because of what I experienced in Germany, I'm no longer youthful and fresh and lively, as I should be as a 15-year-old. As a matter of fact, sometimes I feel like a very old spinster."[12] As one of the only teenagers in the group who had grown up in Germany, she felt like no one else could truly understand the gravity of the situation there, and she feigned a lighthearted attitude with them. If there was anything she didn't want from the members of this group, it was pity.

Which social class she belonged to now and which one she would belong to in the future were foremost on her mind. She mulled over the possibilities:

> There was a time, when I longed for a life like, for instance, the life of Mrs. Herzog. Which means having parties, being elegant, to play a role, to have a well-tended house, and to have very little work. At other times I wished for a trade that would be completely fulfilling for me, but would that be ideal? The former is certainly much too empty, that I know. But if being a laborer could ever satisfy me? Can it be that in the long run a laborer will remain an intellectual?[13]

It is telling that Ruth could not conceive of making a living somehow as an intellectual. To her the future seemed abstract, with many options and possibilities to consider, some of which she would not have any control over. Even at age fifteen, she had a foreboding feeling about being on her own for the rest of her life. She wrote, "I guess it is my fate that I have to make my own way, which means that I have to force myself to make a decision. But someday it will come, either to a good or to a bad ending."[14] At other points in her diary, she seemed to know exactly what her fate was: "I admire the people who can do [hard labor] and were not just doing it because of economic reasons and who are in the kibbutz. I think I am much too weak for that. When I will be going to the USA, I will most likely make a very good member of the middle class."[15]

The bright spot in the Hashomer was the camping excursions that Ruth clearly enjoyed. She had high hopes that on the trips she would bond with her "true chaverim." That usually turned out to be a disappointment, but she realized what she loved about these trips: the satisfied feeling she had at the end of a long day of physical labor. Such labor was either a distraction from her overactive, analytical mind or an opportunity to burn up her restless physical energy, and in her diary she tried to explain the calm that would come over her at the end of these days spent at camp. In August, she fought with her parents by letter over an expensive camping trip just over the border in France. She defied their wishes and went anyway, despite the hassle of obtaining a visa and feeling cheated about the surprise extra costs of the trip. She ended up walking with her Zionist friends all the way to Mulhouse, about seventy miles from Zurich. Ruth had fond memories of the exhausting hike and sleeping in a barn next to her friends. She woke up feeling a sense of solidarity with them.[16] Soon after she got back from this trip, Germany invaded Poland, and England declared war. A month later, Ruth would start her long, circuitous journey to the United States.

Obtaining a visa to the United States was a bureaucratic ordeal that she was forced to navigate for over a year, alone as a teenager. She had to reapply every three months to the local "foreign police" for a permit to stay in Switzerland. She had to prove to them that she was in the country only temporarily and on her way to the United States.[17] In February 1939 she found out that her family's US visa application, first filed in Berlin in August 1938, was still valid, but it would take at least eight months or more for her to get it due to the long waiting list.[18] In April, she found out that her Romanian passport would expire soon and she had to apply for a new one.[19] The American consulate in Zurich informed her that her uncle's affidavit to sponsor her family, written the previous August, was invalid now, and Ruth had to trouble him to write a new one.[20] She explained to him that if she could not prove within the next few weeks that she was going to America, her permit from the Zurich city police would expire and she would have to leave the country.[21] Throughout the summer, she worked on submitting to the consulate required documents, such as her birth certificate, a certificate that she had lived in Germany, letters from her parents stating that she would be going alone to the United States, and health questionnaires. In September, she finally received a summons to appear at the American consulate in Zurich to finalize her visa application.[22]

Although her parents were restricted from coming to the United States by the low quota for Romanian citizens, Ruth was considered under the US Immigration Act of 1924 a citizen of Germany, which had the second-highest quota after Great Britain. It is unclear why Ruth received a visa when so many others were denied one at this time. Perhaps she was just next in line to be approved, but she may have received favorable treatment because she was under eighteen and her uncle Carl was wealthy.

In October she finally obtained her visa and made plans to leave for the US from Holland, the only open port in Europe at that time. Ruth's mother sold her piano to help her buy a ticket for her voyage on the SS

Veendam.[23] On the train ride from Basel to Leipzig, she claimed, she "led learned conversations about Madam Curie, youth league, and women's issues."[24] She stayed with her parents in Leipzig and made preparations, which included sewing and shopping. Just getting from Germany to the SS *Veendam* would be an ordeal, one that left her confused about the travel plans and when and where the ship would leave for the US. She was turned away at the border of Amsterdam for arriving before the ship was in port, and it appears she stayed overnight in Oberhausen and spent a day in Duisburg trying to straighten everything out at the American consulate in the Netherlands, the Romanian consulate, and a travel agency. She had to backtrack to Leipzig without a valid travel pass and claimed she had to live in hiding for a week before returning to Holland, although she did not explain more about what that entailed.[25] After staying briefly in Rotterdam, she finally left from Antwerp for the United States on the *Veendam* on October 28, 1939. Looking back on how she made it through this time in her life, she explained her transformation into an assertive person who had to advocate for herself. She argued that it was simply the result of the events that had happened and of her forcing herself to rise to the challenge, whatever the circumstances were: "My whole behavior is strictly existential. Meet what comes."[26]

~

After presenting a paper about Ruth's work to an international library conference in Lyon, I went to Zurich for a few days to find out more about Ruth's year there. I switched trains at Mulhouse, where Ruth had walked from Zurich to the Zionist camp. As I waited for a delayed train, an older man sat beside me on a bench and we struck up a conversation. He was an American who had grown up in Afghanistan, where my boyfriend, Greg, happened to be on a deployment at the time. The older man's wife had recently passed away, and he had decided to take a long trip through Europe to visit their favorite places. He couldn't wait to get to Prague, which she had loved. We talked for a long time about the war in Afghanistan, and later, on the train, he asked why I was going to Zurich. As another person who had fled a repressive regime, he was enraged when listening to Ruth's story of escaping Germany.

In Zurich I stayed at the Hotel Otter, which had a raucous "western bar" on the first floor. In a cowhide-covered booth, I ate my breakfast of hardboiled eggs and yogurt before heading to the public library. Once I arrived, I stood for a while in the lobby and grand stairwell of the old building, soaking in the solemnity of the space and imagining a fifteen-year-old Ruth walking up the steps. I spoke with a librarian in special collections about the library's history and viewed older photographs of the building. I sat at one of the desks in the new modern wing, impressed with the fact that it was completely packed with students on a weekday afternoon in August. The next day I navigated a maze of narrow cobblestone streets, trying to find the city archives, which seemed to be hidden in plain sight. I pored over Zurich phone books from the 1930s, finding the addresses of the Garfunkels, the Röschards, the Herzogs, and the Jakobowitches. An archivist looked up more information for me about each of these families, including their immigration records, the occupations of the men, and the dates their children were born.

At night I walked through a crowded festival and window shopped at the very expensive stores. I went to what I thought was going to be a late-night concert at Grossmünster Church, a concert that also turned out to be a haunting candlelight tour that ended with a climb up one of its tall bell towers. At the Swiss National Museum, there was a film exhibit consisting of many small booths with clips of famous Swiss films subtitled in Switzerland's four official languages. I opened the curtains and sat on the benches to watch a few. In one film the characters joked about the Swiss always welcoming immigrants and refugees, so long as they had money. The people sitting around me laughed at this national inside joke.

I took a train to Bern for the day to visit the Swiss Federal Archives, which has the records of SHEK. I passed by the beautiful government buildings with their window boxes of red flowers and walked over a high bridge that crossed the crystal-blue River Aare. I waited a long time for Ruth's file to be delivered to the reading room and panicked when the archivist told me they couldn't find it. When they searched again and found it and delivered it to me, I marveled at the documents and letters within it—her mother's handwriting, the word *"arrogante"* in a letter from Dr. Keller to Mr. Röschard. It was utterly remarkable to find this small cache of documents that told so much about this single year in Ruth's life. Just an hour before the archives closed, some other files from the SHEK collection that I thought might be relevant arrived in the reading room for me.

The files were housed in large bundled cardboard cases tied with archival string. I skimmed and copied a few documents related to the "300 Kinder Aktion" group. I looked at one last folder, the title of which roughly translates to "Various Cries for Help." I flipped through what appeared to be hundreds of letters from all over Europe, mostly written by parents, but some were from the children themselves. Some had small portraits attached with paper clips. What had happened to all these children? Were these the ones Nettie Sutro was just not able to help? I didn't have to translate these letters to know what these frantic parents all said, very politely, in one way or another: "Please save my child."

Part III:

Your Life Is a Battle,
Your Peace a Victory

SEATTLE, 1939–1945

Chapter 8

Ruth arrived in New York on November 10, 1939, at the age of sixteen, after an exhausting month of travel. She later wrote in her diary about how she felt when she got there: "I had such a joyful feeling such as I hadn't had for a long time. I think that now I was the most restless person on the boat. I could no longer wait to be finished, and I simply had no more calm in me. It was so wonderful to know that I now no longer had to be worried about traveling further, staying overnight, etc."[1] She stood on the upper deck of the ship "dumb, fat, and happy," as she later put it, watching the other families, who were almost all Jewish refugees like her, greet each other in joy and relief. Her uncle Carl and aunt Dora Rubinstein had taken the train across the country to New York and had waited there for weeks for her to arrive. Due to the mix-up in her travel out of Europe, Ruth had no idea who, or even if anyone, would be meeting her in New York. Eventually she noticed a Western Union boy that had been circling the ship with a message and shouting, "Paging Ruth Rappaport! Paging Ruth Rappaport!" When she finally found her uncle Carl, he exclaimed, "What in hell is taking you so long?"[2]

Her father's brother who lived in New York, Irving Rappaport, was also there, and the two uncles met for the first time while waiting for Ruth to exit the ship. He wanted her to stay with him for a while in New York before traveling to Seattle, but she felt like she should go with the Rubinsteins because they had been waiting for so long for her. For one night, they stayed in a nice hotel, and she went to Broadway with her cousins Marvin and Selma, Irving's children. She wrote of her first impressions: "I liked my family a lot. I had expected something as in Witznitz [Vyzhnytsya], outdated, pious, stingy, in particular, different. Modern, refined, simply: I was pleased with them."[3]

The next day she boarded the train with Carl and Dora for the long cross-country trip to Seattle. They had their own first-class suite on a Pullman car, and Ruth had her own bedroom. She remembered about her uncle on this trip:

> The biggest thing he could do for you was buy you an ice cream cone. I don't think he ever ate ice cream when he was a kid. And I don't know if it wasn't kosher in that little village. Or I don't know why he never had ice cream. But you know, if he gave you a hundred dollars as a present, it was nothing, but if he bought you an ice cream snack, he was really in love with you—he really loved you. And every time the damn train stopped, I got an ice cream cone.[4]

Dora, meanwhile, had heard about the digestive troubles of people who had traveled across the Atlantic by ship. While Carl was buying Ruth ice cream at every stop, Dora was constantly giving her Feen-a-mint, a laxative gum. As Ruth joked later, "I nearly died!"[5]

In 1940 Seattle had about 368,000 residents, and Ruth remembered it as "a backwater town in those days if there ever was one!"[6] The Jewish population of Seattle was around 14,500 in 1937, and Ruth would be one of about a thousand who came from Europe in the 1930s.[7] Carl Rubinstein had immigrated to the United States around 1900, via Latin America. He had married Dora, also from Poland, in Fort Worth, Texas, and they came to Seattle in 1916. Carl started a business selling fruit and then jewelry. In the 1920s, he became the president of the Trinity Packaging Company, and when Prohibition was repealed, he became the treasurer of Northwest Distillers and began financing seafood canneries.[8] He was a benefactor of Herzl's Congregation Synagogue, among many other Jewish organizations. Carl and Dora had a son, Sam (nicknamed Sonny), and a daughter, Rose, who were both a few years older than Ruth.

Ruth recounted a family story that probably occurred before she came to Seattle. Her mother's famous cousin, Helena Rubinstein, had visited Seattle in 1934 to open one of her salons there.[9] It might have been during this visit that she asked Carl what business he was in. As it was told to Ruth, he replied, "the salmon business," and Helena said, "Oh, isn't that kind of smelly?" Ruth goes on: "And he looked straight at her and said, 'So's yours.'"[10]

Carl and Chaja's brother, Abraham, had also moved to Seattle in 1916. Abe married a Russian woman named Lenore and had a son, Marvin, who also went by the name Scott. Abe did not join Carl in his businesses but instead worked as a salesman in men's clothing. Members of the family later remember Abe as quiet and scholarly, and he often gave books as presents to his nieces and nephews.[11]

Another brother, Leo, came to Seattle from Leipzig in 1937, an event that Ruth had written about in her diary. Like his brother Carl, Leo was married to a woman named Dora, with whom he had four children who by 1940 had scattered throughout Seattle, Palestine, and Germany.[12] Only their youngest, David, had come to live with them in Seattle. They lived in an apartment on Howell Street, just north of Seattle's Jewish neighborhood.[13] Carl Rubinstein and his family lived in a large house in the Montlake neighborhood. Ruth noted in her diary that on the train from New York to Seattle, she was told she would live not with Carl, as she had expected, but with Leo. She wrote, "If I am being honest, it was nevertheless a very little bit unpleasant."[14]

She had good reason to feel apprehensive. She wrote of Leo's wife, Dora, just a few weeks after she arrived in Seattle:

> From the beginning, she explained to me that <u>even</u> with an Aunt I was not at home. As if I had left my parents behind in Germany with pleasure in order to travel towards "happiness" on my own. Even in Zurich, at someone else's house they said to me: we hope that you feel like you are at home with us. Because the question now was about school, she clearly and precisely made me understand that I could not perch there at her expense and lead a pleasant life, I had to make myself self-reliant and independent as quickly as possible in order to be my own mistress.[15]

Ruth did not find much camaraderie with her cousins either. She liked her cousin Sam, who reminded her of Roger Garfunkel from Zurich. But David, whom she had grown up with in Leipzig, always acted superior toward her. David's son, Michael, stated that his father had long regretted coming to Seattle with his parents and wished he had moved to Palestine with his brother and sister instead.[16] Ruth wrote in her diary that David's mind-set, developed in the Zionist youth groups of Leipzig, made it difficult for him to adjust to Seattle. Rose pointedly excluded Ruth from her circle of friends. Both Sam and Rose were born and raised in Seattle's assimilated Jewish culture. Although they had come of age in the Depression, their father had done well and they had plenty of money to spend on clothes, cars, club memberships, and outdoor activities. Ruth's foreign accent and awkwardness probably embarrassed them, and she was fully aware that she didn't fit in: "I know that I must appear very funny to Rose and Sam here, I can't dance, can't play tennis, don't ride, don't drive a car. Would like to know what they think about me."[17] Near the end of her life, she remembered what seemed like a petty complaint of Rose's at the time, especially compared to what

Ruth had experienced in Germany: "One cousin's biggest unhappinesses . . . she couldn't join the fashionable Christian golf club . . . she had to join Glendale, the Jewish Club!"[18] Even though it might have been easier for her to have lived with Carl's family instead, Ruth was wary of their bourgeois lifestyle: "If I lived with the other Rubinsteins, I would certainly have painted myself up if only in order to look like the others. But in any case, what I do not want to have happen is to become different over time. If I become just like the others I at least want to be conscious of it. Today wearing heels, tomorrow having my nails done, one week later smoking, etc. Either or!!!"[19]

Because Leo made significantly less money than Carl, Ruth was a financial burden on this branch of the family, although it appears that Carl paid for Ruth's new clothing, including a fur coat. Leo's wife complained to Ruth that she had been forced to financially support Ruth's maternal grandfather and her mother in Leipzig and now had to support Ruth in Seattle. Her resentment was impossible to ignore. Ruth wrote:

> Since the first day I have been here I have known that as soon as Aunt saw me she thought: Ruth is here, I have to care for her, and it will be good for her here, and my children have to work hard in Palestine and for a long time have not had the things that they have needed the most, and none of my relatives are here, everything is going poorly for them. Moreover, she must always think: why didn't she stay at her Uncle Rappaport's in Brooklyn? She has often spoken only of that with me, and if she doesn't say it, she constantly lets me feel it.
>
> Hopefully no one will ever read my diary.[20]

Ruth wondered if she had made a mistake in coming to Seattle. Would she have fared better moving to Palestine to live with Mirjam or staying in New York with the Rappaports? At times even remaining with her parents in Leipzig seemed preferable to the pain and exclusion she felt in Seattle.[21]

Chapter 9

Ruth returned to school as a junior at Broadway High School, which enrolled other young German Jewish refugees and a large Japanese population as well.[1] She was irritated that she had missed so much school. After repeating a year of school in Leipzig and losing a year in Zurich, she felt old compared to the other students in her grade, even though they may have been at or near her age, sixteen. She considered whether she should go to a trade school after earning her diploma and wanted to ask Sam how he had graduated high school early. She complained about the large amount of homework she had every night but also noted it was easy.

In January 1940 Ruth wrote that she had already failed three civics assignments and wondered if it was because she was still struggling with English. If she was struggling, she didn't remember it that way in her oral history: "I passed every single [English] college course, high school, and college entrance by exam. The only thing I couldn't pass was Shakespeare."[2] Perhaps with distance she didn't remember how she struggled with English or just didn't want to admit it. Ruth still preferred to write in German in her diary, which she kept regularly until the end of 1942.

She soon came to realize that her earlier interest in Socialism and Communism, or at least in discussing it in an intellectual sense, was out of fashion at Broadway High School. She observed, "In school we are now talking about Communism, and I have such a funny feeling when I hear the others speak about it so disdainfully. At the moment, I myself know too little about it in order to be able to judge."[3] This last statement seems disingenuous considering that in 1939 she claimed that her friends in Hashomer Hatzair in Zurich were impressed with her knowledge of Communism and current politics, but perhaps she was referring to the specifics of the American Communist movement.

Ruth maintained her instinct for social activism in Seattle: "The first thing that happened when I came to Seattle, Washington—I heard about fair housing. And I don't think I'd been in Seattle more than a month and I trooped off to the state capitol, demonstrating for fair housing."[4] As African Americans streamed into the city for jobs at shipyards related to the war buildup, they faced restrictive covenants and quotas in public housing. The local branches of the Urban League and the National Association for the Advancement of Colored People grew exponentially during the early 1940s and relied on help from the Jewish Anti-Defamation League.[5] She probably became involved in this protest either through Herzl's Congregation Synagogue or a local Jewish group, or perhaps she had read about it in the newspaper.

Ruth looked into joining organizations where she hoped to make new friends, but she was pessimistic. She anxiously waited for letters from friends she had met in Leipzig and Zurich (some of whom were now in the United States) and wondered if she would ever have friends like them again. She made plans to attend a German club but remarked that she knew she would feel cold toward the other members.[6] She also wanted to go to Sunday school at the Talmud Torah, Seattle's only Hebrew school. After attending a Zionist lecture with her cousin David and uncle Leo, she wrote that only a few other young people were there, but at the end of the meeting the group had decided to start a Zionist youth organization. She was unclear what her role would be and wondered whether this would be a true Zionist bund, since she doubted that anyone else in Seattle wanted to immigrate to Palestine.

But she enjoyed meeting the other girls who were interested in starting the group, especially Hilde Schocken, who was a few years older than Ruth and had grown up in Bremerhaven, Germany, and spent the past year in Switzerland before immigrating to the US at the end of 1939.[7] It is unclear if this group actually got started, and if so, what it was called, but later in the summer of 1940 Ruth joined the local chapter of Junior Hadassah, a Zionist women's group.

In January 1940 Ruth's cousin Rose announced her engagement to Julius Jacobs, known as Jay.[8] Ruth did not understand why the Rubinsteins opposed the marriage. Little did they know that he would later own Jay Jacobs, a successful national chain of clothing stores for teenagers. Ruth was concerned about the upcoming wedding because she did not own an appropriate dress to wear for the occasion and would have to ask for one. She also didn't know how to dance and agonized over whether she should try to learn beforehand. For her there was one possible upside to the wedding: Rose would move out of her parents' house, freeing up a bedroom. Perhaps Carl and Dora would then ask her to live with them. Ruth had apparently decided she could overlook their bourgeois tendencies. Ruth reported a month later, "It was a wonderful wedding. I should have tried to dance, I certainly would have been able to do it. There were certainly enough people there who wanted to dance with me."[9]

Ruth constantly worried about her parents and sisters because she heard so infrequently from them. Even when she received a letter after her first two months in the US, she felt unsettled:

> Yesterday I finally got mail from my parents. Everything seems so bleak to me. Poor Papa is sick again. I am so afraid for him. I do not think I will see my parents in America. 1. because of the war and 2. because of the laws.

It is so frightfully far away, because everything seems so bleak to me.

I don't know, here I have everything I need so far, I know where I am living, go to the school, have clothing, am busy here, safe from the war and from the police, and yet I have never been so unhappy as here. I felt much happier in Switzerland.[10]

She soon realized that her uncles probably would not be able to help her parents get out of Germany, and she conveyed to them that she understood "the circumstances" and that "they can't help anything and have other cares."[11] But, thinking of how her own family was no doubt suffering in Europe, she seethed whenever she saw her uncles spend lavishly on clothing, trips, or weddings for their children. In April 1940 her sister Clara had a baby, Guy, in Paris. When Ruth found out sometime later, she worried even more about how her sister's family would survive in France. Even though Dora bought many new things for her, Ruth clung to what she had brought from Germany: "It is funny that the things that Aunt Dora buys are costlier, more beautiful, and better than the things that I brought with me and in part cannot wear. But nevertheless, I keep them, because I know they are from my parents and because I have always had them with me."[12]

Ruth's anxiety about her parents and her loneliness in Seattle began to affect her ability to concentrate or to spend her time productively. She wrote:

I have never dawdled around so much as I did now. I sat there for a long time and did nothing, or something dumb and useless, but didn't sit there for a long time reading or doing something sensible. That means, I am getting better at reading, and am also getting up earlier than I did at the beginning, but I am not spending the time well. Even when I read I sometimes read the words on the page, but not their sense.[13]

Reading had always been her escape. English novels were more cumbersome than she was used to, but once she got over this hump, she returned to her old "ferocious" pace. In 1941 she noted that for school she had been reading Pearl S. Buck's *The Exile*—a memoir with a feminist tone—which was about Buck's mother and the sacrifices she made to be a missionary wife in China. Ruth also described her difficulties writing an essay for a school assignment about a book that had been very special to her:

> This week in English with Miss Ohlson, we had to write an essay and I wrote about the book that I will never forget, I chose Rachel's poems. Before I started I thought that I wouldn't be able to write something worthwhile about a book, as it's more something I feel than analyze. And because I have an emotional history with these poems and know about "Rachel's" background, and the poems sometimes vocalize what I am feeling in such simple but wonderful language, I thought it would be too sentimental/idealistic for an essay in an American school. But I thought we won't have to read it out loud and Miss Ohlson will maybe like it because it is so different from all the other essays. But to my horror, she gave the essays to the class to correct and evaluate, and of course no one was interested in my essay, plus the fact, and maybe I should be happy about this, that probably nobody could actually read it.[14]

"Rachel's poems" were written by Ra'hel Bluwstein, the first famous woman poet in Israel. An immigrant from Russia, she suffered from tuberculosis and wrote much of her poetry in the last years of her life before she died in 1931. They were published under only her first name in the Israeli newspaper *Davar* and became very popular, especially among Jewish women. Her poems had first been published in German in 1936, when Ruth was thirteen; perhaps they were first recommended to Ruth by someone in her Habonim youth group. Rachel's poems are known for their simplicity, because they were written in Hebrew, a language Bluwstein struggled to learn, and address topics such as forbidden love, biblical figures, the land of Israel, and her love of nature.[15]

Ruth probably went frequently to the Seattle Public Library, both its main downtown location and the Yesler branch in Seattle's Jewish neighborhood. The main library, a large, beautiful Beaux-Arts building, was built in 1906 with money from Andrew Carnegie, who was donating his fortune to the construction of new library buildings across the country at the time. During the Depression, the Seattle library and its branches were teeming with unemployed men, while budget cuts forced the libraries to scale back their hours and book purchases. In 1932, librarian Natalie Notkin, head of the foreign books division and a Russian immigrant, was fired for supposedly offering Communist books in Russian. Notkin was offered a job at the University of Washington libraries, where she worked for the next thirty years, but the foreign books division of the public library suffered in her absence. Luckily, by the end of the 1930s, the library system had received funding from New Deal programs and a new Friends of the Seattle Public Library organization, both of which helped the library system hire more staff, buy more books, and paint its aging main building. However, with the onset of the war, ordering books from Europe became virtually impossible.[16]

Although German books would have been relatively scarce in Seattle, Ruth was part of a network of other German refugees who lent each other books. She traded and discussed books with Mrs. Sarkowsky, a family friend of the Rubinsteins who had left Germany in 1934. Ruth wrote about how much she enjoyed reading the American novel *What*

Makes Sammy Run. Written by Budd Schulburg, the book is a caution-
ary tale about a young Jewish man from New York who achieves success as a Hollywood screenwriter through backstabbing and plagiarism.
As Ruth became more fluent in English, she gained access to a whole
new genre: the American Jewish novel. These books often addressed
European immigration, refugees, and anti-Semitism—issues that Ruth
herself faced daily—against the backdrop of assimilated Jews' dramatic
rise to success in the United States. When she lived in Leipzig and
Zurich, she had found comfort in reading about the struggles of Jews
in Europe; in Seattle, she would seek out books by and about American
Jews, in hopes of making sense of her new situation.

Ruth enjoyed going to the movies too, another form of escapism
that also helped her learn English. She mentioned seeing *Tevya* with
her aunt Dora, uncle Carl, and the Sarkowskys, their friends. This film
was an early version of *Fiddler on the Roof*, and it sparked something
deep inside her:

> It was the first time that I sobbed watching a film in several
> years. But I could really empathize with everything that I
> saw. I know that it is a film taken from real life. A typical
> Jewish tragic film. An old story.

> When I saw the film, I automatically thought of a book—
> "Der Pojaz—Carl Emil Franzos."

> The Jewish girl Hawa, and Fedja, the Muschik, loved each
> other soo much, they both read a lot—Gorky—and yet
> there was something like a wall between them—something
> that I think destroys all mixed marriages. [17]

That night, she also saw a Palestinian film called *The Land of Promise*. It brought back memories of her life in Zionist youth groups and led her to question what exactly she was doing in the United States:

> I felt like I was back in my old element—marching, uniforms, Jesus sandals, tents!!!! And yet how far away I am from everything—

> red nails

> red lips

> high heels

> finger waves!!!![18]

> All the pretend, fake, dumb social aspirations!!!

> If I would be happier in Erez, [Palestine,] I don't know! Can people ever be content?[19]

Chapter 10

Over the summer of 1940, Ruth moved into her uncle Carl's home on Montlake Boulevard, as she had hoped she would. At some point in 1940, Sonny married Gladys Seidenverg, leaving Ruth as the only one living with Carl and Dora. Although she felt her life was improving, she also felt unease with her other aunt Dora. Ruth pointed out that this aunt was prejudiced against Germans, having emigrated directly from Poland decades earlier.[1] Although Ruth was not a German citizen, the fact that she had been born and raised there marked her as a German in Dora's eyes. Ruth felt increasingly awkward and as if everything she did was wrong. Whether she stayed in her room and read or offered to help around the house, either choice was wrong. She agonized about having friends over and how to introduce them to her aunt. Even trying to decide whether they would eat in the kitchen or bring food up to her room filled Ruth with dread.[2]

In October she heard from her parents that they were considering immigrating to Shanghai. Ruth knew this would not likely happen, but she also felt that they would "feel very lost" if they came to America. In November the Interclub Council hosted a special dinner for Seattle's high school girls who were from Europe, and Ruth attended. Starting to feel more welcome in the city by her one-year anniversary of living in the US, Ruth wrote:

I have already been here for over a year, but nevertheless how I have changed. In school I am already at home, know many people with whom I chat, boys and girls, behave relatively freely, and thus as if I had always been here, and I gladly belong here. On the outside there is no more difference between me and the other kids, but forever? I myself do not know![3]

Ruth graduated from Broadway High School in June 1941. She was disappointed that the Rubinsteins did not host a party for her, but Sam gave her a nice fountain pen. Her grades had not improved over the year and a half she was a student there. During her last semester, she took courses to prepare for careers appropriate for a woman in the early 1940s, including bookkeeping, shorthand, and typing. Her senior yearbook is full of good wishes from friends she had made at Broadway, an indication that Ruth had indeed made an effort to come out of her shell. Across her photograph, Ruth had signed her name but then blacked it out. Her activities were "Restroom Committee" and "Friendship Representative."[4]

After graduation, Ruth enrolled at Seattle's Metropolitan Business College, and Carl paid for her tuition. She finished courses in accounting and stenography quickly, in half the usual time. She also acquired an apprenticeship at a law firm called Dillon and Carney, where she worked about one hour a day. She aspired to get a full-time job as soon as possible in order to send money to her parents. She knew they had lost everything and was not going to count on the Rubinsteins to send them anything. That summer she read an article in *Life* magazine about Helena Rubinstein. Ruth wrote that it was "about how she worked her way up, how she now lives, about her character, and that she has twenty-five million dollars. It seems entirely impossible, but nevertheless she is Mother's cousin."[5] As Ruth was starting out her own career from the bottom, she had at least one role model in Helena, both a woman and a relative.

The longer she lived in Seattle, the more Ruth became determined to be financially independent as soon as possible. Staying with the Rubinsteins long term was not an option, but how could she earn a living, and where would she go? Much of her optimism the previous year had vanished by the fall of 1941. She wrote:

I have simply had enough of living with Uncle and Aunt. I know that I have it really good here, that I have a nice room, eat well, can in theory, at least, do what I want. I have better clothes than many other people, am going to school, and can pay for books, and nevertheless I am not happy. As long as I am dependent upon Uncle, I will not feel free…

And it makes me so dreadfully sad. There goes Rose, making a friendly face towards her mother and getting a house for ten thousand dollars, and with Uncle helping her with five thousand dollars, of which he had promised a few thousand to help my parents out of the hell in Germany. No, he says, he doesn't have any more money.

Is it any wonder, then, if I am becoming harsh and indifferent, and secretive and cold. Mirjam and her husband in Palestine with hardly anything to eat. [Salomon] when he is still living in a concentration camp in France. [Clara] and her child with not enough to eat. My parents in Germany. Should I then be happy when Aunt is so merciful and buys me a slip (which I don't like and which she bought on sale)![6]

She believed that Carl's wife had an ulterior motive when she bought new clothes for her: "The way Aunt outfitted me, I realized how much I seemed like an overdressed cow which someone is sending to market. I had the definite feeling that she hopes that I will get a 'boyfriend' if I am better dressed!!!!"[7] Dora assumed that the only way Ruth would ever move out of the house would be through marriage, but Ruth had no interest in marrying, at least not at this point in her life: "I know that Aunt hopes that I will soon get married and leave her house for good—and if I also felt as I now do that might happen—but it isn't what I want—<u>I want to be free</u> and not to go into a new imprisonment—and that is how I now feel and therefore I don't know what I will now do."[8] How Ruth came to this conclusion about marriage at age nineteen is somewhat of a mystery, but regardless, she knew she would not compromise in her firm belief that marriage was not a way out of her unhappy situation. In the meantime she rebelled by staying out late with friends (including Gentiles, of which her aunt disapproved), drinking, and smoking, a habit that would soon develop into a multiple-packs-a-day and nearly lifelong addiction.

In March 1941 Carl gave $700 to the Washington Émigré Bureau, an organization in Seattle founded by Jews to help European refugees, to facilitate Ruth's parents' immigration to Seattle through the Transmigration Bureau, a national organization that facilitated the transportation costs for Jews trying to leave Europe.[9] The money was refunded, however, in November when it became clear that the organization could be of no assistance. On December 3, Ruth wrote in her diary that Carl was going to put up $600 to help her parents obtain visas to Cuba. He paid the Dickstein law firm in Washington, DC, as Ruth remembered it later.[10] She wrote in her diary, "Hopefully it is not too late. So many ships have already come that I am losing hope that everything will turn out well."[11]

Unfortunately, Ruth's fears came true. As she explained in her oral history so many years later, "December seventh killed it all." The day after the Japanese bombed Pearl Harbor, she wrote, "Today Japan declared war. What before was unthinkable has happened. . . . No hope of ever seeing my parents again—truly the greatest joy has gone out of my life—while what lies in front of me is only a cursed, unhappy, and hard fate." The night before, she had gone out dancing with a man named Bert Lang and the Sarkowskys' sons. She and Bert, whose parents were also in Germany, consoled each other. She speculated, "Who knows, perhaps tomorrow America and Japan will be at war with one another and I will be sent to Japan as number 287342 with many other people or someplace else, to return not at all or as a cripple."[12]

A few days later, when the United States entered the war in Europe, Ruth was not only fearful but also outraged and numb:

Now practically the entire world is involved in the war. Mass murder without end! And nevertheless, I have the feeling that many people like the excitement and the sensation and feel particularly well when they feel like martyrs and can feel sorry for themselves.

Since Sunday I have been going downhill with the boredom—I don't have any close friends, walk around like a sleepwalker—and I am so frightfully indifferent about everything.

I constantly see my parents' tedious, hopeless life in front of me, no longer a hope that they will get out of Germany—Cuba declared war on Germany today. They are probably hearing only outrageous stories from here on the radio and are very, very, dismayed. I am afraid that I soon won't have any parents anymore, because if it isn't a bomb it will be illness as well as the living conditions in Germany that will take them.[13]

During the winter, even though the world was in turmoil, life seemed to go on in Seattle as if it were untouched by the war, which only made Ruth angrier. Hanukkah and New Year's celebrations went on as planned, but Ruth didn't see any reason to celebrate. If anything, America's entry into the war steeled her resolve to find a job, move out of the Rubinsteins' house, and achieve real independence. In February 1942 Ruth reported on her new job at the Sun Vacuums Store in Seattle:

> I have had my position for 4 weeks as of tomorrow, and I feel rather important, because I came into what you might call a "responsible position"—that is, if one looks experienced—but most of all, I enjoy my work—and I don't have any time to let myself get bored, because my work is so manifold, and I actually do the work of 3 people. I have fun acting as bookkeeper, secretary, cashier, and telephone girl.[14]

She enjoyed getting to know her new boss and coworkers, who welcomed her into the business and invited her out to dinner. However, Ruth was uneasy with some incidents she observed at the store. She noted that the customers frequently lied, which made her uncomfortable, but she aimed to find the courage to speak up about it. Furthermore, she didn't think that the store was necessarily doing anything illegal, but something about her boss, Goldie, reminded her of the con-men types who had come to the restaurant where her mother worked in Leipzig.

She summed up how much she had changed since moving to America, finishing school, and landing her first job:

> When I looked at myself through "German eyes" I feel very low.

1. I smoke too much
2. I have a crazy modern hairdo
3. I wear fake jewelry[15]

Even though she enjoyed her new job, she knew it wasn't satisfying and that she couldn't work there long term. A few months later she wrote of her ambitions for the future:

> I am always dreaming about doing something with my life, but I am lacking a plan. Today I had the thought that I would like to become a libraryan [sic]. If I can summon up enough energy to work for this, and to use the money that I earn better, perhaps I could take a course in "library work"! [...] I don't want to spend my entire life in a vacuum cleaner business.[16]

Clearly, both the Zurich and Seattle public libraries had left a lasting imprint on her. When she visited to pick up books or to read and lounge in a space that was not one of her uncles' homes, she must have noticed and admired the librarians there. They would have been single, educated women, and perhaps they exuded a sense of satisfaction with their work. This dream would not become a reality for Ruth for another seventeen years, but the seeds were planted when she was eighteen years old, if not earlier. In this same diary entry, Ruth listed her eleven goals to improve herself, including "to speak more concisely and precisely" in English and "to do some intellectual work and to read serious books." She concluded:

> To become my own person and to keep my sights on what
> is written in my poetry album:
>
> > Your life is your battle,
> > Your peace a victory.[17]

More than a year earlier, on New Year's Day 1941, Ruth had decided that she wanted a boyfriend who would take her out dancing. She wrote, "Rationally, I am still against an American 'boyfriend,' but emotionally I long for one."[18] Although she chafed at her aunt's efforts to send her "off to market," Ruth started going on dates but was not seriously interested in any one boy. She still pined for Roger and wondered what he was up to in Zurich. One of her first dates in Seattle was with a man named Larry, a double date set up by her friend Mila so they could all go to Seattle's Russian Ball. Ruth knew that he was a Christian and married, and she tried to mumble his name when introducing him to her aunt and uncle so they would not suspect he wasn't Jewish. By 1942 she was not at all seriously interested in Larry, but the experience made her think about Christian men differently and question the stereotypes she had acquired about them:

> Sometimes I have asked myself whether I would go out with young Christian men—and I thought now—because I have always imagined Christian boys to be only rougher, coarser [...] rather brutal and backward—full of male intentions, simply a Goy—without Jewish background— and when I saw Larry Fealham, 100% Aryan—how did I like him? Better than most Jewish young men—how determined he was—simply wonderful. I simply do not think that the Jews are better.[19]

Ruth explained how she was sexually harassed at least a few times. She met the brother of a Mrs. Schneider, Kurt Hamlet, who asked her out to dinner. She described how he groped her on this date, but she resisted and left. She fumed, "If he needs a whore, he should go downtown and buy one for money."[20] Mrs. Sarkowsky's husband, Irving, also groped Ruth. She wrote:

Mr. Sarkowsky—a married man with 3 sons—every time he can get me alone he takes me in his arms and presses me to him so hard that I am afraid he is going to break my entire body, and then he tries to kiss me—and to pass his thick hands under my dress—it has already happened 2 times, and I do not know what I should do—because it happens only when I am alone at home—and he is so strong that I can't do anything about it—and he is also such a good friend to Uncle and Aunt—if they only knew how he bothers me—and his wife—she is an example of a fine lady—and I hate him more than I do anyone else.[21]

But Ruth dated several other men who greatly respected her, and she enjoyed spending time with them. When she met Felix Gruenthal, another émigré from Germany, she was surprised to learn that he also had spent time in Zurich and had even known the Herzogs, the second family she had stayed with. Ruth wrote of when they first met, "Strange, how it sometimes goes—you speak 2 or 3 words and feel like old friends." They had a "European evening," as she put it, filled with interesting conversation but no necking.[22] After a few dates, she invited him home to meet her aunt and uncle and observed, "Funny, everyone thinks that Felix is my 'boyfriend' and that I am his 'girlfriend'—and that we are 'going out' together. And the strangest part of the entire thing is that everyone—boys and girls, as soon as they know that you have a 'boyfriend' they behave entirely differently towards you."[23] But she was certainly willing to admit, "I like him a lot!"

Young men and women were streaming into Seattle, both as workers for war industry jobs (especially at Boeing, which was building new bomber airplanes), and as newly enlisted troops waiting to ship out to the Pacific. Ruth's friends from Germany had to obey the new curfew, but because Ruth had her Romanian passport, she was not classified as a suspicious alien.[24] The young people she had met in high school and at

Herzl's Congregation Synagogue were now scattering across the country and the world. Her cousin Sam left to join the Army Air Forces and would become a second lieutenant specializing in bombsight maintenance in the Pacific.[25] Ruth went to dances at the USO and took photographs with men in their uniforms. In one group of poignant photos from April 1943, she and a friend, Esther Lowinger, goofed around among the cherry blossoms of Green Lake Park with Esther's husband, named Richard, and Mike Perlgut, both in uniform.

Although dances and parties could distract her sometimes, the reality of the war hit home each time she listened to the news on the radio or read in *Hadassah Magazine* of the atrocities committed against Jews. And even though she had fled the Nazis as a persecuted Jew, she still was saddened by the news that America and England were now bombing Germany. She wrote in anger:

> My entire life strikes me as being so false—everyone so deceitful—how can an educated person rejoice that England bombed Cologne—the city of Cologne didn't want the war—it is the people who wanted war—it simply pains me to see the city walls destroyed—"fighting" for the country naturally, I would say that the United States has won—but it seems such a waste and so senseless, there must be another way out from this chaos—I simply can't condone the war my parents are suffering in Germany— Papa's sisters in Poland and Romania, Clara, Salomon, and Guy in France, my sister in Palestine, and I sit here every day afraid that I will get news that they are already dead.[26]

Chapter 11

The summer of 1942 would bring new opportunities that would both energize Ruth and give her some solace. Two years earlier she had joined Junior Hadassah, a division of Hadassah, the Zionist group founded by the American Jewish woman Henrietta Szold. A worldwide organization, Hadassah (also known as the Women's Zionist Organization of America) initially raised money for the Hadassah Hospital in Palestine but soon branched out to provide funds for immigration to the country, the American war effort in World War II, and educational opportunities for Jews worldwide. Ruth became more involved in Junior Hadassah when the West Coast division of the group held a conference in Seattle in July. Ruth was selected convention chairwoman and planned much of the conference. She gave the welcome speech at the Friday night dinner at the Benjamin Franklin Hotel and introduced the invited speaker, Dr. James, who spoke on racism and anti-Semitism and encouraged attendees to think hard about their own prejudices. But more importantly that night, Ruth was reunited with a rabbi she had met years ago, when her Habonim group in Leipzig had taken a trip to the neighboring town of Gera. For the Habonim group, it was the first time these teenagers had "met a rabbi who was strong, Zionist, and understood the problems of young people."[1]

This rabbi was Fritz Cohn, but he now went by the name Franklin. After his stint in Gera, he had lived in Berlin for three years, trying to help Jewish children get out of Germany. In 1939, with his wife and two-year-old daughter, he escaped to New York, where he lived with his brother and sold ties until he found a position at a synagogue in Walla Walla.[2] Rabbi Cohn spoke at the conference that weekend and inspired the West Coast women of Junior Hadassah with his songs (some of which Ruth remembered from Gera), humor, and deep belief in Zionism. Later he helped the women write their resolutions and gave a special speech for the new officers, which included Ruth. She had just been elected the Pacific-coast regional secretary and the treasurer of the Seattle branch.[3]

Two weeks later, Ruth explained how this convention dramatically changed her life:

> When I then became "Convention Chairwoman," I really hoped that I would meet more people that way. But I was entirely overwhelmed with how many people I really got to meet!
>
> 1. I know many more people than I did before and if you asked other people what they thought of me it would be "she is an active girl, good worker, ran the convention," etc.
>
> 2. Although it is just a small thing, and I shouldn't pay much attention to it, it nevertheless doesn't make any difference. I saw my picture in the newspaper, which naturally amounts to a lot of people having respect for me— and not to go on being as disrespected as I was before, rather more, should I say, "personality" or a small "big shot." The whole change in my current "social life" is in part probably due to this mention of me and also my having changed somewhat. I step out more self-confidently, am not as timid, talk to everyone and do things as if I know what I am doing.[4]

Just before the conference, Ruth's uncle Carl had asked Ruth if she had heard of a Rabbi Franklin Cohn. Looking back on the strange coincidence, she explained:

> One of my uncles was the President of the Conservative Synagogue…. and their rabbi was leaving and they were looking for a replacement. This is where it gets funny…. uncle comes home one night for dinner and asks me if while in Germany had I ever heard of a Rabbi Franklin Cohn! I nearly laughed in his face…. nothing seemed funnier at the time than to think of a German Jewish Rabbi to be named Franklin…. however, common sense took over and I suggested he ask the applicant if his name was Fritz Cohn and if he ever had a congregation in a little town not far from Leipzig called Gera. It so happened, as a ten-year-old I was impressed with a Rabbi Fritz Cohn, you won't believe this, because he rode a bicycle…. and he used to take some of us kids on Sunday morning bicycle trips instead of having Sunday school! And lo and behold…. yes indeed…. he was the guy who applied for the vacancy and obviously, how could uncle resist my good common sense and my persuasive powers…. and he got the job![5]

Ruth was thrilled that Franklin would now be the rabbi of Herzl's Congregation Synagogue. Less than a year earlier, she had described her disgust with the former rabbi and synagogue leadership: "I simply could not understand how these grownups could stand up and speak in front of 300 people about a God in which I haven't believed in 10 years and then speak praises and bless each other, and tell people who have absolutely no clue to stand up and say something in order to seem important."[6]

Cohn would soon become a mentor and a father figure. He seemed to be the only adult in Seattle who really understood her. Ruth confided in him about how sad she was that she didn't fit in with the Rubinsteins, especially her aunt Dora: "I told Rabbi Cohn all the things that are going on with me. It could be good—and it could be not so good—in any case, if anyone can understand me, it is Cohn—and if I can speak openly to anyone, it's also him."[7] Less than two weeks later, she wrote about how nice it was that her aunt was being friendlier. She asked Cohn if he had spoken to her, and indeed he had. Ruth wrote, "In any case, it seems to have helped! Who knows for how long?"[8]

Hillel Cohn, Franklin's son, who also later became a rabbi, was just two years old when his family moved to Seattle, but he has vivid memories of Ruth. He recalls that she used to come over to the house frequently for dinners and holidays, often with a group of German Jews who grew even closer during the war. At the request of Rabbi Cohn, Ruth started teaching Sunday school even though she felt she was unqualified. Hillel recounted a notorious story about his older sister, Aviva, who was assigned to Ruth's class. When Ruth chastised her, a rabbi's daughter, for her bad behavior, Aviva slapped Ruth across the face. Hillel is happy to report that Aviva eventually outgrew her infamous stubborn streak. Hillel and the Cohn family remained in touch with Ruth until she died.[9]

Through her work in Junior Hadassah, Ruth found a tight circle of female friends. The president of the branch, Shirley Berliner, and Ida Fink, who had been president in 1937, took Ruth under their wing and invited her out with other members to eat at restaurants downtown, where they often talked about Hadassah until after midnight. She described one of the organization's meetings: "On Sunday morning Shirley Berliner had about 20 girls to breakfast to talk about the Hadassah. As it turned out, girls who don't come to meetings come when they are invited to breakfast. And if you sit next to them, you can inspire enough enthusiasm and strength of will. We had met what you could almost call a successful leader."[10] Although on the surface she was starting to feel comfortable with these new friends, her emotions underneath were roiling:

It makes no difference how funny I am in company here or how good my "company" is and how much fun we have together—as soon as I think back to my time in the Bund—I feel my old wounds deeply—and I feel foreign here although I have "friends"—and I know that many people like me and have consideration for me—I perform for them—and no one notices that it is "done" and isn't natural. I often feel ready to stop and start bawling—but I don't think that anyone would believe it [...] but after a short time one begins to live the role and becomes a different person until it's no longer just an imagining—that's how it goes with me!!![11]

With her job, her commitment to Junior Hadassah, and a full slate of other Jewish-related activities, Ruth was extremely busy, which she previously noted meant she didn't have time for writing in her diary. When she last wrote of Felix at the end of September 1942, she described her ambivalence toward him: "What disturbs me is that he is so steady—never overjoyed, never angry . . . I simply can't tolerate mediocrity—either good or bad—witty—happy or sad—for my entire life I have avoided 'the golden middle'—and here I can find a perfect example."[12] In her appointment book on October 4, she wrote: "Felix left on Coventry."[13]

In November the Seattle branch of Junior Hadassah started a study group under Rabbi Cohn's tutelage. Meeting bimonthly, the group learned basic Hebrew and about Jewish history, culture, literature, as well as the role of Palestine to protect Jews fleeing Europe now and in the future.[14] While this group would have added even more meetings to Ruth's busy schedule, she enjoyed the opportunity to learn from Rabbi Cohn and show off her own rigorous knowledge of Jewish and European writers she had studied since childhood. Because Ruth was not attending college, this class surely filled an intellectual hole in her life.

Over the next few years, Ruth would have many different jobs, some of them part-time. After Sun Vacuums, she worked at the Washington Quilt Company, which made sleeping bags.[15] With a new government contract to produce them for the military, the company was hiring many new employees. She had heard about an opening as a secretary at a local Zionist organization.[16] This would have been her dream job, she admitted, but her family would not have approved of this line of work, and it was too late to apply anyway. In the meantime she would settle for earning money in businesses where she didn't really see a future for herself in the long term.

Although the war prevented any substantial communication between Ruth and her parents, they sent brief messages through the Red Cross. In October 1942, Ruth wrote: "Everybody here well and sending regards to you. Thanks for your letter of early fall. Please let me hear from you soon."[17] They responded the following January: "Letter delighted. New apartment Gustav-Adolph-Strasse 7. Great longing to come to you. Undertaking all possibilities."[18] This address was Ruth's Jewish high school, which had been converted into an incarceration center for Jews, known as a *Judenhäuser*.[19] According to Leipzig's city directories, Ruth's family's apartment was vacant for about a year but was later occupied in 1943 by a family named Meier. What exactly happened to her family's furniture and belongings is unknown, but Jewish property across Germany was confiscated and distributed to German citizens as a vehicle to establish their loyalty to the Nazi state. Around 1942 Chaja became a forced laborer for the Leipzig fur company owned by Alfred Kielert.[20] In April 1943 they sent the last surviving letter to Ruth, informing her that they had moved yet again to Packhofstrasse.[21] The same month, *The Transcript*, Seattle's local Jewish newspaper (formerly titled the *Jewish Transcript*), featured an article on the front page about the recent statement from the Inter-Allied Information Committee that Jews in Europe faced certain extermination in 1943.[22] Although her concern for them surely grew as they were forced to move around Leipzig and she read increasingly terrifying news, Ruth channeled her energy into her Zionist work. If she couldn't directly help her parents or sisters in any concrete way, at least she could contribute to current efforts to assist Jewish refugees and build the new Jewish homeland, where hopefully in the future they could all meet again.

On May 19, 1943, all the endless meetings, fundraising, dances, and seminars paid off for Ruth when she was elected president of Seattle's Junior Hadassah. In *The Transcript* she made a brief statement about her plan for the year: "'Twice as much in wartime,' the national slogan for [J]unior Hadassah workers, will be stressed here, Miss Rappaport stated, adding that there will be no summer recess in the work of the group, but that dances, picnics, fundraising affairs and study groups will be continued throughout the year."[23] Her photograph appeared in *The Transcript* in June along with an announcement of the installation ceremony for the new officers. Just a few weeks later, *The Transcript* announced that the Junior Hadassah branch was being placed on the national roll of honor for fulfilling and exceeding all its fundraising quotas over the past year.[24]

Ruth had big shoes to fill, but she was up to the task. In addition to being elected president of Junior Hadassah, she was elected in the summer of 1943 as president of the Seattle Zionist Youth Commission. This appears to have been an umbrella group that coordinated events among Seattle's various Zionist youth groups, which had proliferated during the war. The first event she planned as president for both groups was a youth breakfast with Judge Louis Levinthal, national president of the Zionist Organization of America, one of many events held in his honor while he visited Seattle.[25]

Since May the national president of Junior Hadassah, Naomi Chertoff, had wanted to visit the West Coast to check up on the growing branches there.[26] Ruth got to work planning many events for Chertoff's Seattle visit. A letter from Ruth to Chertoff was the first of many in her collection of papers at the United States Holocaust Memorial Museum that, beginning in 1943, reveal her mastery of English, her wordplay, and her emerging screwball sense of humor. Responding to Chertoff's profuse thanks to Ruth for planning such a good tour and being a gracious hostess, Ruth wrote, "Trying to make a good conceited egotist out of me? Sorry, you just can't do it. I criticize others as well as myself too severely." She thanked Chertoff for all she had learned from her in such a short time. Chertoff would be one of many older Jewish women, often single, who would guide and influence Ruth during her Zionist work. They would also serve as role models to her for how to navigate the working world as a single woman.

In this letter, Ruth also wrote a detailed summary of the chapter's business and explained the friction between herself and Shirley Berliner, the former president:

> I am having no end of trouble with her. I guess I should give the chairmanship to someone else, but, 1st of all, I don't have anyone capable for the job right now, and secondly, prior to Shirley's regional presidency, that is at the nominating meeting she made a faithful promise not to let the Seattle membership suffer. Well, you had all the girls keyed up, and as far as I am concerned they are much more cooperative when I ask for something, but membership, which I decided to leave entirely to Shirley's responsibility…I can honestly say I have tried to cooperate, and be tactful, and your letter really came as an SOS to keep me back from doing something drastic…Because Shirley complained to Rabbi Cohn about me, and he definitely is one of my severest critics, since he knows I can take it, and he felt that I was right in whatever I said or did. Shirley just hasn't come down to earth yet… I just can't think of a possible remedy any more, than maybe, to always let Ida talk to Shirley when I want anything done.[27]

She closed with a dejected comment that Seattle's Zionist community was at an all-time low, with bickering among the different groups. She hoped she would be able to attend the upcoming national Junior Hadassah convention, if she could find the money for it.

Ruth went to the convention, but she had to quit her job (probably at the Washington Quilt Company) in order to go. She traveled to Cleveland, her first major trip since moving to Seattle. In addition to meeting up again with Naomi Chertoff, Ruth met the rest of the national officers, as well as Zionist leaders, including Rabbi Abba Hillel Silver. The program included mass meetings on underground Zionist groups in Europe, ideas for branch activities, screenings of Zionist films, and Palestinian music programs. Ironically enough, Shirley Berliner chaired a luncheon honoring branch presidents.[28]

Perhaps most importantly, Ruth connected with other young, serious-minded women for whom Zionism wasn't just a vehicle for teas and dances. During discussions, she would have felt free to speak her mind on this topic that she felt so passionate about, instead of trying to suppress her outrage and urgency just to not offend anyone, like she did in Seattle. Remarkably, she was able to reconnect with a childhood friend from Leipzig, Ruth Reicher.[29] Reicher may have also belonged to the Habonim there. Besides the two Ruths, there were other European refugees at the convention who were able to convey to the American-born members what they had gone through there as children or teenagers and how vital a new Palestinian state was for the fate of European Jews. Ruth no doubt had a thrilling time at the convention, and this opportunity to network with such influential Jewish leaders might have made all the local grunt work worth it.

While Ruth was at the conference, Zeanna Berliner (likely Shirley's sister or cousin) was appointed acting president while Ruth was away, and sent letters updating her on the progress of the Seattle branch. She wrote that she and the acting membership chair, Edith, had plans to recruit fifteen new members. Although she told Ruth that she'd do anything she needed, Zeanna also reassured her how much she loved being president, how good she was at it, and how Ruth had nothing to worry about.[30]

After the convention in Cleveland, Ruth visited Rappaport relatives who had moved from New York to Washington, DC. Photographs she captured of her aunt Bertha and cousins Marvin and Selma show the family exploring the Lincoln Memorial and Mount Vernon. Ruth probably still had twinges of regret that she hadn't lived with the Rappaports—they seemed to have had a relaxed, fun time together. When she returned to Seattle, Ruth looked for a job while she helped care for one of her ailing aunts. As she reported in a letter to a friend, when she got back the whole town was "in a mess" about recent bills in Congress concerning Palestine. The various Seattle Zionist groups could not agree on whether to support them.[31]

Ruth took a new job in April 1943 at the Medina Baby Home, which had been founded in 1921 as both an orphanage and a home for unwed pregnant women.[32] In a series of five articles written for the *Seattle Times* over 1944, reporter Anne Swensson detailed the huge rise in unwed pregnancies during the war and how Seattle's adoption agencies were overwhelmed. Stable families who wanted to adopt were difficult to find in wartime, and doctors and even classified ads facilitated adoptions that agencies couldn't assist with.[33] Ruth described her job as "wonderful, fascinating."[34] Even though she was still just a typist, she sometimes helped with casework by visiting homes of adoptees, a task that gave her a vastly different work experience than she had had at her previous jobs.

Ruth wrote to a friend about another new job as the private secretary for the owner of Grunbaum's Furniture Company. She described her new boss:

He is of "GERMAN JEWISH ORIGIN" strictly REFORM, strictly AUTOCRATIC, in a group of 250 employees I believe I am the only one who is not afraid of him, and talks right back to him when I feel I am right (I can afford it for two reasons, I don't give a damn about the job and he is a friend of my uncles). However, he is the most alert man I know at the age of between 65 to 70. No error escapes him. He still talks either German or French to me. He is strictly anti-Zionist, but helps finance an exclusive Jewish Golf and Country Club in Seattle, thinking he is a philanthropist.[35]

Ruth wrote that many of the employees were refugees from Europe, and she was ashamed of their petty behavior, jealousy, and gossip. She genuinely liked one woman who had lived in Berlin and Switzerland and had Zionist leanings. Although the job was good experience, with convenient hours and location, if any other more interesting job came along, she'd take it. After the excitement of the convention, getting back to real life seemed like a letdown. "Seattle seems so dull to me now," she complained, "or rather you always feel like bumping your head in a stone wall."[36]

Ruth updated Ruth Reicher on the Seattle branch. She had to appoint an almost entirely new group of officers and board members after many had to leave town because of war service or sudden marriages. Shirley Berliner had resigned as membership chair, Ida Fink (perhaps her one true ally) had left to try to make it in the radio business in Hollywood, and another member left to return to the family business, a waffle shop on the beach. Ruth's new appointees were "willing," she wrote, but had "no background whatever in Zionism, Judaism, organizational work or anything else for that matter."[37] Remarkably, membership had increased to fifty-six from thirty the previous summer. On top of that, Ruth had recently been recruited to be the secretary of the new Seattle Zionist Emergency Council. She informed Caroline Ruelf, the chair of the national Youth Aliyah whom she had met in

Cleveland, "This year, we, the Seattle Jr. Hadassah have definitely established our reputation locally. No one can say that they haven't heard of us. Wherever, and whenever anything is going on in town we are approached, either as guests, or helpers."[38]

Months later, Ruth wrote a long letter to her friend Esther Elbaum, a former Seattle Junior Hadassah member who now lived in New York. Ruth explained that she had declined to be nominated for another term as president and that, naturally, Zeanna Berliner stepped up for the nomination. Ruth wrote:

> Had a long telephone conversation with her, and it was most distressing. She told me that to her Zionism is not what it is to me. She won't force the girls to do anything, she won't be a slave driver, and whatever the girls want she will do. She has picked a board of totally inexperienced girls, and made me fund-raising chairman, of all things. She is not in the least willing to cooperate. Admitted that she primarily is concerned with personalities, and not Hadassah, and since that fire-side at my house she decided that neither you nor I are human, and that of course leaves me out. The rest of the kids of course want me to be active, but.......[39]

Ruth asked Esther to stop by the national Hadassah office to tell them what was really going on in Seattle, as surely they wouldn't know from any official communication what was up.

She updated Esther on her personal life too. She had recently quit teaching at Herzl's Congregation Synagogue's Sunday school and hadn't talked to Rabbi Cohn in weeks. She revealed her concerns about her family in Europe:

Had a letter from my sister in Paris yesterday. It was dated February 9, and about all she could say was "Nous allons très bien" [We are doing very good]. My brother-in-law is evidently working in a coal mine. That is, she said, Pere, but I believe she means the father of her little boy, as I can't possibly imagine that she means my father. However, I can't be sure, and have no way of checking until this blasted war is over.[40]

She was optimistic about a big change she had made that summer. A few weeks earlier Ruth had enrolled in college, finally setting in motion a plan she had dreamed about for years. Like her cousins and friends had, she enrolled at the University of Washington, just over the Montlake Cut, a few blocks from the Rubinsteins' house. She either walked over the bridge or took the bus up Montlake Boulevard to the campus, a foggy hillside of stone buildings and cherry and fir trees. She was surprised that she already knew so many people there and seemed to fit in easily. The change was good for her, she noted to Esther: "Since I've been back at school I have been much less nervous, much more calm, better poised, more humorous, not more hysterical, am not so upset (as with Hadassah)."[41] She mentioned that she often studied at the campus library in the evenings. Ruth was referring to the Suzzallo Library, built in 1926 and famous for its Gothic style. In 1935 a new wing had been built, doubling the building's size. Ruth had found yet another library that not only provided her with books she needed and a space to study for her classes but also served as a hideaway when she couldn't stand to be at home.

That summer Ruth took a class in sociology, which she would later choose as her major. She also took a speech class and honed her persuasive speaking skills on her favorite issue, as she explained in a letter to Naomi Chertoff:

In one of my English classes (where I am the only Jewish student) I have given a number of speeches along Zionist lines, and honest I felt very happy about the reaction I received. Some of the kids actually asked for references, and then gave speeches illuminating one point or another that I had stressed, as f.e. American Oil in the Near East. It really boosted my morale![42]

Her new persuasive writing skills had developed so well that she received a prize in August from the American Zionist Youth Commission and the American Zionist Emergency Council for an essay she wrote on Zionism. Her winnings were fifteen dollars in war bonds.[43]

In her letter to Chertoff, Ruth couldn't help including a dig at Zeanna Berliner, who had recently quit as president of Junior Hadassah to go on a trip to New York. The vice president of the group refused to take over. "You can see what a mess it all is," Ruth wrote. A month later, she wrote to Alice Bernstein Jacobson, Junior Hadassah's executive secretary, to explain that Marian Elyn, "a girl with a level head and her two feet firmly on the ground," was now president. Ruth believed that with some help (from herself, likely), Marian would do fine and the group would get back on track.[44]

That fall Ruth enrolled as a full-time student and took six courses, including English Composition, a survey of American literature, Introduction to Philosophy (which she almost failed), Introduction to Psychology, a sociology class titled Problems of Social Insecurity, and a gym class. Still working at Grunbaum's furniture store through most of the fall, she was overextended and exhausted, even if she had pulled back on her Zionist work. In November, Ruth quit both of her jobs, at Grunbaum's and the Medina Baby Home. She was now working as the assistant to the director of volunteers at Seattle's USO and the United Seamen's Service (USS), both busy organizations that ran service clubs and programs for troops passing through Seattle.

In January 1945 Alice Bernstein Jacobson wrote to both Ruth and Marian Elyn. Despite Ruth's efforts, she seemed not to have really disengaged herself from Junior Hadassah. Jacobson was at the end of her rope in dealing with Marian and Ruth, both of whom, it seems, had written letters complaining about the lack of interest among the Jewish women of Seattle in joining Junior Hadassah and the lackadaisical attitude of current members. Jacobson chastised them for holding three-hour business meetings, not guiding new members appropriately, and running to the national office about every little incident. She drove her point home: "I want you to study ways and means of helping yourselves. You get the working material through what we send you—but you have to figure out how to put it across so that it will be accepted! You are on the scene; no one can tell you how to do it."[45] She pleaded with them not to be mad at her for her sharp words. In a separate enclosed letter to Ruth alone, Jacobson—acknowledging Ruth's reality as a restless, outraged refugee—asked for patience regarding Marian: "This young American girl is something special we have to deal with—and she requires much, much patience—And Humor."

Jacobson's letter was representative of how other people saw Ruth: she was so driven, so detail oriented, so outspoken, and so judgmental of others she thought of as lazy or indifferent that she exasperated many people around her. However, if Ruth had been a man, she likely would have been admired for her strong leadership. Even though others implied that she should stop caring so much about her Zionist work, she knew that her efforts were making a difference, even if it was a small one, even if it was in "a backwater town" like Seattle. Through her work with the Junior Hadassah, the Seattle Zionist Youth Commission, and the Seattle Emergency Zionist Commission, she had increased membership, educated Seattleites on the plight of European Jews, and raised substantial funds to help start a new homeland for Jews. It may not have brought her much satisfaction, but it was all she could do while waiting out the war in Seattle.

In March 1945 Ruth wrote another letter to Esther Elbaum, telling her how much she was enjoying school. "Burying my head in Plato's Republic, Poli. Science, Abnormal Psychology," she wrote. "Ha, joke's on me." She described how the previous semester she had written a paper for her sociology class that was her "autobiography under the title of 'social insecurity.'" "The whole department is crazy about it," she went on. "Got me an A and a lot of gasping how do you do's from prof."[46] Ruth had no doubt written about her own insecure life, from her status as a noncitizen in the country where she was born, to the persecution of her family, her flight to Switzerland, and her bounces from family to family there. And even though she was safely ensconced in Seattle and living with her privileged relatives, that didn't necessarily bring her or her family in Europe any security for the future.

The process of writing that essay might have prompted Ruth to think harder about her status in the United States. Once it looked like the war could end soon, she had to plan for her next step. She still had a visa, and her status was "alien." In February 1945 Ruth had decided to apply for citizenship. On February 21 she was notified to go to the United States Immigration Station and Assay Office and bring two citizen witnesses who had known her for the past five years, her alien registration card, and eight dollars for the filing fee.[47] She insisted in hindsight that the ceremony was no big deal: "It was really simple. My uncle was a friend of the judge's, and we just went to the judge's chambers, and I swear for five minutes and I was a citizen."[48] She received her naturalization certificate, declaring her an American citizen, in April.

When asked later if she felt like she was "very German," Ruth responded, "Hell no. I never felt German. I was a Romanian." But she explained that she didn't "feel Romanian" either: "I mean . . . sort of between and betwixt. I had a passport from a country I barely knew. I lived in a country where I didn't have a passport . . . I was just kind of floating."[49] At some point in her life she began to not just speak and read in English but think in English as well. She admitted, "Now if I want to, if I switch to German, I have to really push a button. I really have to make a switch and force myself. I mean, I can think in German but it's a conscious effort."

Ruth claimed that she didn't feel any different after becoming a citizen: "I felt at home from the day I got there . . . I was fluent in English. I had good friends. I was sort of generally accepted."[50] In that one phrase, "sort of generally accepted," Ruth glossed over the deep pain and alienation she had felt in Seattle over five long years. At age eighty-seven, she blustered that gaining American citizenship hadn't meant anything to her, that she had felt at home in Seattle since she had arrived there. For someone who had never been a citizen of any of the three countries where she had lived, achieving citizenship actually must have brought her both relief and a sense of security. She knew she didn't feel at home living with the Rubinsteins, or even in Seattle really, but she recognized that the United States was her home now and in the near future. There was no way she was going back to Germany, or even Europe, now that it was completely destroyed by war. Although she didn't agree with US politics and it hadn't done enough to save other Jews like her, including her parents, she at least had the security of American citizenship. For now, anyway, Ruth had proof on paper that she belonged somewhere.

~

Greg and I flew to Portland to visit my family and drove up to Seattle for a short research trip. We stayed at a cheap hotel near the university and spent our first night walking around the student neighborhood. Nearly every block was under construction, with cranes looming in the dark above new high-rise condos. Ruth's "backwater town" had grown to be a huge and very prosperous city.

In the University of Washington library's special collections, I pored over more of Ruth's papers, most of which were related to her time as a high school and college student. I flipped through an endless number of add/drop slips, which included a laundry list of excuses Ruth had for why she couldn't attend class or finish her assignments. I perused her high school yearbook and read some essays and letters she had written. In other collections, I found and read issues of the *Herzl-Gram*, the newsletter of Ruth's synagogue, and skimmed oral history transcripts of people Ruth had mentioned in her letters and diaries.

While I was in the archives, Greg explored the city. I gave him an assignment to visit the cemetery where the Rubinsteins were buried, and he took diligent notes and photos for me. We drove to the Montlake neighborhood and found the Rubinsteins' old house. We walked down the street to see the Montlake Cut, and I imagined Ruth walking down the sidewalk, where I knew she went at night to sit by the water and think. We visited the old Herzl's Congregation Synagogue, which was now a community health center, and walked inside to see the lobby.

On our last night there, I exited the Suzzallo Library into the dark fog and circled the library complex trying to find Greg and became a bit disoriented among the fir trees. Although she made attempts to conceal it, Ruth struggled to adjust to life in Seattle. It was a completely different environment from the one in which she had been raised, and she found it difficult to shed her past and her personality just to fit in. But, like she always had, she pushed through. After she moved away and reflected, she said Seattle felt like a dream, a fairyland. As I stood there among this mist and these trees, it certainly was.

~

Part IV:

Don't Bet on It

SEATTLE AND SAN FRANCISCO, 1945–1947

Chapter 12

The people of Seattle were not certain how to mark the Allies' official victory over Germany. The announcement had come through the Associated Press on May 7, 1945, but not yet from the government. Leaders of the city had imagined a large celebration in anticipation of the end of the war, but revelry did not fill the streets, neither on that evening nor on the following day.[1] Ruth might have listened to President Truman's address, then gone to her classes at the University of Washington in the morning. She probably went to her job at the USO, where perhaps she celebrated with other volunteers and men stationed in Seattle or on leave. Herzl's Congregation Synagogue held special services that evening. With Truman's nod to Mother's Day in his speech, did she wonder about her own odds of reuniting with her parents? She had read the reports earlier that year of the destruction of Leipzig. Her old neighborhood, the Graphics Quarter, had been bombed, which destroyed not only the buildings but also one million books.[2] She had seen in the newspapers the photographs of liberated concentration camps. The news was too stunning for most Americans to fully comprehend, but for someone like Ruth, who had witnessed Kristallnacht and followed closely the reports in Jewish publications of what is now called the Holocaust, it may have been no surprise.

In May, shortly before her twenty-second birthday, she had come down with the measles and had decided to finally quit Junior Hadassah. The angst of watching the organization she had built up now fizzling away under Jewish girls who were indifferent to Zionism was finally too much to bear. She wrote her letter of resignation to Alice Bernstein Jacobson, the executive secretary of Junior Hadassah in New York. Jacobson wrote in reply, "Ruth, I do not think you expect me to reply about your decision to withdraw from unit activities for awhile. You know what is best. On the other hand, I want you to know that we appreciate what you have done for the past few years and we feel sure that your deep concern for the Zionist movement will never waver."[3]

In the spring of 1945, Ruth was invited to speak at three forums sponsored by the Joint Anti-Fascist Refugee Committee (JAFRC) in order to raise money for refugees from Spain. The title of this program was "A First-Hand Account of Fascism," and Ruth spoke about her experience in Germany and what her family across Europe was going through.[4] At this point she knew that her father and brother-in-law, Salomon Rosner, had been deported to concentration camps, but it is unclear if she knew the specifics of where they were and what exactly happened to them. JAFRC had been founded in the early 1940s by Dr. Edward Barsky to unite various fundraising groups for victims of the Spanish Civil War. Barsky went to Spain in 1937 with the Abraham Lincoln Brigade and served as a pioneering surgeon, developing methods there that would be used by American army medics in World War II. JAFRC's funds aided Spanish refugees in France and Mexico with medical care, housing, food, and clothing.[5]

At the beginning of June, Ruth wrote with a darker tone to her friend Esther Elbaum, apologizing for a hasty telegram that she had sent the day before. Ruth had seen a blind job ad that she suspected was for a position at Hadassah headquarters, where Esther now worked in New York, and she desperately wanted it. Ruth wrote:

You know that I have never really been happy in Seattle, mainly because I want to do some real work, something that is close to me, and it is impossible to find that work in Seattle. Since I have my citizenship papers and am free to travel around without having to be afraid, I feel that if I could just land a job in New York my life would be much better adjusted and run more smoothly. You know that I have a lot of excess energy which I tried to use up by doing Zionist work out here and studying, however neither one of the two alternatives are really satisfactory. The Zionist work is [too] petty and the school is too poor. I don't get out of my courses and teachers what I want, and would rather live in New York and take a few night courses. Also, by being right in New York I might do more in locating my family than by hibernating on the West Coast.[6]

Ruth still lived with her uncle Carl and aunt Dora. They went out of town often, but she still longed for a place of her own, which she probably couldn't afford. She was desperate to get out of Seattle to make her own way in life and end her dependency on the Rubinsteins, even though they had been largely benevolent toward her. Esther responded that Ruth shouldn't get too "het up" about the job because she'd be working with a woman who was "a driver and a sourpuss." Esther explained the headaches of working at Hadassah headquarters; a position there likely wouldn't give her more satisfaction than the work she had done in Seattle. Esther offered to go across the street from her New York office to the American Jewish Congress headquarters to help Ruth search for her parents.[7]

In the immediate aftermath of the war, American Jews seemed uncertain of how to go about finding relatives who had been left behind in Europe. Who was responsible for coordinating these efforts? For the American and Russian armies, the Red Cross, and Jewish organizations, the first task was to rehabilitate concentration camp survivors, who were eager to leave for Palestine or the United States. Jewish organizations compiled lists of survivors and dispersed the lists throughout the Jewish diaspora. On May 28 an announcement appeared in *The Transcript* that some survivor lists were already available at the Washington Émigré Bureau. Max Schneider, Ruth's brother-in-law in Palestine, made the first inquiry for Mendel and Chaja Rappaport.[8] Ruth probably contacted Clara and Mirjam to hear how or whether they made it through the war and to inquire if they had heard from their parents. She anxiously followed the news from Palestine, where Jews were fighting the British to allow more displaced people, known as DPs, into the country.

Ruth decided to take a break from school. The end of the war might have brought too much turmoil for her to keep concentrating on her studies, but she continued her job with the USO and the USS. The Seattle branches of these organizations would soon see a flood of soldiers returning home and would be busier than ever. In August the *Seattle Times* noted that women's volunteer work for the war was not over yet. Concerning the USO, Aileen Hicks Finley wrote:

> More than 1,000 feminine volunteers work at the Seattle U.S.O., according to Mr. William D. Martin, manager. These women man the Snack Bar, Information desk, Hospitality desk, cashier's desk and program office, where they distribute razor blades, tooth paste and other creature comforts to the men. They run the switchboard every day after 6 o'clock and on Saturday evenings and Sundays. A special group sews buttons on uniforms and mends holes . . . Mr. Martin believes the club will see a sharp increase in patronage with so many service men leaving the Pacific as well as inductees leaving from here for that area as occupation forces.[9]

In August, Ruth applied for a secretarial position with the JAFRC. This job would have been a chance for her to officially work for the causes she believed in, but she didn't get it. Likely disappointed, she continued with the USO through the end of the year. In October, Ruth helped plan a special event commending the USS's 325 Seattle volunteers for their accomplishments over the past year, including placing eighteen thousand pounds of magazines and game chests on 360 ships at the Port of Seattle.[10] Ruth was still eager and ready to move to a paying job within the Jewish community, working for some kind of cause she deeply believed in.

Chapter 13

In January 1946 Ruth began working for *The Transcript*.[1] During the war a string of young women edited the paper due to the shortage of men. The weekly newspaper was usually four to six pages and on its front page included national stories from the Independent Jewish Press Service and the Jewish Telegraphic Agency. Most of the rest of the issue reported on local Jewish events, including organizations' meetings, speaking engagements, and a social column. Ruth could now put her childhood "reporter" instincts to good use. She would not be allowed to vocalize her opinions on Zionism through her work at the newspaper, but she could observe and write about the community she had grown, if somewhat begrudgingly, to see herself as part of. Even if this job consisted of tasks such as compiling notifications of marriages, births, and routine meetings rather than hard-hitting reporting of the international drama concerning Palestine, it was a start on Ruth's slow climb to a career that resonated with her.

She was appointed acting editor for the March 4, 1946, issue.[2] On the front page, she featured an Associated Press article about President Truman's recent meeting with representatives from the United Jewish Appeal (UJA) concerning the Nuremburg trials and the obligation of the US to admit Jewish DPs. She also included the Western Union telegram that was sent from the UJA to Al Shyman, president of Seattle's Federated Jewish Fund, to report on the meeting with Truman. The issue included a notice of the newspaper's new office hours in the morning rather than the afternoon, presumably a change meant to accommodate the new editor's schedule. She no doubt was proud to see her name on the masthead, if only for one issue. Beatrice Sussman became the new editor for the next three months, and then Ruth took over permanently. The prolific engagement and wedding announcements of local Jewish couples competed for space in the paper against dramatic international headlines on the aftermath of the war and Palestine. As her friends began to pair off and have children, Ruth could finally say that her career was getting off the ground. As she put it, "I was a living encyclopedia on Jewish affairs in Washington, British Columbia and northern Oregon!"[3]

Ruth reenrolled at the University of Washington in the summer of 1946, taking her first journalism class on newswriting and one on economics.[4] She seemed to be hitting her stride in her newfound career, making new connections along the way. A few years later Ruth explained in her diary how she met her first love around the time that she became editor of *The Transcript* in 1946. Riding on a bus in Seattle, she noticed a man who appeared to be Arabic. She spent weeks trying to find out who he was: M. Gamal Mostafa, also known as Jim (Ruth also sometimes spelled his name as Jamal). Five years older than Ruth, he had been born and raised in Egypt and had earned a bachelor's degree in engineering at Cairo University in 1943. When he met Ruth, he was a student at the University of Washington, working on his master's degree in civil engineering.[5]

On one of their dates, Ruth took him to the Washington State Press Club, where she was a new member. In advance she had asked the club if it was all right for Jim to join her, since, she said, "his skin color was a darker shade than ours." In the Pacific Northwest, racial discrimination routinely occurred in social clubs, and Ruth was well aware of it. She was told, however, that it would be fine to bring Jim, so they attended the club together on July 30, 1946. When they arrived, one of the waitresses was "extremely rude" to Jim. After talking to other wait-resses, Ruth was assured that it would not happen again. Ruth and Jim came back to the club about a week later. The doorman and two other people "in a very crude, blunt, tasteless and tactless manner, and these adjectives [described] their attitude only very mildly and inadequately, accused Mr. Mostafa of not being 'white' and therefore refused to admit him." The next day Ruth wrote an irate letter to the club, detailing what happened. She argued that the club should welcome Jim, considering his accomplishments and the fact that he had been accepted by other social clubs in Seattle. She accused the club of "Jim Crowism" and asked that they "rectify, if possible, the blunder [they] made."[6]

The Washington State Press Club had recently been taken over by a new group of young reporters back from their war service. Known initially as the Ale and Quail Society, this group had aimed to get on the club's board of governors, which was dominated by an older genera-tion of reporters.[7] This new cohort seemingly had no use for the loud Jewish woman who was the new editor of *The Transcript*, a minor local paper, or her Egyptian boyfriend. Dudley Brown, the president of the Washington State Press Club, wrote back to Ruth: "The matter of your letter was read before the Board of Governors, and, on its instruction an amount equivalent to your unexpired balance of your membership is enclosed. Evidently you are not in sympathy with the manners and operations of this Club and the Board feels that in view of that fact it would be best to accept your resignation." A check for $1.87 was enclosed.[8]

Chapter 14

Over a year after the war had ended, Ruth had still not heard from
her parents or from anyone concerning what had happened to them.
It had been almost seven years since she had seen them in person and
three since their last letter. In July 1946 Ruth wrote to Leipzig's recently
reinstated Jewish community organization, the jüdische Gemeinde zu
Leipzig. It might not have been the first letter she wrote to search for
them. A copy of this tattered letter, handwritten in German, is included
on the microfilm of the organization's records:

> I do not know who to turn to, so I am writing to you in
> hopes that you will help. When I left Germany in October
> 1939, my parents, Mr. and Mrs. Mendel Rappaport,
> remained in Leipzig. My parents lived at Salomonstrasse 18.

> Sometime later I received letters via the Red Cross in
> which they listed their address as Packhofstrasse 1 or
> Packhofstrasse 5. The last letter I received from Leipzig
> was dated August 17, 1943. At the time, the address of my
> parents was Gustav-Adophe-Strasse 7, which I believe was
> where the Jewish High School was. Since that time I have
> received no messages, despite all my efforts. I would very
> much appreciate it if we could get some information. If

my parents are no longer in Leipzig I would like at least to know what happened to them—

My father, Mendel Rappaport, was a furrier in Leipzig, and has lived since approximately 1913 there. He was born in Rostoky (in Romania), and he was a Romanian citizen. My mother, nee Chaja Helena Rubinstein, was born in [Mielec] (in Poland). I am willing to give you more information if necessary and would be very grateful to you for any information.[1]

On August 27 the organization wrote a short letter to Ruth:

We received your letter dated 07/08/46 and must notify you to the fact that your father, Mendel Rappaport, died in January 1944 in the Buchenwald concentration camp, where he was sent in October 1943.

Your mother was deported to the Ravensbrück concentration camp, from where she has not returned, so unfortunately, it is presumed that she was killed by the criminals of the SS.

We are sorry to send you this sad news.[2]

Ruth had expected the worst, and now the facts were laid before her. She had probably also found out by this time that Clara's husband, Salomon Rosner, had died in Auschwitz in June 1943 after being deported from the Drancy internment camp near Paris. He had initially been sent to the South of France to a work camp and had tried to escape to Spain with other Jews when Germany invaded. But he was arrested and sent to Paris.[3] Her cousin Deborah, Leo and Dora's daughter, had been institutionalized in Germany for schizophrenia and was also murdered in a concentration camp, but which specific one is unknown. Michael Rubinstein, the son of Ruth's cousin David, was shocked when he found out about Deborah. It had remained a family secret for decades.[4] In her oral history interview, Gail Schwartz attempted to ask Ruth about the moment when she found out what had happened to her parents. When Schwartz remarked that the news about Ruth's parents must have been devastating, Ruth answered, "Obviously, but . . . ," and trailed off. She had nothing more to say about it. Like many others who had lost family members and friends in the Holocaust, Ruth never really wanted to discuss her parents or how they died. Many people who worked with Ruth through the years or were later friends with her knew nothing about this part of her life.

Mendel and Chaja were both deported from Leipzig on October 11, 1943.[5] Like most Jewish couples, they were split up by gender as they boarded separate trains or trucks bound for different camps. Chaja was sent to either Ravensbrück or, as Ruth remembered in her oral history, Thereisenstadt. Chaja's file at the International Tracing Service, the organization that documents Holocaust survivors and victims, suggests that she could have been sent to Thereisenstadt.[6] Other women from Leipzig were sent there, so it remains a possibility. But there is no surviving record of her arrival at any camp. Her story ends there, when she left Leipzig. She seems to have vanished into thin air. In 1964, for the purposes of restitution, she was given a death certificate with a date of March 31, 1945, and Ravensbrück as her place of death.[7] Mendel arrived at Buchenwald, just an hour west of Leipzig, on October 12, 1943.[8]

~

I visited Buchenwald with my parents after I completed my research in Leipzig. We drove an hour west through the pristine German farmland, passing by huge modern wind farms. The name Buchenwald translates as "beech forest," and the thick woods still surround the camp for miles. In the parking lot, we saw German teenagers exit a bus and enter the visitor's center on a common, and required, field trip for those raised in the country. The Buchenwald Memorial offers guided audio tours, and I downloaded the Buchenwald app on my phone. My guide, a male voice with a slight German accent, steered me through the camp on a bitterly cold day, October 13. Mendel Rappaport had arrived here almost exactly seventy-three years earlier.

Buchenwald was one of the first concentration camps in Germany and opened in 1937. Others besides Jews were sent there, including disabled people, homosexuals, foreigners, subversives, and prisoners of war. The camp imprisoned primarily men, and in total about 280,000 people passed through it before it was liberated in April 1945. Built before the "final solution" was conceived and implemented, Buchenwald was used as a work camp and holding station for prisoners who were waiting to be sent to other camps either in Germany or out of the country. About fifty-six thousand people died there, primarily from illness, but there were also many deaths as a result of medical experimentation and executions.[9]

The recorded voice led me past many buildings that served as barracks for guards outside the perimeter of the camp, and past the site of an abandoned zoo that had once entertained SS guards. It was certainly the most bizarre—and unexpected—aspect of the camp. I walked along the barbed-wire perimeter fence toward the main gate, which had a sign that read, *"Jedem das Seine."* The phrase translates to the idiom "To each his own" or, more accurately, "Everyone gets what he deserves." Through the gate, the wide-open camp slopes slightly down a hill. It is nearly all gravel, and the buildings that were destroyed are marked by rock and cement borders. The first thing I passed in front of the gate was the small memorial for all victims of the camp.

Because Buchenwald was one of the camps in which records were not completely destroyed by the guards before it was liberated, the International Tracing Service has a file on Mendel. It includes documents from the camp while Mendel was a prisoner there and the records of inquiries that were made about him after the war. His prisoner number was 9281. In addition to being imprisoned for being Jewish, he was classified as a political prisoner. One document lists what he wore when he arrived: a cap, coat, vest, trousers, two undershirts, underwear, a pair of shoes, two pairs of socks, a collar, and a tie. Another document lists the contents of his suitcase: six shirts, three pairs of underwear, eight pairs of socks, two ties, two scarves, one pair of gloves, one pair of pajamas, two handbags, one sleeping bag, one blanket, and one rucksack. Mendel signed both papers to verify the inventories.

For about three months Mendel lived in block 22, the barracks assigned to Jews. Like most prisoners, he probably worked in the rock quarry there; this might have been what Clara was referring to in her letter to Ruth when she said that "Pere" was working in a coal mine. The work was brutal, and Mendel died in Buchenwald on January 13, 1944, of heart failure. This may have been a generic cause of death assigned if it could not be easily ascertained. Buchenwald did not have gas chambers, so it is clear that Mendel did not die as so many other European Jews did.

After Mendel died, a document certified that none of his belongings remained in block 22. It was signed by the *Blockältester* (block elder), Carlebach, and the *Blockführer*, in an illegible scrawl. Carlebach was Emil Carlebach, a relative of Ephraim Carlebach, the rabbi who had led Ruth's synagogue. Emil was from a Frankfurt branch of the family. Imprisoned at Buchenwald for joining the Communist movement in 1938, he was a leader of the resistance movement at the camp for years and led a mutiny in April 1945. He survived an execution attempt and was hidden by his fellow prisoners until the camp was liberated. He was chosen as the spokesman for the newly liberated prisoners, and he went on to serve on the Frankfurt City Council and own a newspaper there. He remained a committed Communist until his death in 2001.[10]

I walked farther downhill to the Little Camp Memorial, a notorious site of many deaths and where prisoners were held temporarily before being sent to other concentration camps. To the left was the infirmary; perhaps Mendel had been there when he died. Buchenwald includes a large museum in the former train depot at the bottom of the hill; the first floor is a stark, empty cement space with a haunting, looping video about the camp. The second and third floors are filled with exhibits containing documents, photographs, and artifacts from the people imprisoned there and their captors. A remarkable array of well-known people passed through Buchenwald or died there: writer Elie Wiesel, theologian Dietrich Bonhoeffer, French prime minister Leon Blum, as well as many other writers, politicians, artists, actors, doctors, and members of the resistance from across Europe. I scanned each exhibit case hoping to find something, anything, about Mendel, but I never saw his name.

Outside the museum lies a tree stump known as the Goethe Oak. An enormous tree, it is believed to be where Goethe wrote some of his famed poetry. The tree was famous before the camp was established; in fact, originally the camp was to have been named Ettersberg. But due to its association with Goethe and other writers and philosophers from the Weimar area, the name was abandoned in favor of the more generic Buchenwald. Although this tree was cherished by prisoners—as a reminder of the famed writer and the world outside the camp—it was also a site of many executions. During the Allied bombing attack of the camp in August 1944, the tree went up in flames. Many saw it as a sign of what was to come: if the tree fell, so would Germany.[11]

Near the former Goethe tree are memorials dedicated to the various populations of prisoners held at Buchenwald. I stopped at the memorial for murdered Jews: a long, simple, rectangular pit of stones. Along one side reads Psalms 78:6: "So that the generation to come might know, the children, yet to be born, that they too may rise and declare to their children." For Mendel, I left at the site three stones representing his three daughters that had scattered across the globe. On the way out I made one last stop at the crematorium and found a room full of bouquets of flowers. I assume that Mendel was cremated here, but there is no way to know for sure.

The next day I went to the Leipzig City History Museum. I learned about the early founding of the city and its history as a center for publishing and music. Near the end of the exhibit is a section on the city's Jews. I was surprised to see a wall that listed hundreds of names, although Ruth's and her parents' were not there. But I sat down at a touch-screen directory to search for them, and there they were. Mendel and Chaja are memorialized on this digital screen, but there is no permanent, tangible marker anywhere in the city, no proof that they had once existed here.

In the 1950s Ruth applied for restitution for the deaths of her parents and provided the meager documentation that she had about them.[12] She may have received in the mail more records related to her father's imprisonment and death during this process, but I am unsure if she ever saw the documents held at the International Tracing Service, as Peter did not find copies of them with her other papers after she died. Near the end of her life, she claimed, "I'm not sure I wasn't avoiding it but I wasn't trailing the Holocaust. I mean, I was future oriented, not backwards. What happened, happened."[13] Did she ever see the list of Mendel's belongings? Did she know he died of heart failure? Did she ever read about Buchenwald to learn what happened there? Maybe she decided she didn't want or need to know.

~

Chapter 15

In September 1946 Ruth threw herself into work and college, enrolling in Russian Literature, Introduction to Theater, and a sociology class on race relations. She may have been inspired to take this class after the incident with the Washington State Press Club. Jim may have helped her through this extraordinarily difficult time. She remembered:

> The only time I did not want any more than what I had, that I was deep down inside of me happy and contented was with Jim, in spite of all the unhappiness and misery his love had attached to it—when I was with Jim I did not want anybody else, I was happy, I was content—I stopped looking for the indefinable, I did not care where we went, what we did, what I wore, what people said or did—he was all I needed and yet, maybe one can or should not live like that all one's life—maybe it should just be an episode, a happy interlude to draw strength from, something beautiful tucked away in memory? Who knows?[1]

She remarked that Jim was possessive of her, and she did not mind. She had dated many Jewish men in Seattle, but none of them had excited her the way Jim did. Dating an Arabic man probably shocked her friends and family. Ruth noted later her pattern of falling in love with men who were somehow off limits; these relationships were always doomed. Ruth and Jim had discussed marrying but knew it was impractical, not only for social and religious reasons. He would graduate in December 1946 and had been accepted as a PhD student in engineering at the University of Minnesota, to start in January. She remembered the holiday season of 1946 as probably the best one of her life:

> 2 years ago, Xmas 1946, I had Jim, uncle and auntie were out of town & Xmas vacation at school was just one round of gayeties, parties, etc. Aziz Sedky came to town, & between our house, the Transcript office & Jim's house we were having some wonderful times, though somewhat saddened by Jim's impending departure. Also Gail gave a big Hanukkah party and Jim & I went, & Hillel had a party, there were not only people, there were friends and New Year's Eve, we all had a marvelous time—I was so much in love with Jim then, anyplace where we could be together was heaven—and in November & December of that heavenly winter we were together 24 hours of the day.[2]

It had to end, of course, and in January he left for Minnesota. Why didn't Ruth go with him? It was impractical to marry at the time, with both families probably against it and Jim still in school. Ruth probably also wondered what she would do in Minnesota. She would be unlikely able to find a job as fulfilling as her work at *The Transcript*. They promised to stay faithful to each other, and she hoped that he would return to Seattle after graduating.

Ruth continued as editor of *The Transcript*. She was obviously lonely during this period, although she remained busy with more classes, including another on Russian literature. She remembered walking over the Montlake Bridge near her uncle's house to the University of Washington Golf Course (later taken over by the sprawling university hospital) on the other side of the Montlake Cut. She had walked there frequently at night with Jim; now she went by herself, probably to think about her past and future.

Over the winter term, Ruth took a few more classes but had to withdraw from two of them. At the beginning of 1947, her uncle Carl began to get sick, and Ruth listed his illness as the reason she had to withdraw from those classes. This term would be her last at the University of Washington, and she had passed just enough classes to be considered a sophomore. Carl died in March, and Ruth probably wrote his obituary for *The Transcript*.[3] In the *Seattle Times* his obituary listed his many memberships and positions in local Jewish organizations.[4] An announcement of his estate in the *Seattle Times* a few days later revealed that he had amassed $540,000 (about $6.14 million in 2018 dollars).[5] Ruth was given $10,000, and the rest would be divided among his wife, Dora; his son, Sam; and his daughter, Rose Jacobs. Rose's husband, Jay, had already opened a women's clothing store that would eventually become a chain in the northwest called Jay Jacobs. Sam would take over his father's business, expand into new ventures, and become a well-known Seattle philanthropist. Ruth's $10,000 was put into an account or trust managed by Sam, who distributed portions to her over the next few years. She had never expected to be taken care of financially; from the time she arrived in the United States, she knew she was on her own. But the inheritance was enough for her to finish college or get started on a new adventure. She chose the latter.

She recalled her twenty-fourth birthday on May 27, 1947: "Last year I had such a wonderful birthday in Seattle—my interview with Zev got me a job in Frisco, for the first time I had a birthday cake with candles, after working late at the Transcript [Rabbi] Franklin picked me up, we went out to eat . . ."[6] Zev was W. Zev Bronner, the Pacific-coast director of the Zionist Organization of America.[7] She later reflected on this new opportunity:

> The American representative to the UNSCOP commission [UN Special Committee on Palestine] was Bartley Crum of San Francisco....so, someone established a "Zionist Emergency Council" to support and feed Bartley....they had one person to set up the office (a childhood friend and class mate of Teddy Kolleck, the famous mayor of Jerusalem) and he needed help....somehow he heard about me and came to Seattle and recruited me and I went to SF to work for the Zionist Emergency Council which again put me in a position of meeting all SF Jews with and without money, all the rabbis, lay leaders....you name them....I dealt with them. Another fun part of the job was that frequently I was the "escort" officer for visiting dignitaries (Schlichim?),[8] fund raisers, etc.[9]

Similar to Seattle's Jewish community, San Francisco's was deeply divided among assimilated Jews who had succeeded in business and a small enclave of those who had recently emigrated from Europe and were supportive of Zionism. San Francisco was considered the most strongly anti-Zionist city in the nation at the time. Before Ruth arrived in 1947, Rabbi Saul White and Morris Lowenthal had led the city's Zionist movement and organized against the city's complacent, wealthy Jews that had joined the American Council for Judaism (ACJ), an anti-Zionist group. They had also convinced Bartley Crum, a well-known San Francisco lawyer, to join their cause in 1945. In what was described as a civil war, the city's Jews had turned on each other until the stark news of the Holocaust forced members of the ACJ to open their hearts and wallets to the Jewish National Fund and its efforts to coordinate national fundraising for DPs and Palestine.[10]

Crum was not, however, a member of UNSCOP, as Ruth remembered. The committee, established in May 1947, included delegates from "neutral" countries, which did not include the US.[11] Crum had served on the Anglo-American Commission of Inquiry on Palestine from 1945 to 1946 and had visited Palestine and Europe and advised Truman to urge Britain to allow more Jews into the country. In 1947 Crum published the popular book *Behind the Silken Curtain: A Personal Account of Anglo-American Diplomacy in Palestine and the Middle East.* That year, he devoted much of his time to speaking at fundraisers and events for the Zionist movement. Meanwhile he was defending himself against a smear campaign and was under daily surveillance by the FBI, suspected of Communist ties due to his work to establish the Progressive Citizens of America and his disagreements with the State Department on Palestine.[12]

Ruth was the office manager of the San Francisco district of the Zionist Organization of America (ZOA).[13] She would also work closely with the local Zionist Emergency Council. The American Zionist Emergency Council had been founded just a few years earlier and had established local branches that were largely run by ZOA staff members like Ruth.[14] She would be involved with nearly every Zionist event in San Francisco and meet everyone who passed through the city related to the movement, as well as get to know the movement's local leaders.

In June 1947 Ruth moved to 725 Pine Street on Nob Hill, right around the corner from an alley later named for Dashiell Hammett, who had lived there in 1926. San Francisco was in a housing crisis, as people streamed into the city looking for jobs and a new life after the war. Ruth remembered wandering around, sometimes on her own, lonely for Jim. She described one specific evening: "I had just moved into my Pine Street apartment, everybody had left town, Aziz & the boys, and I felt just as low & lonely as tonight—I called Jim several times, finally about 9pm I talked to him—after that I could not stand being alone any more, I went to the International Settlement, in the

St. Moritz (3 little Swiss). The waiters were astonished to see a young lady unescorted come into such an expensive place . . ."[15] She may have found it amusing to eat at this restaurant named after the city she and her mother visited so long ago. Ruth seemed to be mulling over the past when she first moved to San Francisco, but she couldn't for long. Her days and nights would soon be consumed with events, parties, planning, and socializing with the city's Jews.

In July, Esther Elbaum wrote Ruth a long, thoughtful letter, advising her about both her love life and career. Concerning Jim, she cautioned:

> The contents of your last letter described a situation that I assume is past history, for you would certainly not have gone to the rainy city of hills and UN's birth if your romance with this Egyptian had culminated in any permanent kind of relationship. I, of course, did not react as you seemed to expect—with condemnation and disapproval. I only felt, when I read your letter, that it was unfortunate that you should be in the grip of an infatuation with what sounded like an utterly charming person who is completely unsuited to your lifestyle. Make no mistake about it, Ruth, it is very difficult to live with anyone who has views diametrically opposite to yours on politics or any kind of issues which excite great emotional overtones and loyalties. Not that you must marry a far-brenteh [ardent] zionist, but to consider marrying a man who is accustomed to a different treatment of women, and an entirely different outlook on life from yours in that important respect is inviting trouble . . . I only have this to say—when you do marry, don't marry a man to change him, marry a man whom you think you can like as well as love, and one who shares your opinions on such basic

117

matters as politics, religion (or the lack of it) and the place of women in society.[16]

Ruth probably already knew that Esther was right, but she seemed to have taken her advice seriously; she would never marry a man just for the sake of security or in the midst of blind passion. Despite her private pining for Jim, she would continue to be wary of most men and to refuse to sacrifice her own career, her opinions, and her freedom at the altar of the postwar rush to marriage and family life.

In the same letter, Esther also advised Ruth not to get too caught up in her new job: "Now that you are working for a Jewish organization you might become very cynical at what you see about the vast gap between the very un-idealistic behavior of the people who work for idealistic causes. It requires a great deal of faith in humankind to work for one of the Zionist organizations and yet keep to Zionist ideology." This advice might have not yet meant much to Ruth, as she was just starting out at her new job, but it would surely mean a lot to her in the near future.

Ruth had longed for a job with meaning and one that would bring her some public recognition—ideally connected to the Zionist movement—and now it was actually happening. She later described her work with the ZOA in a résumé: "supervising 2–3 clerical employees; correspondence with regional offices and outside agencies; report writing; writing publicity releases; arranging press and radio interviews; record keeping; planning meetings and conferences; community relations."[17] Looking back, she reflected on not only her hard work but also the recognition she was starting to receive: "Morris Schwarz put it very aptly when I left Seattle, saying 'here you are a big fish in a little pond—why go & be a little fish in a big pond?' at the time very confident I thought I could go & be a big fish in a big pond—well, it was a hard struggle in S.F. but looking back I think I was on the way [to] becoming a big fish there."[18] In San Francisco she was continuing to meet powerful people, although her job in many ways was still a lowly secretary. Rabbi Cohn wrote to her in September, with his notorious sense of humor: "I am happy to learn that the office in spite of your presence is working efficiently. I hope that by the time I shall be again in San Francisco you shall not have become Executive Director, but kidding aside, Sam Tarshis told me you are doing a grand job, which does not require any raise in salary."[19] Ruth responded to Rabbi Cohn, explaining, "All I can say is in all my life I haven't worked as hard as this . . . Such a mad-house is incomparable to anything or anyplace I've ever had occasion to see or be."[20]

Chapter 16

Zionists claimed a series of victories in the fall of 1947, both internationally and in San Francisco: in September the UN Special Committee on Palestine published its recommendations to support a new Jewish state; in October the United States, backing the majority decision of UNSCOP, announced at the UN its support for the Partition Plan, a resolution declaring that a new Jewish state in Palestine should be established along with an Arab state and international control over Jerusalem and Bethlehem. The San Francisco district of the ZOA announced the results of its election on October 13, with George Edelstein as the new president and fifty-four board members. The chapter also noted that it would raise a minimum of $25,000 for the Jewish National Fund during the next Jewish year and that a thirtieth-anniversary celebration of the Balfour Declaration would be held at a rally on November 2.[1] These victories were immense for San Francisco's Zionist community, which had barely existed just a few years earlier.

Rabbi Cohn wrote to Ruth again in October, informing her that he was moving to San Francisco for a new job as regional director of Histadrut, the Zionist labor party, and asking her to help find an apartment for him and his family, noting, "Eventually, it would be a good idea that we take over your apartment and put you out on the street. I am sure that some other guy will pick you up from the corner."[2] After a frantic search, Ruth wrote back to him, "'Where do we go from here?'

. . . Germany, Seattle, San Francisco . . . in the future let's coordinate our plans? . . . All joking aside, and very seriously, I've tried my damndest to find you a place to live . . . no soap . . . it's the toughest assignment."[3] Ruth had moved into a better apartment on Hyde Street that she shared with a few other Jewish women, but the housing situation was even worse than when she had moved to the city in June. Besides working night and day for the ZOA, Ruth was planning for her future. She had applied to the University of California at Berkeley for admittance in the spring.

The Balfour Declaration anniversary celebration was a resounding success, and Ruth no doubt helped pull it off. Held at the Fairmont Hotel, it included a breakfast event, awards by the ZOA for recruitment of new members, and evening speeches by national leaders in the Zionist movement, both Christian and Jewish.[4] The flurry of activity that fall came to a head when the UN passed the Partition Plan. Around the world, Jews leaned in close to their radios to hear the votes called under strict rules of silence at UN headquarters. In San Francisco that evening, Mr. and Mrs. Jack Verdi hosted a celebration at their house with over a hundred guests, including leaders of the Zionist community such as Saul White, Morris Lowenthal, George Edelstein, W. Zev Bronner, and Rabbi Cohn. In the long list of guests announced in the *Jewish Tribune*, Ruth Rappaport was the only woman listed as a "Miss."[5]

Ruth often recounted a story of the moment while she was living in San Francisco when she was inspired to go to Palestine. She claimed that Golda Meir came to the city for a fundraising trip that Ruth helped plan. Feeling sorry for Golda, whose schedule was always hectic and exhausting, Ruth combined two separate functions into one and took her to the top-floor bar at the Mark Hopkins Hotel. While having cocktails, Golda told Ruth, "You are a Zionist and you mean well . . . but we don't need any more of your kind of Zionists . . . What we need is for young people with education and training, people like you to come and help us build our country! But you won't come . . . you'll raise money for others with less education, less experience, less training to come!" Ruth responded, "Don't bet on it."[6]

~

When I first heard this story, I wondered if it was really true. Of course Ruth would want to be associated with this famous woman, the "Iron Lady of Israel," a feminist hero to women around the world, despite her questionable leadership in the 1960s and '70s. But in the 1940s, Goldie Meyerson, as she was then known, was not famous outside Zionist circles. A leader of the Jewish Agency, a worldwide organization founded to assist Jews who wanted to move to Israel, she visited the United States on several fundraising trips in the 1930s. Was she actually in San Francisco between July and December 1947, when Ruth was living there?

My mom and I met up for another American Library Association conference in 2015, this time in San Francisco. We arrived early and stayed in Berkeley for two days. While I went through local Zionist collections at Berkeley's Bancroft Library, she looked through microfilm in the basement of the Doe Library next door, scanning PDFs of the *Jewish Tribune* for me. I told her to look for Golda Meir's visit, but she didn't see her name, even under her former name of Meyerson or Meirson, during the right timeframe. The next day we headed downtown to the conference, where I manned my station at the Library of Congress booth in the exhibit hall and she ransacked the free books and giveaways. One evening we decided to go up to the Mark Hopkins Hotel. Trudging up Nob Hill, we stopped at Ruth's first apartment on Pine Street to get a photo, then pushed farther on to the hotel a few blocks away. We took the elevator up to the Top of the Mark, where a jazz band played and people shimmied on the dance floor. We were seated in the corner with a magnificent view of the south side of San Francisco. We ordered a cheese plate and wine and mulled over this riddle of Ruth's.

I was certain they had met later in Israel, but Ruth had recorded in her diary there that she "was very impressed by the speech given by Golda Meyerson whom I heard for the first time."[7] Did that mean the first time in Israel? Or had she met her before but hadn't seen her give a speech? What if she was misremembering in old age, and they had met for the first time in Seattle, not San Francisco? Could she have confused the Mark Hopkins Hotel with some other rooftop bar in Seattle? Ruth later worked occasionally for Zionist organizations in San Francisco when she returned in the 1950s. Could she have met Meir then?

So, what did it mean if she actually hadn't met Meir before 1948? Was Ruth an outright liar? Had she inadvertently created a false memory, after so many people had probably asked later if she had ever met Meir in Israel? Her memory was so specific and so rich in detail that it seemed like it must have happened, in some way.

"To Golda and Ruth," my mother and I toasted.

When I returned home, I scoured the *Jewish Tribune* myself and confirmed that Meir was not in San Francisco in 1947. Her biographers were also in agreement: she was definitely in Palestine at that time, although she had embarked on a successful barnstorming tour of the US in early 1948, after Ruth left San Francisco for Palestine, the two passing each other like ships in the night. However, I came across an interesting story on the front page of the *Jewish Tribune*. A woman named Yehudith Simchonit, a Pioneer Women delegate from Palestine, was scheduled to speak in San Francisco on November 30:

> Mrs. Simchonit comes on an urgent mission as the representative of the 70,000 women organized into the Working Women's Council of Palestine . . . An outstanding leader of the Women's labor movement in Palestine, Mrs. Simchonit has devoted more than 25 years to pioneering among the workers in the colonies and towns of the Jewish Homeland.[8]

Was this the woman who inspired Ruth? There is no doubt that they would have met in San Francisco while Ruth performed her duties, which included escorting dignitaries around the city and planning their speaking engagements. Coming just a day after the UN's vote, Simchonit's talk may have been overshadowed by all of the excitement, perhaps a perfect time for the two women to slip away and go get a drink. Because Simchonit had a similar background as Meir, perhaps Ruth mixed up the two women in her mind later in life. Or more likely, Ruth the raconteuse just wanted to tell a great story, even if it was a fib, to captivate her friends and neighbors.

As I scrolled through the *Jewish Tribune*, I came across a heartbreaking article on the front page of the first issue of the new year, January 2, 1948. I already knew the story, but it was no less shocking to see it in print.

Ruth Rappaport to Palestine

When her brother-in-law was killed at Holon December 23, Miss Ruth Rappaport, currently with the San Francisco Zionist District, decided to return to Palestine. She is leaving here by plane on Saturday, January 3, en route to Lydda Field, Palestine.

Miss Rappaport is going to see her sister, Mrs. Miriam Schneider, whose husband, Max, was killed in the fighting at Holon on December 23. Mr. Schneider, a native of Germany, went to Palestine in 1933, and lived in the collective of Givath Hashlosha until 1938, when he and his wife moved to Jerusalem. Since that time he has been actively engaged in home defense.

Holon was one of the towns where the British disarmed all Jews, members of Haganah and the home
guard, when fighting started some days ago.

Miss Rappaport is planning to stay three months, and
will live at House Ettinger, Kirath Shmuel in Jerusalem.

Prior to coming to San Francisco last June, Miss
Rappaport was the editor of the Transcript in Seattle,
where she was active in the Zionist work of the
Community. She is past president of the Junior
Hadassah and secretary of the Seattle Zionist Council.

Max Schneider, 31, a brother-in-law of Ruth Rappaport,
a member of the Haganah home defense force, was
killed in Holon, Palestine, a settlement where the
British disarmed Jews. He had four brothers, all in
Haganah service now.

~

At the end of December 1947, Ruth's sister Mirjam sent a telegram
to her asking if she would come to Palestine and stay with her while
she grieved for her husband. On December 26 Ruth wrote a resignation letter to George Edelstein, president of the San Francisco office of
the Zionist Organization of America, and apologized for her sudden
departure.[9]

In her oral history, Ruth did not mention her brother-in-law's
death as her reason for going to Palestine. There was her Golda Meir
story, of course, but she said also that she went as an "advance party
of one" for the Zionist Emergency Council, to "have all the rich San
Francisco Jews go on a mission—now they call them 'missions.'" She

went on: "We were going to have all the people who gave money and time to work towards partition. We were going to have this publicity flight: DP! Destination Palestine. Oh, weren't we clever . . . And I was dispatched."[10]

Regardless of the exact reasons Ruth went to Palestine, it was a chance for her to finally see it for herself and to live out her ideals as a Zionist. She had never desired to live on a kibbutz, but she thought that perhaps Palestine could be an opportunity to advance her career while placing her at the center of a momentous event in modern history. She had ambitions to travel around the country, learn more about the people there, and keep an extensive diary that she might use to write a book or go on a speaking tour later in the United States. If anything, she could probably pick up work as a journalist or photographer and meet other people in this field who would give her leads or help her climb the ladder to a position she felt was worthy of her intelligence and skills. Only a very small number of Jewish American women made the commitment to go to Palestine in 1948.[11] Most of them were single and deeply committed Zionists. Historians Shulamit Reinharz and Mark A. Raider have noted, "Those who did emigrate were seen as heroines or, just as often, incomprehensible."[12]

Unsure of how long she would stay in Palestine, Ruth left San Francisco for Chicago on January 3, 1948. W. Zev Bronner, Rabbi Franklin Cohn, roommates Zamira and Sharon, and others had a going-away party and came with her to the airport to see her off. From the Palmer House Hotel in Chicago, she wrote of her shame that she was hoping that her ex-boyfriend Jim would come to see her in Chicago. After calling him but realizing "he was out sleeping with some other dame," she finally reached him. He said he might come if he could find the money. She complained, "I don't know why I waste my thoughts, time and money on him. Except that I cannot forget him. I sure know how to mess up my life." Jim did not come to meet her, and the next day she sent him a telegram in which she wrote, *"Enta Iben Kalb,"* roughly translated from Arabic as "You are a son of a bitch." Ruth met up with a friend she had known in Zurich. She informed Ruth that her first crush, Roger Garfunkel, had gotten married. Ruth decided, "Well I got over him, maybe I'll get over Jim too."[13]

From Chicago, Ruth flew to Washington, DC, where she stayed with her uncle Irving Rappaport, aunt Bertha, and cousin Marvin and "found out who all is left in Viynita [Vyzhnytsya]"—in other words, which of her father's relatives had survived the Holocaust in the Ukraine. From Philadelphia, she flew to Newfoundland, Ireland, and Paris, where she visited her sister Clara and her nephew Guy for just a few hours. Ruth also stopped in Geneva on the way to Cairo.[14] But for "political reasons," she wrote in a letter, they landed not in Egypt as planned but in Lydda (today Lod), a predominantly Arabic town southeast of Tel Aviv. Because of gunfire, Ruth and other travelers were stuck overnight in the airport. Her arrival wasn't glamorous, and it wasn't what she had expected, but after pondering, imagining, and waiting for this moment her entire life, she had finally made aliyah.

Part V:

It Is All Such a Vicious Circle

PALESTINE/ISRAEL, 1948–1949

Chapter 17

The day after her arrival in Palestine, Ruth took a short flight to Tel Aviv, where she was finally able to reunite with Mirjam. They traveled to the home of Mirjam's sister-in-law, Hadassah, in Holon, which was in the middle of guerrilla warfare. Although both Jews and Arabs had been fighting against the British in resistance movements for decades, now Arabs were launching attacks against Jewish settlements in protest of the Partition Plan. The Haganah, which was undergoing a transformation from a paramilitary organization into an official army, retaliated against these attacks, and now a new civil war was underway.

Ruth and Mirjam had not seen each other since 1936, when Ruth was thirteen and Mirjam came back to Germany for a visit after making Palestine her permanent home in 1933.[1] Although they had probably written letters to each other, their ten-year age gap, being half sisters (or "stepsisters," as Ruth sometimes put it), the upheaval of World War II, and spending their formative years in two such vastly different places would define their relationship. While Mirjam had married young and committed herself to a spartan Orthodox Jewish lifestyle in Palestine, Ruth had taken a different path, partly by chance but mostly of her own free will. Although a committed Zionist, she had fully immersed herself in American culture, taken some college classes, and eventually held several different challenging and interesting jobs as a single woman both during and after the war.

Ruth stayed with the Schneiders for a few uncomfortable weeks. Besides Hadassah, the family included Max's brothers Fred and Ben, who lived in Jerusalem. Ruth explained the conditions in Holon: "One never quite [knew] if a bullet would come into the house or not. In the morning it became a steady routine to look at the bullet holes on the outside of the house."[2] It saddened her that Hadassah's children played with cartridge casings instead of marbles.

Reflecting on her two weeks in Holon, she commented on Hadassah's "proletarian poverty" and how everyone had been so depressed about Max's death that she was motivated to leave after two weeks. She did not feel very close to Mirjam or believe that she could really help her. Fred, who spoke English very well, escorted Ruth around the city and to Tel Aviv, where she visited with the parents of a few friends from the West Coast and tried to seek out a job. Fred soon fell in love with Ruth. She admitted that she had some initial attraction to him but that it ended for her there: "It not only became burdensome for me with his overpowering emotion, adoration, servility and concern, but it enraged Miriam who in her state of nerves became extremely jealous of [me] and [intimated] that I was robbing her of the last bit of Max!"[3]

Ruth left for Jerusalem, where Mirjam, Fred, Ben, and Rita, Ben's wife, were living. A mixed city of Christians, Jews, and Muslims, it was a symbolic place for all three religious groups and the center of an intensely violent struggle for territory. The Old City was divided into sections according to religion, and recently arrived Jews had settled in West Jerusalem, outside the Old City's walls. Ruth hoped to find stories to write there as a correspondent. On a harrowing bus trip into the city by convoy, the British troops searched Ruth and the other travelers, then watched as Arabs shot and threw grenades at the bus and other cars a few miles outside the city. Also on the bus was the chief rabbi of Palestine, who recited the Tehillim (Psalms) for the other passengers.[4]

Ruth lived with Fred in an apartment on King George Street, and Mirjam may have lived in the same building. "Under normal conditions," she described the building they occupied, "[it] would be a lovely place . . . one of the most modern of Jerusalem's six-story apartment houses. My balcony faces the Old City . . . Citadel of David etc. etc."[5] Although she had a view of the Old City, she could not visit it. Jews were banned from that part of the city, except for a small number who lived there and who would soon be forced out. The situation in Jerusalem was even worse than in Holon. There were constant firefights, and Ruth described her furniture as riddled with bullets. Living in Jerusalem at this time tested the limits of her ability to survive under traumatic and stressful conditions. She explained:

> Since we have a critical water shortage, we have to go down each day and buy four gallons of water, when it is available, that is, and since there is no electricity, the elevator does not work, so I have to carry my buckets up six flights of stairs… and there is no gas or petroleum either, so I cannot cook anything, but then there are no groceries available, so I don't have to worry about not being able to cook them, and since there is no mail, I need not worry about no electricity, for there is nothing to read.[6]

She wrote to W. Zev Bronner in San Francisco: "It is hard to adequately put into words the hopelessness and [ugliness] and sordidness of the situation to anyone who has not seen it in person. And yet, I do not wish it to anybody to live here under present conditions . . . I am beginning to feel as if living in San Francisco or Seattle was living in a fairy land compared with this nightmare here."[7]

On February 22, Ben Yehuda Street was bombed, just a few blocks away from where Ruth lived. She wrote an article describing the wreckage and the tragic story of a five-year-old girl who survived but lost her family. She enclosed it in a letter to Victor Bloom, the owner of the *Jewish Tribune* newspaper in San Francisco, asking if he was interested in publishing a weekly dispatch from her and requesting that he send press credentials.[8] Although she didn't hear back from him and had no idea if he had published her article, she sent more. Another article of hers did appear in the *Jewish Tribune* in March under the title "Jerusalem, a Besieged City," along with her letter to Bloom.[9] This one described her visit to a newspaper office and how one hour afterward the man she had spoken with there was shot on a bus. Ruth wrote that the British did not report or count his murder or the murder of other civilians in Jerusalem. She closed her letter to Bloom with a plea to the *Tribune*'s audience: "I do hope that the article will convey something to your readers, and help to move them to action, or if they are active, to more action."[10] Ruth was also unsure of whether the "Destination Palestine" trip sponsored by the *Jewish Tribune* would happen.[11] As she remembered it later, she sent a telegram to those planning the trip that said, "War broke out, stay home."[12]

As in Leipzig, Ruth once again faced a dangerous situation and, instead of avoiding it, wanted to witness it and describe it to others. Reflecting on this much later, she stated, "People sort of sometimes say . . . I seem to be war-prone. And I frequently get this business of, aren't you scared? And you know, I'm not scared. You know why? I pretend I'm a spectator. I'm not in this war; I'm watching this war. And that gets me off the hook—I don't have to worry."[13] Ruth lamented the constant gunshots, bombings, rationing, and the depressed mood of Jews in Palestine. The frequent battles frayed her nerves, but she never felt as though she would be killed or hurt. She told her friends that she hoped the US would get involved in the conflict and that every American Jew should do more to support the new state.

Because she had departed so suddenly from San Francisco, Ruth had left many of her belongings in her apartment, but she had planned on her friends and roommates sending her some things and packing and shipping the rest to Seattle. Ruth ultimately lost many items and grew frustrated with people whom she had trusted to carry out these tasks. Her letters also reveal her demanding personality: asking friends to do laundry lists of favors, including shipping food to her sister Clara, developing her negatives, contacting the IRS about her new situation, and shipping clothing and supplies she could not get in Jerusalem. She always enclosed blank checks or offered to reimburse any expenses and encouraged friends to send items that she could sell for them in Jerusalem at a big markup. At least one friend responded exasperated that Ruth expected too much and had left a mess for others to pick up. Coupled with many letters lost in the mail, Ruth began to doubt if she had any real friends in San Francisco.[14]

Ruth had accumulated substantial savings along with her inheritance from her uncle Carl. But due to the high cost of living, she was losing money quickly. She was soon desperate for a job and inquired around Tel Aviv and Jerusalem for journalism positions. Before she left the US, many people had given her names of people in Palestine to contact about jobs, but these opportunities did not pan out. She did not know Hebrew, and many employers did not want to hire during the uncertainty of the war. She also blamed Fred for holding her back in her search for a job.[15] In the spring of 1948, she was planning on coming back to the US in July unless she got a permanent, decent job. In April, Ruth was offered a trial job to replace an Acme United Press photographer who was killed in Jerusalem. She wrote in her diary about this opportunity: "It pays very little, but promises to be interesting—although I know so little about photography it is not even funny—but then, I did not know anything about the Transcript job and got it and kept it."[16] She was also concerned that she would not be able to keep any of the negatives or prints she shot, which she hoped she would be able to use later for a speaking tour. She made plans to photograph a Haganah training camp for Acme United Press, but worried about her decision: "All seems to be settled, except that something in me is too apathetic for me to pull myself together & to become enthusiastic. I think I'm scared of this job, I don't feel equipped for it. I am not afraid of the danger but of the flopping."[17] But she managed to confront these fears and took photos of which she was proud. She attended press conferences in Jerusalem where she met other journalists and leaders of the Jewish forces.

These war correspondents were part of an international network of men who had covered the Spanish Civil War and World War II. Many of them were leftists, if not outright Communists. They had traveled the world and risked their lives to capture images and stories of some of the most tragic and poignant moments of the twentieth century. They had seen their acquaintances and friends—and as in photographer Robert Capa's case, also their lovers—killed in action. Many in this group no doubt suffered from post-traumatic stress disorder. Many others likely felt an emptiness after World War II had ended. Some had tried to cover regular civilian life or Hollywood, but they yearned to get back to documenting another world event. The war in Palestine proved to be what they craved, and in the case of Capa and other Jewish journalists, it would have a deep, personal connection to their lives.[18]

Capa had taught Ruth how to use a camera.[19] They may have connected over their Jewish childhoods in Europe, and she was probably aware of his famous photo of the death of an American soldier on a balcony of an apartment in Leipzig, but she mentioned him only twice, briefly, in her diary.[20] Ruth could go toe to toe with these journalists, and her quick wit and willingness to go out drinking and dancing with them helped her gain acceptance in their circle. But she could never shake the feeling that her skills were not quite up to snuff, that she didn't have their worldly experiences, or that they saw her only as an obnoxious hanger-on, a woman who was not a true equal.

In May 1948 Ruth went on a press trip with forty other journalists and photographers to Katamon, an Arabic section of Jerusalem where there had been recent fighting.[21] The group was not allowed into the area, however. Ruth later went back by herself and discovered that "a friendly smile to a commanding officer means much more than dozens of press cards."[22] The officer showed her around and allowed her to take photographs. Ruth realized she saw a dead Iraqi lying in the grass, the first dead body she had ever seen.[23] She was disgusted but took a photograph of it. After discussing it with her Acme United Press editor, Dave Boyer, she realized that the photo was evidence that Jews had violated the Red Cross rules against abandoning casualties. For two days she panicked, fearing her press card would be revoked and that she, the officer, or members of the Red Cross would be in trouble. She found out later that the Red Crescent (Arabic Red Cross) insisted on removing their own bodies but that the Jewish forces had not allowed them in—"Typical Jewish bungling," Ruth wrote. The incident caused her to realize the serious ethical and moral issues that war journalists faced: "Everything is confused, blunders are made, information leaks quickly, & is apt to be given out without being conscious of it. Extreme care must be used, and chances are [that] the source of the crazy military rules and prohibitions that do not seem to make sense are quite necessary."[24] Ruth realized she still had a lot to learn about war journalism, and although she was eager to succeed at this new job, the experience she had gained in Seattle had left her ill prepared to cover such a fraught and dangerous situation.

On May 14, British troops officially left Palestine and Jews declared independence, creating the state of Israel. Ruth wrote of her increasing alienation from these landmark events, "Well, this is supposed to be the historic day—Independence day—The Birth of a Nation—the beginning of the Jewish State, only being right on the spot the glamour is lacking."[25] The same day, Ruth wrote about the continued fighting and how she had taken pictures of the boys manning the Spandau machine gun on the roof of her apartment building. She observed, "It is all so unreal[,] almost like a cheap book or movie thriller."[26]

She continued to worry about "flopping" at her job. Despite the momentous events taking place in Israel, Ruth admitted she had done nothing for two days and should have gone to Tel Aviv but either could not or would not leave, because the city was still under siege. She explained in her diary the new political situation: "In Jerusalem we now have martial law—well, rather Jewish martial law, [which I'd rather have] over my head than foreign. America already recognized the Jewish State. Perhaps we shall get some help from there. It will soon be over with victory or no hope! The sun shines, the birds sing, and the bullets whizz while the cannons roar."[27] When the British troops left, Jews took over the official buildings for their new government. The Jewish Agency took on the role of providing information to the press. Due to her proximity to people in power, Ruth was beginning to pull back the curtain and realize that Jewish governance did not guarantee an ethical, fair system that could guarantee basic security for its citizens. She grew increasingly concerned that the residents of Jerusalem were being sacrificed to make a larger point to the world. She was outraged: "Things are not going so well, and . . . there is a terrific censorship in the country! Easy enough for the bigshots to say if necessary they will turn Jerusalem into a second Stalingrad—but who will survive it? And afterwards—who will get Jerusalem? Not the Jews! So why all this sacrifice?"[28]

Ruth had to battle Israel's inaugural spokesman, Gershon Hirsch, to obtain a new press pass. He claimed he needed to confirm her status, even though her Acme United Press colleague, Leo Turner, had already done so. Hirsch also joked it might take her five years to get a pass and asked why she needed one anyway if she was a photographer.[29] It is unclear why he gave her so much trouble, but it appears likely that it was because she was a woman. When she was locked out of one press conference, she passed the time in another room with another woman, Shoshannah Rothblatt, a correspondent for *Hadassah Magazine*, who might have also been barred.[30]

In her diary Ruth admitted that her strongest desires were professional success and recognition. As she worried about her job and whether she should go to Tel Aviv to seek out a new opportunity, she wondered if coming to Palestine was a mistake and if she could have done better by staying in the US:

> Palestine and Jerusalem are a smaller pond even than Seattle, but after 5 months I have not even started to swim—I have had a few splashy dives, but that is all—now I'm afraid I'm going to drown. Tel Aviv or Haifa are my last hope—either I do good or I go home defeated. I guess I crave recognition and being known more than anything else—especially since I tasted it in Seattle.[31]

As Ruth waited to get her press pass, she mostly stayed at home, because it was too dangerous to go out. To pass the time, she read many books, including the German translation of *I, Claudius* by Robert Graves. She missed going to the press conferences and panicked as mortars hit her apartment building and bullets flew into her room's open windows. Her isolation and boredom spiraled into depression: "I don't know, I have the blues and have them badly—I have never felt so sad and alone and lonely, so low—it's more than just a bad head cold, or no food for 5 months, I feel as if I carried the sadness of a thousand years on my back."[32] She began to question the point of it all. A week after Israel declared its independence, Ruth prophetically explained, "I shudder to think of the aftermath[,] when all the casualties, dead and crippled are going to be known, the poverty & the hatred that will follow, both among the Arabs and the Jews. I wonder if it will really have been worth all this to get a state."[33] Even her belief in Zionism was beginning to crack. She had built her life and her identity around this cause, and she wondered whom she would become if she could not continue her support in good faith:

> The way I feel about Palestine and have felt about it ever since I first came here really means a disillusionment of

many years' belief, and even to myself I am not ready to admit it, I keep thinking these are abnormal times, I have not met the right people, etc. ... if I go back home now I could not possibly continue being a Zionist, and after all these year[s], it would just be as if part of my life were missing if suddenly I would say nothing any more about Zionism, the great Jewish experiment, the solution of the Jewish problem—oh, it is all such a vicious circle—where does it start and where does it end, and what is going to become of me?[34]

She admitted that she did not celebrate Jewish holidays. In her diary there is no mention of her attending a synagogue, although she did write that she missed American celebrations of both Jewish and Christian holidays, if only because they came with parties and feelings of connection with friends and relatives. Ruth seems to have led a completely secular life in Jerusalem and questioned her identity as a Jew and her allegiance to other Jews: "Sometimes I begin to wonder, maybe the Jews deserve what they are getting here. I know this is wicked, but they are such little mean people, taken up with their own importance, everybody mistrusts everybody else, everybody cheats everybody else out of their last penny, everybody tries to get the better of everybody else, everything is based on 'Protektia—protection' that is all."[35] She had always defined herself as a Jew first. She hadn't always gotten along with other Jews, but the fact that they could treat each other so horribly in this new environment—finally, a Jewish state—was a shock to both her identity and worldview.

Ruth repeatedly wrote that Fred would come into her room and "paw" at her in bed and described other acts that we would now refer to as sexual harassment or abuse. The fact that Fred was a relative made the situation worse, as the boundaries between family, friendship, and sexual relationships began to blur. Jewish tradition held that when a married man died, his brother should marry the widow. Mirjam probably could not have conceived of marrying Fred after Max's death, but perhaps Fred looked toward Mirjam and Ruth as his only options. Ruth lived with Fred because she seems to have had no other place to live, and she could not escape his constant presence in her own home. Initially Ruth questioned why she was not attracted to Fred and why she felt guilty about it. Was it that she just wasn't over Jim? She realized that maybe she was acting toward Fred the way Jim had toward her. She mulled over ways to explain to Fred that they just weren't suited to each other, deciding to tell him that she was an extrovert and he was an introvert. After months of trying to be polite, Ruth decided she had to be firm. She wrote, "I hesitated & then decided that since this utterly foolish relationship and behavior must stop sooner or later it might as well be now. I had intended to do it painlessly, but that won't work—so—it must be done with 'Ach & Krach' [by the skin of my teeth]."[36]

Fred had grown increasingly jealous of Ruth's interactions with other people, especially men. As she began to meet other journalists and new and old friends in the city, they recognized her on the street and would often stop to chat. Strangers stared at her nice clothes, and she went out to cafés and bars, as she hated to sit at home. These interactions left Fred fuming, and Ruth complained about his outbursts, crying, and sullen moods. His standoffish attitude toward her new friends and colleagues was downright embarrassing to her. Ruth wrote about what once happened after she came home from a party with other journalists: "[Fred made] a quiet, but nonetheless terrible scene, quietly sobbing away. So I gave way, with the result that he did not let me sleep a wink, kept on pawing and pawing me, until I almost screamed. I was so tired and strained I thought my nerves would burst."[37] Even though she projected an outward image of an independent, confident single woman, Ruth still struggled to say no to Fred.

Jim Pringle, a fellow journalist, asked Ruth on a date to a party at the Sebria, a restaurant and bar.[38] When they arrived, she was surprised that Carter Davidson, head of the Associated Press bureau in Jerusalem, knew who she was. She also met journalist Roy C. Carlson, who had written the bestseller *Under Cover*, in which he described his infiltration of right-wing American groups with pro-Nazi leanings before the war. Carlson was actually the Armenian-born Avedis Derounian. Roy C. Carlson was one of many pseudonyms he used for his investigative work. When Ruth met him in 1948, he was infiltrating the Arabic neighborhoods in Jerusalem for his book *Cairo to Damascus*, which would be published in 1951 under the name John Roy Carlson. In the book, he admits to sneaking over to the Jewish side of Jerusalem to sleep at the YMCA, since there was no comfortable lodging in the Arabic neighborhoods. At the party, Carlson monopolized Ruth's attention, to the point where she felt she had committed a faux pas with Pringle. Carlson even invited her to come along with him to take photos. After drinking, dancing, and having a good conversation, Ruth later wrote, "[I] had a swell time—the kind of time I am used to & that one can have every place if one knows the right people."[39] But when she got home, Fred told her, "If you want to be a public whore, at least don't let the whole house know it by returning at 3 a.m." He had also read her personal letters to Jim. Ruth was "too crushed and disgusted" to say anything and went to bed but comforted him later that night anyway. It would not be the only time during her two years in Israel that she would be called a slut or prostitute. As a single woman who often traveled without an escort, socialized with men in bars and restaurants, and had her own money, Ruth was vulnerable to these gendered insults.

About two weeks after the party, Ruth again ran into "the great" Roy C. Carlson, as she sarcastically called him. She realized he was spying for both sides and getting paid for it. In their conversation Carlson admitted that if he had known earlier that Fred was her brother-in-law and not her "lover," he would have given her food and cigarettes. Ruth expressed her outrage at this presumption: "If he thinks he has a chance to sleep with me, then I can get things [from him]—God—what has the world come to. Am I just waking up? Have I been completely naïve and asleep all these years?"[40] This was only one of the many, in fact almost daily, humiliating propositions she would be on the receiving end of throughout her time in Israel.

At the end of May, Fred attempted to commit suicide by hanging himself in the kitchen of their apartment. The rope broke, and when Ruth came home she found him lying on the floor.[41] She claimed that she was really through with him and that it was clear he was mentally ill. Two days later Fred joined the Israeli air force, and Ruth hoped that the experience would be good for him.[42] Over the next few months, Ruth would take steps to cut Fred out of her life, although she would run into him occasionally. In letters to friends, she referred to Fred's suicide attempt as an example of the awful dating scene in Israel. Disgusted with him, she would remind herself repeatedly to not behave toward any man the way that Fred had toward her: as an obsessive stalker manipulating her with all kinds of efforts to win her over, even with pity.

On the eve of her twenty-fifth birthday, Ruth summed up her general dissatisfaction with her life:

> What achievement? Nothing! My own life disorganized—not finished with school—not married—no job—no place to live because I want to or like it! In San Francisco? Half washed up with my sudden departure! In Seattle? Who knows, maybe forgotten or half? In Palestine not a friend outside of Fred—whose friendship is too much of a burden to be enjoyable. My sister? Not giving a damn, but then, I don't either, really! Jim? All washed up—Fred—soon to be washed up! My money? Soon spent—Next what? Rather a poor inventory, Rappaport, at 25 you might have managed better! Oh, what do I know—no place at home, no place happy, nowhere satisfied? So, what is the difference then where I am or what I do. Why feel so sorry for myself?

> Papa used to say "Wie man sich bettet so schläft man"
> [you've made your bed, now lie in it]—o.k. so I do, then
> why must I feel so sorry for myself? Oh hell, I'm so miser-
> able and lonely and lonesome, it's more, it's almost frus-
> trated, dissatisfied—but with what? Myself? The war? My
> inability to make an adjustment here in Palestine below
> the surface?[43]

Ruth seemed to blame herself for all her problems, and in her many complaints across her journals she seemed to understand that being a Jew and a woman was at the heart of her troubles, and slowly a consciousness of the discrimination she faced began to emerge. The allusion to her father is just one of two brief mentions of him in her voluminous diaries across two years in Israel. She had learned of her parents' murders in concentration camps two years before, but she never wrote about it, even in her diary, unless those pages did not survive or Ruth later destroyed them. Her loneliness, while possibly the result of her lack of friends or a boyfriend, may also point to her grief about her parents, which may have seemed unspeakable.

Ruth grew increasingly concerned that she was still single at age twenty-five. She regularly received letters from friends who updated her on their weddings, new babies, and houses. Surely she must have felt somewhat left behind as they entered these new stages of life. She was not immune to the enormous pressure of the American postwar drive to settle down into a steady life of family and job security. But she questioned if that was what she wanted anyway. When she contemplated a future with someone like Fred, she wrote, "I don't know why I cannot just be happy living a quiet life without trying to be something or somebody. Why do I keep complicating my life so much?"[44]

In June 1948 Ruth met Viktor Radnicky in a café in Jerusalem and "something went click."[45] He was a Communist Czech photographer on an assignment in Israel and a friend of Robert Capa's. Later at the Press

Information Office, a division of Israel's Ministry of Foreign Affairs, he told her that he was going to Tel Aviv. She wrote, "Already then, though not deliberately, I wanted to hurry to TA to get to know him better." Desperate to get away from Fred a few days later, she hitchhiked to Tel Aviv by herself without saying goodbye to him. She made it to a friend's house, where she showered and ate, then went to see Hadassah in Holon and another friend, where "both acted as if they saw a ghost coming up."[46]

Ruth had lost thirty-five pounds while in Jerusalem and often wrote of the intense hunger, food rations, and awful food she subsisted on. At her memorial service in 2010, many friends reminisced and joked about her food-hoarding habits and her repeated requests for friends to drive her to Costco. One woman said that she had once asked Ruth why she did this, and Ruth had replied, "I was hungry once. And I never want to be hungry again." The woman presumed Ruth was referring to when she had jumped off the train in Switzerland, but Ruth more likely was remembering her experience in Jerusalem.[47]

Chapter 18

In Tel Aviv Ruth not only began to recover physically from her weight loss, but she also started a months-long binge of frantic dancing, drinking, and dating while she despaired about never finding a job. She met up with Viktor several times, and after she spent the night with him she noted, "When he did not do any more than I let him I knew that I really loved him and that he could get out of me whatever he wanted." She hoped that Viktor could finally make her forget Jim, but unfortunately he would have to go back to Prague soon. Ruth admitted she "went to bed with him," but that she had her doubts: "In the middle I realized it was another Gamal [Jim] affair, here today, gone tomorrow and myself knee deep in it, and like a fool I started crying and could not stop . . . sometimes I think he loves me too and is just waiting for me to take the lead, and then again I think no I'll just make a fool of myself for he is not serious."[1]

In between seeing Viktor, Ruth had many job interviews and lunch dates, visited Fred, who was now in a hospital in Tel Aviv, and tried to get settled in this new city. She wanted to marry Viktor and strategized about how to make it happen. When other women showed up at his apartment while she was there, she acted like she didn't care, but she also cried like a "complete neurotic" while on another date with him, on the beach. She wrote a long diary entry while waiting in his apartment for him to come back from a trip to Jerusalem, with his roommate, Walter, singing French love songs to her and proposing to her. She asked, "Why is it that all the wrong men are running after me, and the one I want I cannot seem to get[?] This is really ironic . . ."[2]

Ruth did not believe in learning to love someone over time. She was instantly attracted to Viktor and explained why in her diary, comparing him to her ex-boyfriend Jim: "He too is soft on the inside, also much like a boy, proud to be a man, his career more important than anything, his own life and his idea. The good differences between the two are that the things Vic. stands for are the same to a big extent as what I stand for."[3] She knew deep down that she would never be satisfied in a relationship unless it was a true partnership of intellectual equals. She wanted more than just a warm body to financially support her and share a home: she desired a sparring partner to bounce ideas off and someone to help her better understand the world and her place in it. She had an obvious disdain for men who tried to overpower her or looked to her to save themselves from their depression or loneliness.

On Viktor's last night in Israel, they discussed their feelings:

> I also got it across to him that I was not quite as much of a butterfly as he thought I was, and in the end I told him that I loved him. I knew he was being honest when he told me his emotions were very mixed up. He liked me very much but did not know if it was love. That he hoped we would meet again some day, and that perhaps I just met him at the wrong time. He was married once and afraid to do it again, etc. etc.[4]

After going with him to the airport the next day, she reflected, "Maybe I'll meet him again someday, and maybe I'll even marry him . . . If he had asked me to marry him, I would have said yes, but even if I could I would not make him, for I don't want to mess up his life, and I don't know if I am strong enough to lead his kind of life, although I admire it. He takes his communism seriously, he knows what he wants to do and how to do it. That is the difference between him and me."[5]

After Viktor left, Ruth continued to get settled in Tel Aviv. She bought new clothes, gained back the weight she had lost, visited friends, and tried to find a job, which grew increasingly discouraging. She knew she needed to learn Hebrew in order to be employable in Israel and debated spending serious time to learn it. She was depressed, writing frequently of her bouts of "the blues." Even though she longed for Viktor, she went out on dates with different men almost every night. Just two weeks after Viktor left, she wrote:

> True I had the worst blues yesterday, but after stooping so low that I let Diskin make love to me I decided I must take myself in hand. I feel really ashamed of myself at this rate. If it continues I might as well become a prostitute and the cold thing is I hate it…these boys…not only mean nothing to me, but I have not even respect for them. Finish—out—and I am not going to sleep myself into a job here—it is hideous.[6]

A week later, in the same fashion, she admitted of a man named Sigie, "[I let him] make love to me last night partly because I had drunk a lot[,] partly because I liked him, I wanted to be cuddled, etc., etc." When he came by the next day and Ruth refused him, he said that someone told him that she had slept with Viktor also and that he was not actually divorced. Ruth agonized, "It is all so queer & crazy it gives me the creeps sometimes how everything gets around." She also reflected on the fact that her dark side, which she worked to control, was emerging in these chaotic circumstances: "My obviously long suppressed desires to lawlessness, adventure, my love of playing with fire seem to more & more gain the upper hand, but if I have it in me to come out as the victor, or if I[,] like so many people here[,] will go under[,] I do not know."[7]

Ruth went out with Sigie again, though, but did not want him to come into her apartment. On another date, he "promised to behave," so she allowed him in. "First we had a big talk," she wrote, "[and I] told him exactly that he cannot make love to me . . . that it was not fair to wear down my resistance with persistence . . . He then made love to me by force, I got mad . . . & went to spend the night alone on the beach. If I had not left I could have created such a row the whole town would have awakened."[8] The phrase "date rape" would not become a familiar term to describe these kinds of experiences of women until the 1990s, but it is clear this is what happened to Ruth. She exhibits a proto-feminist consciousness when she wrote of her feelings about the incident with Sigie, and possibly with other men: "During all these happenings, I think I also found part of the clue why I loved Jim & Vik. They are both men—all others are <u>males</u>—no matter how much they want a woman, they will only try up to a certain point. When [men] see [a] no go without force they are man enough not to use the cheap advantage of strength, & not to get mad and have hurt pride and never see her again."[9] Although she was disgusted with Sigie, his charm and manipulative cycle of apologies and flowers were hard for her to resist.

She went out with him again a week later and suffered through another humiliating spectacle when she refused to let him come in and he screamed at her outside her rented room and threw stones at her window for hours.[10] Her upset landlord, Mrs. Sprung, ordered her out the next day. Ruth sought refuge with a new friend, Gad Pollack, who promised she could stay with his mother temporarily. It turned out his mother was out of town and Gad expected that Ruth would give in to his overtures in his bedroom. She was annoyed and refused him but was glad that he at least didn't force himself on her. The next night she moved into the hotel Viktor had stayed in, although she could not afford it.[11] Her move to Tel Aviv that summer was just the beginning of a never-ending revolving door. She would spend the next year and a half packing her bags over and over, getting kicked out of rented rooms, sharing apartments, and finding herself in hotel rooms for a litany of circumstances beyond her control. As in Zurich, Ruth had a constant dark feeling of homelessness and ached for a quiet, permanent place of her own.[12]

Sigie and Gad were not the only men she went out with during these early months in Tel Aviv. She made more than one date per day or evening and brought home many different men. Looking back months later, she alternated between embarrassment at her reckless behavior and a refusal to feel ashamed about it, mentioning it many times in her diary and often referring to it as some other state of reality: "[Gad] closed a rather brief but the more eccentric and not very nice period of my life—and yet—I'm not really ashamed—though my behavior was all but conventional or admirable—in a peculiar [way] I felt cleansed, revenged or something—it was all like a trance[,] not really me—it was as if my soul had left my body & my body was fending for itself."[13]

Mirjam had grown increasingly worried about Ruth's reputation and how it would reflect on the Schneider family. She asked Ruth if she planned to go back to the US, which Ruth found insulting.[14] This postwar frenzy in Israel that Ruth participated in was probably similar to what was happening around the world as survivors of the unspeakable horrors of World War II sought to drown their traumatic memories in alcohol, sex, and mindless distractions. In September 1948, Ruth wrote to Rabbi Cohn, explaining her disgust at the men in Israel:

All, and I repeat this, all Palestinian males think if they pay one drink for a girl, she must go to bed with them! Otherwise, why waste 20 piasters! There is one way of getting a good job, that is sleeping your way into it..... sorry.....I do not believe in getting a job that way. Worse, even if you go out and pay your own way, and say no to a proposition[,] you are called a bitch, etc. etc. This goes for people in Histadrut, Sochnut, Army, Air force and government. I guess that too is a reason for my getting such a lovely reputation here....for men don't go around telling people that I slap their faces in the middle of the street on the way home, and go home by myself, nor that

I always pay my own way whether that be for dinner, drinks or dancing.[15]

Most days, she met with friends and acquaintances who gave her promising job leads. Some of these led to an interview for a secretarial job with strings attached—sexual favors for married men looking for a diversion. Ruth was also up against stiff competition for white-collar jobs that were often given to people with stronger connections (*Protektia*) than she had.[16] She danced with men who name-dropped their powerful bosses or fathers and implied they could get her a secure position in the government. In a letter to Rabbi Cohn, she vented her frustration with the list of job contacts he had given her: "Bancover I met at a Histadrut reception, and pardon the vulgarism, he practically tried to make me at the reception while Golda Meyerson was giving a speech. Later he asked me to see him at his office, and the minute I entered he locked his room, but while trying to come close I whackingly boxed his ears."[17] This was the same speech she wrote about in her diary, complaining about this man who had harassed her: "Sunday afternoon I got to the Histadrut reception—was very impressed by the speech given by Golda Meyerson[,] whom I heard for the first time—also by some of the other people but very disgusted with Bancover."[18]

Ruth was very excited about a position as an army photographer. After a good interview at the Press Information Office, she later went back to inquire again about the job but was told that the department could not hire women.[19] Unemployment was starting to drive her stir-crazy. It wasn't only the lack of money or desire for success that drove her to find a job; she also craved a sense of usefulness and structure to her days. Being busy and accomplishing tasks was how she burned her excessive energy, connected with like-minded coworkers, and kept her mind off depressing thoughts and memories. Israel was supposed to be a place where she could flourish in her career and where Jewish women were supposedly going to be treated as equals, but she had spent the last eight months barely treading water.

Chapter 19

Sometime in October, Ruth finally joined the Defense Army of Israel and got a position in the photography unit of the Press Information Office (or the PIO, as she called it), the same office where she had applied for the photographer job.[1] In her oral history, Ruth claimed that she had landed this job through her "old friend" Golda Meir. In her letters and diaries, Ruth did mention seeing her give a speech in August, but she was not writing in her diary around the time she got the job a few months later. She later claimed that she went to Golda's office and declared she wanted to join the army to learn Hebrew while working in the kitchen. Golda responded, "No, if you're working in the kitchen, you'll be learning how to peel potatoes."[2]

After Ruth started the job, however, she was very disappointed. She sarcastically explained:

> Photography? Ha, ha, what a laugh! Office work, ha, ha! A pleasant and decent boss??? Ha, ha. This time I have really outsmarted myself. Cannot I ever learn to take my loss in good time, before it is too late....this whole trip started out wrong, I should have known it would come to no good end. But could I admit defeat and go home like a sensible kid??? No. Or could I go to camp, and though uncomfortable, at least meet Palestinians, get some

"Chawershaft" [camaraderie][?] [N]o, I had to be ambitious and different.....PIO.....ha, ha, fancy.[3]

She complained that her job could be done by a child, that other employees could get away with wearing civilian clothes, and that her wages were less than what she was paying for rent. She may have loathed the job, but she couldn't just quit. Joining the Israeli army was a serious commitment, even though she retained her American citizenship and never sought Israeli citizenship. It was a temporary, six-month position, and then she would be offered a discharge with various options. Ruth did not get along with her boss, Lieutenant Colonel Moshe Pearlman. She knew that her coworker Alisa Cerf hated her and feared that she was after her own job.[4] Once again Ruth felt trapped into being no more than a menial worker as she toiled away writing captions for photographs, increasingly alienated from the events documented in them.[5] In a letter to a friend the following March, she described her five basic job duties: arranging and captioning thousands of photos, selecting photo series and captions for journalists, and occasionally taking photos herself and helping out with developing them in the lab.[6]

In other letters, she explained that the PIO served as a headquarters for English-language journalists and photographers. It was located in the Ritz Hotel, which had a restaurant and bar in the building and a terrace that faced the Mediterranean. She often stayed at the office until midnight, eating, talking, and drinking with them while working or writing letters.[7] She vividly described it in another letter:

> I am spending my days being ritzy at the ritz (Hotel). It's really quite a place... the official hangout for foreign correspondents...with such "notables" in the field of journalism as Luter from Life and Time....Bilby of the New York Times...Rosenfeld of N.Y. Post....Robert Miller of the United Press [...] They and their friends hang around

the Ritz, which has a big lobby-press room where all official press conferences are held, where everyone works on
their own little desk, dotting the w[hole?] of the place...
including a post-office, censorship office...a fine restaurant, especially clean, fast and fancy service at the lowest
price in town (Propaganda!) a bar, and upstairs offices and
downstairs photographic laboratories. There I sit from 9
a.m. until 12 midnight many a time....there I am happy,
and there I am sad! There I fight with the errand boys,
and there I listen to Shertok. There I work, and there I get
intoxicated (oh, please, don't frown).[8]

Her pay was simply not enough to cover her expenses, even though
she was now sharing an apartment with several roommates and kept
meticulous account books. To make ends meet, Ruth began to take on
freelance jobs, mostly typing and German translation. She explained the
satisfaction she got from one of these jobs: "Went to do some work for
Spencer Irving of Cleveland—and really enjoyed it—it always has given
me a happy feeling to work real hard and well and get a lot done—and
especially if someone on top of that recognizes it."[9] Her expertise on
Israel and world affairs proved useful for many of these positions.

Sixty-one years later she would look back at this job at the PIO
with pride. She explained, "I think my biggest contribution to this
whole English publicity bit was, I took a very firm stand and I said,
'The pick-and-shovel days are over. Israel needs big-time money to get
off the ground. You don't get big-time money in support of paving a
road with a pick and ax.' And so I said, 'Get away from this dumb
publicity of the pioneer who does everything, and get with the people
who are starting a state.'"[10] She was very proud of a campaign she developed to publicize the Jaffa orange industry. Many years later, she would
receive a certificate from Israel acknowledging her work as the state's

first photograph archivist and thanking her for her contributions to the country's founding.[11]

Soon after she started her job, she went out to celebrate a successful air raid with the famous (but very small) 101st Squadron. "A pilot named Lee," she recounted, "[who] has never taken me out, or spoken to me[,] walked in drunk and wanted to know who invited me to the party . . . also adding that I had sponged drinks off everybody in town and that I had slept with everybody in town . . . Well, I got so sore, I just stood up and [slapped] his face in public."[12] Even though she was no longer at the behest of potential employers, she would still have to regularly fend off passes, often from married men. She continued to mull over in her diary the sexism she faced in Israel. One galling incident on a beach particularly set her off:

> Here it is the 20th century. An era of emancipation and modernism, and yet human beings and society are as interwoven and perhaps even more restricted because of their very freedom as in the Middle Ages. Especially for a girl. It is rather pathetic, just because a woman walks along the beach alone in the evening people get suspicious, turn around, want to strike up a conversation or want to pick her up. And if a girl comes to a new town, unless she has an escort, she can go to but very few places without at least attracting attention, that is usually unfavorable attention, if not men!

> What if people want to be alone? [...] What if one does not want to be dependent on a friend or husband? Could one really defy society and manage alone? [...] It is a vicious circle. Even if one knows no one, everyone knows one......if with wrong company they frown, if alone they

ask questions. Cafes are even worse than the bars and restaurants here, as each has "Stammkundschaft [regulars]."

At least in Seattle I could sit by myself in a coffee shop on the Ave, a drug store downtown, and have no one bother about me. Or go for a walk late at night without arousing suspicion.[13]

Ruth knew that to gain control of her life she needed to find more quiet time by herself and, especially, to focus on reading. In May 1949, she wrote in her diary: "Must sit down & make plans to stop drifting— Must find out what makes me always want to 'get someplace' [and] 'be somebody' when I know I have not the stomach to fight for it! Hell, we are all twisted up and jerky—must start doing some organized reading!"[14] She listed the four books she was reading, including *Prodigal Women* by Nancy Hale and *Strange Fruit* by Lillian Smith. *Prodigal Women* was a 1942 bestseller. In 2014 Caitlin Keefe Moran wrote that it "is a strange, giant, wonderful book, full of desperate, sad, sometimes wicked, sometimes pitiable, women." Moran went on to describe the character of Leda: "Leda is deliciously unlikeable. She is described as 'frantic with self-consciousness and envy and desire'; she exclusively 'hated people, or envied them, or scorned them.' She schemes for social power, she carries on affairs with the husbands of her friends, and above all she feels no shame."[15] *Strange Fruit* was censored in the United States in 1944 due to its frank portrayal of a southern interracial romance. Reading books like these, one about women who broke the boundaries, another that spoke the ugly truth of racism, Ruth continued to find comfort in stories that spoke to her own experiences or opened new worlds to her. No doubt, books by women writers helped Ruth define and analyze the experiences and difficulties she herself faced as a woman.

When she thought about her future, Ruth most often thought about Viktor, but she wondered if he was just a psychological crutch for her. She hadn't heard from him in months, although she had run into reporters who had been to Prague and seen him there. Finally she sent him a telegram on his birthday. Soon after, she received a five-page letter from him in which he asked if she would like to meet him in Paris, which lifted her spirits.[16] She struggled to decipher what this actually meant: Did he want to get married? For the next few months she did not hear from him, and her hopes were dashed when Robert Capa returned from Europe empty-handed, whereas Ruth thought he might have brought a letter or message from Viktor. Throughout those agonizing months, she thought about various options: Could she marry him and live in Prague? Would he come to the United States with her, and could he be happy living there, in such a materialistic and dog-eat-dog society? There were so many options of where to live and under what circumstances—marriage or perhaps living together or separately—but Ruth carefully combed over and weighed each of them in minute detail in her diary.

She dreaded going back to the United States without Viktor. She craved the freedom of the United States and the stability she had experienced in Seattle but hated the idea of going back and feeling like a failure, or worse, begging the Rubinsteins for money. She knew that the United States was her best shot at a fulfilling career but detested the compromises that came with it in this new postwar society: the complacency and ignorance about what was happening in the rest of the world. In the spring of 1949, she pondered:

> Made a rather odd discovery today—talking about the States & looking at American magazines—it all hardly seems real any more—it is almost as if it never was—& when f.e. the question of my return comes up—return? It's something unreal too—almost like my first migration there. Sure I can mentally think back on all the various even minutest experiences—but it is more like a book I

once read—not like something that has really happened to me—in fact—some books seem much more real![17]

For months she created lists for and against returning to the US or remaining in Israel. This was a strategy she used often in making decisions throughout her life. Even after she retired, she would carefully weigh her options before any major decision. List-making created order in the chaos of her mind and reminded her that logic and reason should always guide her path. Even so, when thinking of returning to the US, she seemed to be facing a brick wall. What would she do there? Would she ever feel like she truly belonged? Would she ever get married? And God forbid, would she be stuck in a secretarial job forever? On June 5, 1949, she wrote her last ever (or last surviving) diary entry in Israel, including one of her lists of options, all of them depressing to her:

Should I go home? The truth is this—

1. If I stay here it is not because I want to stay here, but because I don't want to go home.

   a. I do not have the nerves for the family.
   b. I do not have the strength to start all over again there, especially with the worsening conditions.
   c. The men that might want to marry me there I could not stomach!

2. If I go home, it is because I don't want to stay here.

   a. not real friends
   b. not enough income
   c. no place to live

Both being negative reasons, it really does not matter much what I do—only, when will I stop drifting and know what I want & go after it? Maybe never—perhaps I'm just one of those people who cannot live on their own—

Whatever I look towards is no good—and yet what instead.

> a. a white brick house with a picket fence in Seattle, no—
> b. a furnished room in Israel all my life? No! So there—[18]

By the end of the June, Ruth had been discharged from the Israeli army. She was given the option of continuing at the PIO job as a civilian. Her coworker, Alisa, quit, giving Ruth a chance to take her position and finally run the office how she wanted. Ruth revealed in her diary that when Alisa had been on vacation, she had gotten a glimpse of the "inefficient, slovenly job" she did managing the archive.[19] Ruth continually complained to her supervisors about the disorganization of the archive and had many ideas about how to improve operations to meet its stated mission—to provide relevant photos to both government officials and the public in a timely manner. It embarrassed her when journalists on a deadline requested necessary photos and the PIO repeatedly failed to provide them. She now had the opportunity to overhaul the office into the well-oiled machine she knew it could be.

A month after she started the new position, Ruth wrote a letter to her boss, Lieutenant Colonel Moshe Pearlman, to inform him that she had neither received the authority to make the necessary changes in the archive nor gotten her first paycheck as a civilian. With this letter, she submitted a typed list of "Suggestions for Changes and Additions in Archives Department" that included recommendations for more photographs submitted on certain topics (including women); weeding out duplicates; a triple-reference card index for names, places, and events (no doubt based on the typical library card catalog system); and more accurate and timely descriptions from photographers. To prove that these changes were necessary, she included a three-page typed document of monthly activities, in which she listed all the requests the archive had received and the various reasons why they were not fulfilled in a timely manner.

A copy of a large classification schema that was most likely developed by Ruth to organize the photographs by topic with a call number system from 100 to 5000 is also in her papers at the USHMM. Examples of these broad subject headings, listed on the first page, include parades, diplomats, children and youth, cities and towns, and various headings for military and government departments. Each of these headings was further subdivided by many more topics, each with their own call number, on the subsequent pages. She even included headings for PIO parties and specific journalists in Israel. These documents offer a window into Ruth's sharp mind and her approach to her future work as a librarian. She never saw a job as just a job; she threw herself into her work with unceasing energy and a desire to improve workflows until she was satisfied that every routine task could easily be accomplished.

Writing descriptions, classifying items by subject headings, typing up catalog cards, and the endless, endless filing—the daily grind—were thankless, tedious tasks that have always fallen to the lowest-paid and least valued workers, often women. But without this necessary work, there would be no archive or no library. Ruth understood this and knew that being able to quickly present whatever item was needed, and the resulting gratitude of the requester, gave her an enormous sense of satisfaction and pride. To be able to simply say "Here it is" gives every librarian and archivist a small thrill. It's the prize we all seek in the tedious slog of our everyday work.

In August, Ruth started a business with her friend Lee that they called Lee and Ruth, Your Private Mobile Secretary. Bringing their typewriters and stationery with them as needed, they worked primarily for English-speaking men visiting Israel in need of typing, research, translation, and errands. They printed up their own cards with a form that could be filled out by clients and dropped off at the Hotel Gat Rimon. Ruth enjoyed working on these short-term projects and found that her and Lee's services were in demand throughout the fall of 1949. She was finally able to break even, possibly even save some money. Both Lee and Ruth later moved to New York in 1950 and continued their business there.[20]

In early 1949 Ruth admitted not only to herself but also to friends back in the United States that life in Israel was just not what so many idealistic Jews had envisioned. To her friend Mila, she explained:

> It is all very well to talk of staying in our country, being a Zionist, etc. etc. but after all, life must be faced with a certain amount of realism on the part of an individual. Considering the short time of [Israel's] existence, the struggle it has had and is still having, etc. etc.[,] wonders have been achieved. However, you don't live life, or perhaps I should say, I do not live a day by day life reminding myself [every time] my blood pressure goes up [that] Israel is being created. That does not feed me, nor does it make me less hungry. And while I am perfectly willing to take all that comes along, and a little more about that later, for the "duration," I cannot as yet readily commit myself to take it for the rest of my life.[21]

If Zionism was something Ruth ever truly believed in, her experiences in Israel killed that dream. A homeland for Jews would not protect her from housing and food shortages, low wages, sexual harassment, date rape, nepotism, or job discrimination. She couldn't claim that she had faced difficulty there because she was Jewish, and she now realized the significance of connections and the harsh reality of sexism among people who were supposed to be on her side. The United States didn't promise relief from these problems either, but it did hold one advantage: due to its booming postwar economy, it would be easier for her to build a career there. If anything, Ruth knew that she could make it if she had a steady income and work that she truly believed in and could accomplish every day.

She made a firm commitment to quit her job at the PIO on November 30. She wrote to her friends of her plans to go home, "and by that I mean the States," she explained. She planned to go to Paris, and to possibly stop in Prague on the way if she could get a visa. This trip would finally confirm if Viktor would be a part of her future. In explaining to her friends and family why she was leaving Israel, she sometimes just wrote that she would tell the whole story in person. To Mila she wrote, "Perhaps it is that a certain phase of my life and experience here is closed, and that I don't just want to slide into the next without a break. Perhaps the next is less appealing, perhaps I'm afraid of sliding into a civil service rut, etc. etc. Well, anyway, there are many reasons. Also, I need a bit of distance and perspective to digest the last two years, so . . ."[22]

Ruth spent the next five months in Paris visiting her sister Clara and nephew Guy. If she met up with Viktor, there is no record of it today. She may have received more of her inheritance from her cousin Sam Rubinstein to fund this trip. Many years later Sam wrote a short memoir and briefly explained how his father Carl's estate was divided up among the family after his death in 1947. He mentioned Ruth's $10,000 share and stated that she went back to Europe and quickly spent a lot of money.[23] He made no mention of her two years in Israel, if he had remembered them at all. Ruth never seemed to have been able to clearly communicate to the Rubinsteins that she was not simply squandering away her inheritance on a world-traveling binge.

When Ruth left Israel, she knew that she would be starting all over again. She could no longer look to the Zionist community for her sense of identity, although she would later occasionally work as a substitute secretary for a Zionist organization in San Francisco and would always defend Israel's right to exist. She would return at least twice to visit Mirjam, and in her oral history she stated that Yad Vashem, also known as the World Holocaust Remembrance Center, in Jerusalem, was a more meaningful memorial to the Holocaust for her than the USHMM.[24] She later considered returning to Israel to assist Helena Rubinstein with opening a new makeup factory, a plan that was never realized. But at the end of 1949, Ruth was ready to start a new path. Her two years in Israel had changed her life, but not in the way she had anticipated. It had hardened her, challenged what she thought she knew and believed, and made her realize that her search for a true home and sense of belonging was not over, not yet.

~

I traveled to Israel with my friend Maya, another archivist at the Library of Congress. This was a trip that for years we had talked about taking. Her mother had grown up in Jerusalem, and her sister now lived there. After meeting up at our hotel in the German Colony, Maya and I walked down King George Street and found the apartment where Ruth had lived with Fred Schneider. We walked on just a few blocks more to a construction site for the new museum dedicated to the history of the Knesset, Israel's parliament. Plastered to the fence were photos of Israel's founders, including one of Maya's grandfathers, who served as deputy secretary of the Knesset for many years. Her brother-in-law, a professional tour guide, showed us around the Old City. We walked through the labyrinth of ancient streets, stopping at a hidden garden at Christ Church, the Church of the Holy Sepulchre, and the Western Wall. While Maya went up to pray at the wall, I sat down in a chair and wondered if Ruth, the adamant atheist, had ever come here to pray when she later visited Mirjam. We took a day trip to Tel Aviv to meet up with one of Maya's friends and found another one of Ruth's apartments on Ben Yehuda Street. We huddled in the rain on the beach, and I realized that the Carlton Tel Aviv Hotel that we walked by must have been the Ritz Hotel, where the PIO office was.

Back in Jerusalem, I searched on my phone for information on a figure in Israel's history, Avraham Stern, but the link to his Wikipedia site came up as "Website not available." I got the same message when trying to read a few *Washington Post* opinion articles. Why couldn't I read these websites? It dawned on me that this might be my first encounter with state-sponsored censorship, and it left a sour taste in my mouth and a knot in my stomach.

On my last day in Jerusalem, I walked through the quiet streets on Shabbat to the Israel Museum. I made my way slowly through the Valley of the Cross Park, past the olive trees and the Monastery of the Cross. Ruth often came here to escape Fred, sit on a bench, and write in her diary. At the museum, I saw the Dead Sea Scrolls and endless exhibits of art and artifacts of Jewish life. I walked into an exhibit by Ai Weiwei that featured his sculptures and wallpaper imbued with symbols related to his experiences living under censorship and violent repression in China. Children danced in their socks across a wide, handwoven carpet that Ai had created for another exhibit in Germany, called *Soft Ground*: an exact replica of the tile floor of the Haus der Kunst, the art museum Hitler created in Munich. As I stared at Weiwei's wallpaper, which—patterned in a style that mimicked black-and-white Greek pottery—depicted Syrian refugees, I was overcome with grief for those across the world who still lived under terror and those who took flight and tried to survive as stateless refugees. In the dark lobby of the museum's library, closed for the day, I sat and tried to collect myself, thinking of Ruth's apt phrase: "It is all such a vicious circle."

One ordinary workday, in Washington, DC, I had to take back some archival boxes to our storage area deep in the stacks of the library's Jefferson Building. Contained in the eastern half of the building and under the Main Reading Room are fifteen floors of closed book stacks—mostly in the areas of history and social sciences—and a few storage cages for archival collections, including those for the American Folklife Center. I waved my badge to get through the first locked door, then struggled to push my bulky cart through two more awkwardly placed doors. For whatever reason that day, I looked up at the first aisle of books right in front of me, which I had never noticed before. They were all about Zionism and Israel.

I was in the DS 101–151 range, "Israel (Palestine). The Jews," a simple subject heading for one of the most fraught problems of the twentieth century. I had browsed this subject heading and its many subdivisions in LC's online catalog before, when I searched down the electronic rabbit hole for books that might help me better understand Ruth's experience as a Zionist and temporary resident of Israel. Countless times I had ordered the books through my staff account and waited for them to be delivered to a small office in the Adams Building, five floors above my own office, where I could then check them out.

It was quite another thing altogether to be confronted with these thousands of books in front of me, the result of over a century of people from all over the world arguing about what it means for Jews to have a homeland. Would they be disgusted to know these books were living in perpetuity down here together? I wondered if Ruth ever came down this aisle to browse, to remember what she had seen and felt in Israel, to verify that it had all been real. Did she want to see what new theories, treatises, and screeds had been added lately to these shelves, to marvel at what had become of her "old friends" there? Maybe she never did. Maybe she chose to ignore all the squabbling and shouting in this aisle and sought out new ideas, new books, and new answers to understand her place in the world.

~

Part VI:

What Else Can One Do in This Mad World?

PARIS, NEW YORK, AND BERKELEY, 1950–1959

Chapter 20

Ruth stopped in Genoa on the way to Paris and had a portrait photograph taken. In it her hair is wrapped in a bun on the top of her head to the left, and she wears a large beaded necklace and matching earrings. Although her eyes are half-closed, she appears genuinely happy. Also in Genoa, an artist named G. Giuliani drew a portrait of Ruth at the Hotel Columbia.[1] She is wearing a gray suit and yellow necklace and carries what appears to be a trench coat. The artist drew her in profile and accented her severely pointed shoes. With her glasses and updo, Ruth looks like the serious librarian she would one day become.

Guy Rosner, Ruth's nephew, was just ten years old in 1950, but his aunt made a big impression on him during her visit. She seemed to be zooming everywhere, not just in Paris but all over the world. She was ambitious, he recalled, just like a shooting star. Ruth stayed with Clara for a few weeks, then got her own place on rue de Marignan for about three months. Many journalists and men supposedly showed up at her apartment, but it is unclear if any of them were Viktor.[2] In May 1950 she left for New York and stopped in England on the way.[3]

When she arrived in New York, she met up with friends she had known in Israel. She moved into an apartment on West 108th Street with Alisa Cerf, her nemesis from the PIO job in Tel Aviv.[4] She wrote to a friend in Israel, "About life in the United States in general, I cannot possibly write you, as I would have to produce a book with many more than one volume."⁵ But she provided a vivid description of her new life and living situation, which seemed to be similar to her life in Tel Aviv: "We have quite a bit of company . . . Around the corner from us is an apartment full of schlichim, and any time of the day or night they feel like it they drop in here . . . In all[,] I've kept away from organizations as much as I could, just going to an occasional party with other Israelis. There's now an Israeli cabaret in New York . . . Every time I'm there I run into some people from Israel."⁶ She explained that she was working for several clients part-time, including an art dealer and men from Israel who were in New York temporarily and needed help with correspondence and other tasks. Of one of these clients she wrote, "I am thus working for an author for whom I did research for a book he published 3 weeks ago, and very much enjoyed that job, as it was more like studying than work."⁷

On the same day, in another letter to a different friend, Ruth further explained exactly who the aforementioned author was: "If you read the papers lately you will know the name Max Lowenthal[,] [author of] '[T]he Federal Bureau of Investigation.' I worked on the book all summer and am still with Max part-time."⁸ Lowenthal was a Jewish lawyer with a long career in government service: he had clerked for Judge Julian Mack (and married his niece), joined on the Morgenthau mission to Spain in 1917, and worked with Felix Frankfurter on President Wilson's labor mediation committee. In the 1930s he became one of the major architects of the New Deal, serving as research director of the Senate Committee on Banking, Housing, and Urban Affairs. He was also the chief counsel for the Interstate Commerce Commission, where he became a close friend of freshman senator Harry Truman when they worked together on the Committee to Investigate Railroad Finances. Lowenthal was an informal adviser to Truman when he later became president, and was also credited as playing a major role in Truman's support for Israel in 1948.⁹

For decades Lowenthal had been amassing research on the FBI, which he considered to be a dangerous threat to the civil liberties of anyone tangentially suspected of Communist proclivities. He and his colleagues and friends had been investigated by J. Edgar Hoover's army of bureaucrats for their real or imagined Communist associations. In September 1950, when Ruth was working for him, Lowenthal was called before the House Un-American Activities Committee (HUAC) and questioned about various acquaintances. His son David recalls:

> Max's responses were, in the first place, totally, even maddeningly, disarming. Time and again when asked if he had met so-and-so or knew of links to someone, he said he had no memory of that, but was happy to accept any evidence the committee might have to the contrary. "Anything the committee has that would correct what I say on this or anything else, I will accept. If it is a fact, I will accept it." This meaningless but conciliatory throwaway line, uttered very slowly ten, twenty, fifty times in a deep, sincere tone, drove his inquisitors round the bend.[10]

Hoover and his ally, Representative George Dondero, had ordered this questioning of Lowenthal to threaten the publication of his forthcoming book, simply titled *The Federal Bureau of Investigation*. Lowenthal had trouble finding a publisher, but William Sloane had finally agreed to do it, although the company refused to promote it. Released in November to a storm of mostly negative reviews and editorials, the book was denounced by Dondero, who told Congress that Lowenthal was "a menace to America whose exposure would prove him a Soviet spy more dangerous than any since Benedict Arnold."[11] Also in 1950, Lowenthal's son John, a Columbia University law student, assisted the defense lawyers for the espionage trial of Alger Hiss (also a friend of Max's), likely bringing even more suspicion to his father.

In the Max Lowenthal papers at the University of Minnesota, there are hundreds of newspaper and magazine clippings on the publication of Lowenthal's *The Federal Bureau of Investigation* and his correspondence with the publisher and friends, including Truman, who had enthusiastically read a draft of the book. Lowenthal sent a note to his publisher in August 1950 with revised galleys of the book, stating that more were coming and that "Miss Rappaport will be able to note on them any new changes in blue pencil."[12] In a response to a friend who had asked Lowenthal how he had managed to complete such an enormously detailed book, he explained:

> Some friends sent me clippings from time to time over the years. The reading of official hearings and reports I had to do myself. Probably I missed some recondite items, depending so much on myself. The biggest use of staff, in fact only one, was after the material was in galley proof. I got a number of graduate students to check on every statement in the book, against the sources. Some chapters checked four times. It was eminently worth doing that, though it took rather more energy than I could command at the time.[13]

Ruth was this staff of one and may have directed this effort to check the sources and revise the book over the summer of 1950. Her initials "rr" are in the corner of many documents dated from the fall of 1950, indicating that she typed both lists of names Lowenthal planned to send the book to and the corresponding letters.[14]

Lowenthal's FBI file is over seven thousand pages long, and he was under heavy surveillance in 1950.[15] In a personal letter to President Truman, Lowenthal detailed the harassment of himself and his family by a HUAC staff member:

Some day I hope to tell you the stories of the attempts in the past week to stop the book, through the operations of the staff of a House Committee, one of whose Republican members wants to go to the Senate and perhaps fears that the book's incidental reference to his public record may hurt his chances.

You may be particularly interested in that Committee's staff visit to my home late at night when my wife was alone and undressed, on an apartment floor all of whose other tenants were obviously away, and how a strange man, carrying the Committee's credentials[,] "politely" intimidated her into opening the door, tried to scare the daylights out of her, and then came back still later that night to repeat the performance, possibly after phoning Washington and getting instructions. This was followed by a daytime visit to my publishers, a showing of the Committee credentials, and "casual" comments indicating that the publishers might be unwise in publishing a book written by me.[16]

In all the job applications, résumés, and lists of references Ruth would use later in life, she never mentioned working for Max Lowenthal. But working for him made a deep impression on her at the time. She wrote to her friend Lynn, "I feel what else can one do in this mad world, but to contribute one's time, effort and limited ability to stave off the course of madness, or at least to try. The consequences are still rather uncertain."[17]

Chapter 21

While Ruth lived in New York City, she inquired into going back to school. She knew she could not continue to work as a secretary or typist for the rest of her working life and dreaded performing these mundane tasks that had been designated "women's work." She wrote in August 1950 to her friend Esther Elbaum, "If nothing else pops I shall leave N.Y., as I do finally want to finish school. Have what I think are some good ideas for the future . . ."[1] She asked about starting in the fall or, if she had been too late in applying, the following spring at University of California, Berkeley, which she had applied to in 1947 before going to Israel.[2] She also took an entrance exam for Columbia University and passed. Notified of this on January 26, 1951, she may have already been on her way to Berkeley, where she would be able to transfer her credits from the University of Washington and enter as a sophomore.

If Ruth thought that in Berkeley she would escape the Red Scare, she was sorely mistaken. Robert Gordon Sproul, president of the University of California since 1930, had begun targeting and firing professors and graduate students who openly admitted to Communist Party membership. In 1949 California state senator Jack B. Tenney introduced thirteen bills to root out Communists from state government. The same year, President Sproul forced all University of California faculty and employees to sign a loyalty oath. The faculty senate voted to change the wording of the oath, and after months of negotiations between

Sproul, the senate, and the regents, in the summer of 1950 Sproul fired thirty-one faculty members who had refused to sign it. Two years later the California Supreme Court ruled in *Tolman v. Underhill* that the university had unjustly fired these employees, and they were reinstated.[3]

When Ruth enrolled at Berkeley in February 1951, the university was beginning to contract from its postwar growth in enrollment, when the GI Bill encouraged returning World War II veterans to attend college tuition-free.[4] At twenty-seven, Ruth considered herself to be an older student, a square peg among the silent generation, who had been children during World War II. She had inquired about living at Berkeley's International House but had either missed an application deadline or decided instead to live off campus.[5]

At the University of Washington, Ruth had considered majoring in sociology; it seems clear she stuck with that plan at Berkeley, enrolling in two sociology classes her first semester. Berkeley's Department of Sociology and Social Institutions was considered an upstart, having only been founded in 1946. Although a Department of Social Institutions had existed since 1923, the faculty was opposed to the concept of sociology as a discipline. Under the leadership of Herbert Blumer, who arrived to be the new chair in 1952, it became the number-one-ranked sociology department in the country by 1966.[6] She received Bs and Cs in these sociology classes her first semester, but an A in French.

It appears she did not initially seek out a job to support herself. But paying out-of-state tuition at Berkeley was costly, and the following summer she knew she had to start earning money. In July she obtained a position with the army as a typist and punch-card operator for mainframe computers at San Francisco's Port of Embarkation at Fort Mason, working a night shift. In 1947 President Truman had signed Executive Order 9,835, a preemptive measure to ensure the loyalty (and heterosexuality) of all federal employees. Truman had been accused of being soft on Communism, so his solution was to convince the public that this order would take care of the problem. Besides the creation of a Loyalty

Review Board, it also led to the Attorney General's List of Subversive Organizations, which included not only Communist organizations and fronts but also the KKK and Nazi groups.

This executive order meant that after she was hired by the army, Ruth would have to undergo a name check to verify that she had no Communist sympathies. Over 4.5 million federal employees were investigated from 1947 to 1958 under the order. Of these, 27,000 required a full investigation, and 378 were dismissed for disloyalty.[7] Perhaps Ruth was confident that despite her questionable political activities and associations, no one could prove that she had ever advocated for Communism. Her work for Lowenthal would have certainly prepared her to know exactly what was coming.

The FBI began an investigation of Ruth, but in her file there is no mention of her work with Max Lowenthal or her relationship with Viktor. What was a huge red flag to the investigators was a brief part of Ruth's activist life in Seattle when she addressed the Joint Anti-Fascist Refugee Committee (JAFRC) in the spring of 1945.[8] Edward Barsky, one of the founders of the organization, had joined the Communist Party in 1935, and other members may have been Communists as well. The group ended up on the Attorney General's List of Subversive Organizations in 1947 and became a top enemy of J. Edgar Hoover. The organization refused to hand over its records to the House Un-American Activities Committee and spent years unsuccessfully fighting for its right to exist as an organization. By the mid-1950s the organization had disbanded, and Barsky and other members had served jail time; his career as a doctor was over.[9]

Besides speaking at these events, Ruth had also unsuccessfully applied for a secretarial job at the organization's Seattle branch. According to her FBI file, "The appointee was not considered for the position because it was feared her sympathies were not entirely in accord with those of the organization." In other words, Ruth was not Communist *enough*, or even one at all, for this so-called front organization. Even so, FBI agents in Seattle were ordered to begin investigating Ruth for subversive activities based on her involvement with JAFRC.

More information about Ruth's time in Seattle trickled back to FBI headquarters in December 1951. May Goldsmith, executive secretary of the Jewish Welfare Society, provided a list of individuals for whom the society could vouch as Jewish refugees who were not Communist sympathizers. Luckily, Ruth was included in the list.[10] Immigration and Naturalization Service records in Seattle were checked. The name of Ruth's uncle, Carl Rubinstein, had been put on the JAFRC's donor list, which had been taken from a list of donors to the Seattle Symphony, although he never gave any money to the group. Her uncle Abe was also contacted by the Seattle agents. He gave a lengthy explanation of Ruth's background in Germany and her parents' deaths:

> He said that as a result of this personal loss and her first-hand observation of the Nazi treatment of non-Arians and others, the appointee came to hate Fascists. He said the appointee is definitely anti-Fascist in her sympathies but certainly not in the same sense that Communists are anti-Fascists . . . He said it is altogether possible the appointee may have participated in any anti-Fascist movement or organization without knowing or considering the identity or purpose of the sponsors of that movement.[11]

Her cousin Sam was interviewed and claimed he didn't know Ruth well enough to make any statements about her loyalty. The owner of *The Transcript*, her coworker at the Medina Baby Home, and two acquaintances were also questioned, all agreeing that while Ruth hated Fascists, she was no Communist. The report concluded, "In view of the foregoing, it appears little basis exists for a full-field investigation."[12]

In a January 1952 memo from J. Edgar Hoover to the chief of staff of the army, he explained what had been discovered in Seattle.

Disagreeing with the Seattle office's conclusion, he also noted that Ruth had lived in Europe and Israel recently and was born in Germany, more red flags to him. The army was to take responsibility of this full-field investigation outside the US. The FBI would take care of the domestic half of Ruth's case.[13] What exactly would this investigation entail? The number of people contacted and the breadth of locations is staggering for one lowly army base typist, and it reveals the extraordinary resources the FBI and military put into these Loyalty Board reviews. It is probably not a stretch to say that in the early 1950s, every person in the United States was either being investigated or questioned about someone being investigated.

It all started with a search through the FBI's Identification Division, the system Hoover had dreamed of while working at the Library of Congress from 1913 to 1917. Every US citizen would be identified in a main card catalog, with cross-references to other file groups. Without the work of careful and consistent cross-referencing, the FBI's massive intelligence system would have never grown so large and efficient.[14] When the clerk checked for Ruth's name, it was already in this system, number 965 279 A. She had been given another number, 2374605, when she registered as an alien in 1940. A new number, 12.52.22573, had been assigned to her on October 1, 1951, likely the date that this investigation began. On every sheet of Ruth's eighty-two-page file was another number, sometimes stamped, sometimes scrawled: 121-3452, the code for the FBI headquarters. At the bottom of every page in her file, or sometimes all across the page, was a hodgepodge of initials, stamps, dates, and signatures by who knows how many bureaucrats that had come into contact with Ruth's file.

The first to be interviewed for the full-field investigation was William Bauman, Ruth's former boss at Grunbaum's Furniture Company in Seattle, now in Chicago. He could barely remember Ruth. Next, a special agent verified Ruth's status as a student at Berkeley. A blacked-out name revealed the trouble Ruth had in the fall of 1952:

"[Name withheld] stated that the appointee had dropped her classes due to extreme pressure caused by necessary employment hours and class work. [Name withheld] advised that she has had three discussions with the appointee and volunteered that she considers the appointee emotionally unstable and disorganized."[15]

Seven of Ruth's current and former coworkers in San Francisco were interviewed. Lynn Atterman had worked with Ruth at the Zionist Organization of America in 1947, and the two had become close friends, corresponding for many years. In her letters to Atterman, Ruth had detailed her relationship with Viktor, and although she probably hadn't explicitly said he was a Communist, she had explained he was from Prague and was "stuck behind the Iron Curtain." Ruth had also explained her job with Max Lowenthal to Atterman, but Atterman only reported that Ruth had never discussed Communism and that she would never doubt Ruth's loyalty. One current coworker at the army base stated that whereas Ruth admired a kibbutz in Israel that practiced "true Marxism," she had also said that Stalin's regime was the same as Hitler's. Besides the coworkers, six of Ruth's landlords (including two married couples), a neighbor, and a friend from Berkeley were interviewed in San Francisco.

In Seattle two of her listed references for the army job were also contacted, in addition to thirteen more friends and former colleagues. All of them repeated the same refrain: while Ruth hated Fascists, she was no Communist. In addition to checking all her school and university records, the FBI contacted a local credit bureau and the police to see if Ruth had any records. Another reference in Cleveland, Spencer Irwin, a journalist she had briefly worked for in Tel Aviv, was also questioned. Next, investigators from New York contacted Ethel Waugh, a literary agent whom Ruth had worked for there. Waugh was the only New York employer Ruth had listed on her army employment application, despite the fact that she had worked for many different people there, including Lowenthal. The investigators interviewed seven of Ruth's landlords, friends, and Zionist colleagues in New York. Local Communist informants stated they hadn't heard of her. Memos from the spring of 1952 indicated that investigations were conducted in London, Rome, Paris, and Israel, but apparently only the Paris records survived. On April 24, 1952, Ruth passed the investigation and was deemed "eligible on loyalty."[16]

After all this, it's hard to understand why Ruth would want to work for the federal government, much less the army. She hadn't much enjoyed serving in the Israeli army or working for the government there. She hated bureaucracy, but with the large growth in civilian military jobs after World War II, and particularly with the growth of opportunities for women, perhaps she knew that once she was approved by Hoover himself, the army and the federal government could always be a career option for her.

Chapter 22

On March 10, 1952, Ruth was driving home from her job at the army base when she was hit by an oncoming car. It was reported the next day in the *Oakland Tribune*: "The accident occurred on the 22nd Street overpass leading from Oakland Army Base to the Bay Bridge approach lanes. Miss Rappaport was taken to Cowell Memorial Hospital with fractured ribs and face cuts. A passenger in Gibbs' car, Clydel Kingsberry, of 1454 Ninth Street, also suffered face cuts. Gibbs was cited for driving on the wrong side, excessive speed, and no operator's license."[1]

Two months later Ruth received a letter from the doctors and nurses at the hospital, thanking her for the candy she sent them to thank them for their good care.[2] This accident was the beginning of a string of bad luck. Sometime in the 1950s Ruth also was a victim of a home fire.[3] She apparently also had a gambling habit and admittedly wasted her tuition money in Reno.[4] These problems interfered with her ability to stay focused on her schoolwork, and throughout her time at Berkeley she either failed or had to withdraw from many of her classes. But despite these setbacks, Ruth was determined to earn her college degree, no matter how long it took.

In March 1954 Ruth quit her job at the army base.[5] Working nights had proved too exhausting. She took on a few positions as a research assistant and secretary for several professors. She worked as a housekeeper too, as blogger Bill Hess reported many years later when describing Ruth's relationship with cats over the years:

> For a time she worked as a live-in housekeeper in Berkeley, California in a home owned by a Siamese cat. "The only place that cat wanted to do its business was inside my alligator shoes," Ruth grumbles, more than half a century later. Ruth wanted her own room to be a pleasant place, and so she put some beautiful drapes up on the windows. The cat sneaked into her room and tore the drapes to shreds. Ruth put up another set. Again, the cat played its mischief upon them, leaving them in tatters. Again Ruth tried, with the same result.[6]

Ruth knew she couldn't continue with this series of temporary and dead-end jobs. She took the Strong Vocational Interest Test for Women, developed by Edward K. Strong of Stanford University. Her scores indicated that the top four professions she showed interest in were lawyer, social worker, psychologist, and librarian. Her score on the femininity-masculinity scale reveals that her general interests were more masculine than the average woman. Strong advised the test takers, "Remember also this is a test of your interests. Your abilities must also be considered. Interests point the way you want to go, abilities determine how well you can progress."[7]

In January 1957, after a sporadic eight years as a part-time student (including at the University of Washington), Ruth finally graduated from Berkeley with her bachelor of arts in sociology and a minor in "Oriental Studies." It appears she was still unsure about her professional future. She spent the next few months working around Berkeley as a freelance translator, researcher, and editor for faculty and graduate students. Over the summer, she worked as the assistant to the regional director of the American Zionist Council, where she probably had secretarial duties similar to those she had in so many other jobs.[8] In May she sent a letter to the American Library Association, asking for information about the library profession and entrance requirements to library schools. She also sent letters to eight library schools asking for application information and course catalogs.[9]

She wrote to one of her former sociology professors, Wolfram Eberhard, a specialist in Chinese folklore and a native of Germany who had left in the 1930s to escape pressure to join the Nazi Party.[10] She wrote, "After thinking the matter over very carefully I finally decided that although Sociology will always be my primary interest, for the time being at least, getting a Master's degree in Librarianship might be more practical for me and more easily feasible than continuing my studies in the field of Sociology, and so I am applying to the School of Librarianship."[11] She asked him for a recommendation letter to both the University of Washington's and Berkeley's library schools.

A letter in Ruth's archives seems almost apologetic about her desire to go to library school. It was "practical" and "more easily feasible" than pursuing sociology. Would she have rather pursued a graduate program in sociology? If so, what was holding her back? Perhaps she was aware of the sexism that women professors and graduate students faced in the 1950s or thought her grades were not good enough to get into a graduate program. They were good enough for library school, though. Libraries were on a hiring binge in the 1950s and '60s as college and university libraries greatly expanded, and the rapid growth of publications in all fields created a deluge difficult for catalogers to keep up with. Considered pink-collar professionals since the late 1800s, white women librarians did not face discrimination in hiring except at the management level. If she could get her master's in librarianship, Ruth would not have much trouble finding a job.

The following essay was also part of the University of Washington collection:

XI. Autobiographical Essay

While never directly employed by a library or in library work, much of my previous working experience has brought me in close contact with libraries and their various facilities and personnel. Since childhood I have been an avid reader, and perhaps because of my experiences living in Nazi Germany, where books were burned and banned, I have had a profound feeling and respect for books and their value all my life. The experience of attending a private Jewish school under the Nazi regime and a subsequent one-year stay in Switzerland while waiting to migrate to the United States have made me further conscious of the value of books as a tool for education. I can truthfully say that the most memorable point of my stay in Switzerland was access to libraries and books which opened for me a whole world of new ideas that had been strictly taboo in Germany. Undoubtedly these teenage impressions account for my deep-rooted interest in education and by extension my wanting a profession that in some manner aids education. In my sociological studies, where my interests centered on so-called underdeveloped areas, I was again and again struck by the importance of the printed word and its dissemination. These thoughts have also become reinforced both in my travels abroad and in discussion with visiting educators and other travelers from abroad. As archivist for the Israel Government, though perhaps formally rather poorly prepared, I realized that I was temperamentally suited for this type of work and received much satisfaction from it. My research assistantship with Professor Brady, which necessitated daily work in libraries, strengthened this conviction, not only because of my enjoyment in the work but also because of the comments I received from workers in the field on my adaptability and suitability. Perhaps I can restate this sketchy outline in this manner.

Proceeding from the premise that two of the most important factors in choosing a profession are doing work that is worthwhile, satisfying, interesting and stimulating on the one hand, and on the other, being able to contribute something to the job; having accepted education in its widest sense as a primary value; and recognizing my deep and abiding love of books, it only seems natural to think in terms of librarianship as a career goal. Having travelled widely; being conversant in four languages and intending to study one or two more; and considering my research experience with two authors as well as information work for the Government of Israel, I feel that I have something to give to this type of work above and beyond mere academic training. This would include a certain facility for the administration and organization of work. I am not only interested in books, but also in people and peoples. My career goal in long-range terms, after receiving my formal training and necessary library experience, is directed towards helping to build libraries in some of the underdeveloped areas. By helping build libraries I am specifically thinking of helping establish certain services that have proven so effective and useful in the United States and are not established in other countries, as for example, reference services, which I feel would offer an excellent opportunity to apply one's skill of working with books and people.

I am fully aware that there are many people with greater intellectual or academic achievements than myself, but I do feel that my administrative and organizational abilities may in certain fields of librarianship compensate for some such lack. Furthermore, I feel that my academic record does not truly reflect my academic aptitude because I was fully self-supporting during my undergraduate studies. Lastly I feel that the moral and financial rewards offered by this profession would give me a totally satisfying career and life.[12]

So it wasn't just a "practical" decision after all; Ruth clearly had a sense of idealism when it came to her decision to pursue librarianship. She was willing to reveal her childhood in Nazi Germany to the faculty of Berkeley's library school and use it to boost her chances of admission when her transcript consisted of mostly Bs and Cs. Ruth wanted to emphasize that she was not just another library school applicant who wanted to enter the profession because she liked to read or because she had failed at another career. Books and libraries held a deep meaning for her, and she had the foresight to know that being a librarian didn't mean that you read books all day, a common misperception of the profession. She recognized that it meant interacting with people who sought information and were beholden to its gatekeepers. Ruth knew that the organization of libraries was the key to their success. Her battles in Israel over the sloppiness of the photograph archive were ample training to prepare her for work as a librarian.

In the same folder as this admissions essay (an original folder that Ruth had labeled "Graduate School Records") was a handwritten draft list of books and a typed final version titled "Books Read over Last Six-Month Period." Perhaps another part of her library school application or part of an assignment in one of her library school classes, it is a list of sixty-four titles:

Anthology of Japanese Literature by Donald Keene

The Tale of Genji by Lady Murasaki

The Story Bag: A Collection of Korean Folktales by Kim So-un

The Wall by John Hersey

The Heart Is a Lonely Hunter by Carson McCullers

Selected Stories of Franz Kafka

Dirty Hands by Jean-Paul Sartre

The Respectable Prostitute by Jean-Paul Sartre

Abel Sanchez by Miguel de Unamuno

Mondo Piccolo: Don Camillo by Giovannino Guareschi

The Colors of the Day by Romain Gary

A Literary Chronicle, 1920–1950 by Edmund Wilson

The Secret Agent by Joseph Conrad

Lafcadio's Adventures by André Gide

The Old Man and the Sea by Ernest Hemingway

Across the River and into the Trees by Ernest Hemingway

Bonjour Tristesse by Francoise Sagan

Ten North Frederick by John O'Hara

Farmers Hotel by John O'Hara

Bread and Wine by Ignazio Silone

The Man Who Died by D. H. Lawrence

The Good Soldier by Ford Madox Ford

East of Eden by John Steinbeck

The Short Reign of Pippin IV by John Steinbeck

Disappearance by Philip Wylie

Devils of Loudun by Aldous Huxley

The Bad Seed by William March

Death of a Salesman by Arthur Miller

Miss Julie by August Strindberg

Bus Stop by William Inge

Picnic by William Inge

Tea and Sympathy by Robert Anderson

Borgia by Klabund

Der Kreidekreis by Klabund

Chinesische Gedichte by Klabund

Das Urteil by Franz Kafka

Der Zauberberg by Thomas Mann

Königliche Hoheit by Thomas Mann

Das Gesetz by Thomas Mann

Professor Unrat by Heinrich Mann

Der Gärtner by Rabindranath Tagore

Phantastische Nach by Stefan Zweig

Kleine Chronik by Stefan Zweig

Verwirrung der Gefühle by Stefan Zweig

Sternstunden der Menschheit by Stefan Zweig

Tehilla and Other Israeli Tales

The Literature of Modern Israel by Reuben Wallenrod

Scapegoat of Revolution by Judd L. Teller

The Kremlin, The Jews and the Middle East by Judd L. Teller

100 Hours to Suez by Robert Henriques

What Price Israel by Alfred M. Lilienthal

There Goes the Middle East by Alfred M. Lilienthal

Between Man and Man by Martin Buber

Black Hamlet by Wulf Sachs

Only Yesterday by Frederick Lewis Allen

The Big Change by Frederick Lewis Allen

The Age of Jackson by Arthur M. Schlesinger

Collection of Essays by George Orwell

Homage to Catalonia by George Orwell

1984 by George Orwell

Animal Farm by George Orwell

The Law of Civilization and Decay by Brooks Adams

Toulouse-Lautrec by Gerstle Mack

One Little Boy by Dorothy W. Baruch[13]

This remarkable list offers a window into Ruth's reading life that she only occasionally mentioned in the letters and diaries she left behind. If she truly read every book on this list over six months, she would have completed one about every three days. The list reflects Ruth's wide-ranging nonfiction interests: Israel and the Middle East, Asia, sociology, philosophy, psychology, history, art, and drama. She had included Simone de Beauvoir's *The Second Sex* on her draft of the list but for some unknown reason left it off the final version. The fiction she read was challenging; some of the titles written in the mid-twentieth century are now considered classics. Most of them addressed social issues she was concerned about: censorship, race, gender and sexuality, religious fanaticism, and alienation. Twenty years after she read banned books as a teenager in Germany, she continued to read books by those banned authors, including Hemingway, Kafka, Zweig, Thomas Mann, and Heinrich Mann.

Chapter 23

The person deciding Ruth's fate concerning her admission to library school was J. Periam Danton, known as Perry, the chair of Berkeley's School of Librarianship. The son of two American German teachers, Danton had grown up in China. Michael Buckland wrote in his introduction to Danton's oral history at the University of California Archives, "His undergraduate experience was also highly untypical because he accepted an invitation to join his father in Leipzig for the academic year 1925–26 . . . Leipzig was still in the twilight of its greatness, not yet undermined by Nazism and by the devastation of the Second World War . . . To spend a year in Leipzig was, predictably, a powerful experience. German and Austrian scholarship and librarianship became central to his interests."[1] If he indeed read Ruth's admissions essay, perhaps her opening paragraph would have sparked an interest in her. Whether they ever knew about each other's backgrounds in Leipzig remains a speculation.

Danton had earned his undergraduate degree in librarianship at Columbia University and his PhD in library science at the University of Chicago. With experience at the New York Public Library, the University of Chicago Library, the Colby College Library, and the Temple University Library, he was recruited as dean of Berkeley's School of Librarianship in 1946. His ambitions were to take charge of a small and quasi-professional program with only three professors (including

Chaja and Mendel Rappaport, ca. 1922.

Courtesy of Guy Rosner

Ruth Rappaport, 1929.

Courtesy of Guy Rosner

Chaja, Ruth, and Mendel Rappaport, undated.

Courtesy of Guy Rosner

Ruth Rappaport, undated.

Courtesy of Guy Rosner

Unknown man, Ruth, Chaja, and Mendel Rappaport at a café in Leipzig, undated.

Courtesy of Ben Zuras

Photograph of Clara and Mirjam Rappaport at the Monument to the Battle of the Nations in Leipzig, 1929.

Courtesy of Guy Rosner

Chaja and Mirjam Rappaport on Salomonstrasse in Leipzig, July 17, 1937.

Photograph number 51879, Ruth Rappaport collection,
United States Holocaust Memorial Museum

Ruth Rappaport in the courtyard of her apartment building, November 8, 1938.

Photograph number 51874, Ruth Rappaport collection, United States Holocaust Memorial Museum

Photograph of Ruth Rappaport watching Ursi Herzog climb on her carriage in Zurich, February 5, 1939.

Photograph number 51871, Ruth Rappaport collection, United States Holocaust Memorial Museum

Ruth Rappaport at the Herzogs' home in Zurich, February 4, 1939.

Photograph number 51872, Ruth Rappaport collection United States Holocaust Memorial Museum

Ruth Rappaport's passport photograph, December 29, 1947.

Ruth Rappaport collection, United States Holocaust Memorial Museum

Party in Israel with Moshe Pearlman (fifth from left), ca. 1948–1949.

Photo probably taken by Ruth Rappaport, Ruth Rappaport collection, United States Holocaust Memorial Museum

*Ruth Rappaport in Israel,
ca. 1948–1949.*

Ruth Rappaport collection, United States
Holocaust Memorial Museum

Illustration of Ruth Rappaport by G. Giuliani, Hotel Columbia, Genoa, 1949.

Courtesy of Guy Rosner

Ruth Rappaport, Genoa, December 26, 1949.

Courtesy of Guy Rosner

Ruth Rappaport (right) with other librarians, ca. 1960–1969.

Ruth Rapport Collection, United States Army Heritage and Education Center, Carlisle, PA

Captain Archie Kuntze, undated.

Ruth Rapport Collection, United States Army Heritage and Education Center, Carlisle, PA

Ruth Rappaport, ca. 1960–1969.

Ruth Rappaport and unknown man in library in Vietnam, undated.

Ruth Rapport Collection, United States Army Heritage and Education Center, Carlisle, PA

Ruth Rappaport at the opening of Miller Library at the Vinh Long Airfield, 1966.

Catrine Goska, Ruth Rappaport, Regene Ross, Jurij Dobczansky, Ruta Penkiunas, Irene Roberts, and Catherine Hiebert Kerst (left to right) at the Library of Congress, 1985.

Ruth Rappaport at the Tidal Basin in Washington, DC, undated.

Courtesy of Ben Zuras

Ben Zuras, Ruth Rappaport, and Peter Bartis on Ruth's front porch, August 2010.

Courtesy of Ben Zuras

Photograph of Ruth Rappaport, undated.

Courtesy of Guy Rosner

himself) and develop it into a much bigger school that would include a rigorous master's degree and a PhD program.[2]

In 1954 Danton laid out his plans for the program in an article in *California Libraries*. He noted the school was not a place for future librarians to learn the lower-level tasks often delegated to technicians or assistants, a pedagogy he described as akin to teaching doctors how to empty bedpans. He revealed his frustration with library schools' second-class status:

> A school of the kind we are describing is not a refuge for the individual who has been patently unsuccessful elsewhere—since, in general, the attributes of success have a certain commonness—for the person who seeks escape from the maddening [sic] crowd, for those with "difficult" personalities (you know the kind: "Of course, he hasn't the qualities to make a good teacher but I think he'd be a fine librarian.") or for those whose intellectual ability or what you will, is sub-normal.[3]

He argued that Berkeley should recruit men and women with "the best possible personal and intellectual qualifications" and that the school would focus on the theory, practice, and professional ethics of librarianship. He wrote that schools of librarianship should generally not accept candidates over age thirty-five (Ruth was thirty-four when she applied), because this age apparently revealed that the candidate had failed at other careers. He noted the difficulties of recruiting faculty to library schools: a miniscule number of people had PhDs in the field, and it was difficult to recruit excellent librarians to teach when they would rather advance in library administration.[4]

Despite his mostly admirable ambitions, Danton was not especially well liked during his long tenure at Berkeley. Fred Mosher, a library school professor who was hired in 1950, revealed in his oral history that Danton had divorced his wife to marry the recently divorced wife of the university's assistant librarian, causing a scandal and rift among the faculty and staff of the library and School of Librarianship.[5] In his memoir, *No Silence! A Library Life*, William Eshelman recalled that when he attended Berkeley's School of Librarianship in the early 1950s, the students referred to the school as "Danton's Inferno."[6] Mosher candidly summed up the faculty and students' attitudes toward Danton:

> My impression and the impression of the faculty I admired most was that he was considered to be—that he knew how to keep the paperwork going, but that his relationships with students and his relationship with many of the faculty was not very good. I don't know how to phrase it. It seemed to me that he was interested mainly in himself and not in the school or the students, and that he made many judgments that were against the interests of the students, especially, because of his own personal feelings.[7]

It appears that Danton was not impressed with Ruth. In a recommendation form he later filled out for her first job as a librarian, he wrote—after begrudgingly giving her middle-to-high rankings in the categories and admitting she "has a good mind and is a hard worker"— "Miss R. is a compulsive talker, without any terminal facilities, completely self-centered, not receptive to criticism, was a disturbing force in her class; uninterested in the needs or rights of others."[8] Like other students, Ruth did not get along well with Danton. They both seem to have had strong personalities, and Ruth was unwilling to back down when expressing her opinions and ideas. Perhaps Ruth was truly difficult in class and bulldozed over her classmates in discussions; perhaps Danton was so turned off by an opinionated Jewish woman that he exaggerated this evaluation.

Chapter 24

In the fall of 1957, Ruth became occupied by another matter that surely distracted her from her library school classes. Friends of hers who were also displaced European Jews had begun to apply for restitution, and she decided that she should too. She wrote the following letter to the United Restitution Organization (URO) in November:

Gentlemen:

After contacting the San Francisco [Émigré] Committee, I was advised to get in touch with your organization concerning the following matter.

I was born and raised in Germany, and as so many others, had to leave and resettle somewhere else. Both my parents remained in Germany and died in concentration camps. As far as I know, my sister, living in Israel[,] is taking the required steps for compensation, etc. concerning both of us as heirs. However, I have been told that independently of this claim I am entitled to personal compensation for my own resettlement, loss of schooling while waiting for an American visa in Switzerland (while legally of school age), etc. Could you please mail me whatever forms are necessary for me to fill out and whatever other pertinent information I should have[?] Is it correct that all such claims must be initiated before December 31, 1957?

Thanking you for whatever assistance you can give me, I remain,

Ruth Rappaport[1]

The United Restitution Organization was founded in 1948 as an international legal-aid society to assist Jews around the world with their claims for compensation from the German government. In 1945 the Allies had made a commitment to pursue justice for Jewish victims; the next few years resulted in enormous confusion over certain types of claims and unclaimed property. The four new zones controlled by each of the Allied powers had different regulations concerning restitution. After the unification of the Federal Republic of Germany (FRG) in 1948, the new chancellor, Konrad Adenauer, made a speech to the German parliament in 1951 declaring the new country's responsibility to alleviate the suffering of Jews the Nazis had persecuted. A series of laws passed in the 1950s and '60s, officially called the Bundesentschädigungsgesetz, or BEG, dictated the types of claims and rules for eligibility. The URO established offices around the world, primarily run by German Jewish lawyers, and had a total staff of around twelve hundred people to assist applicants with the complicated forms and interpreting the responses and settlements from the FRG.[2]

Edith Dosmar of the URO's New York office explained to Ruth that she could file for compensation for her parents' deaths, along with Mirjam's claims for the same. Ruth could also apply for a loss-of-education claim and for the money she and her family had spent on her travel expenses to the United States. She instructed Ruth to write a curriculum vitae explaining her education, career goals, and how the Nazi regime had interrupted them.[3]

Ruth set to work gathering the necessary documentation she would have to submit. She wrote out her curriculum vitae, detailing the events in her childhood and young adulthood related to leaving Germany and the loss of her education. She explained how no one paid for her college education, which she had to complete in fits and starts across eighteen years while supporting herself (she made no mention of her inheritance from her uncle Carl, however). She enclosed the documentation in her letter back to Dosmar, in which she stated that she was unclear if she had written it correctly. She also expressed her frustration that she knew so little about her parents' financial and business dealings and what had happened to them after she had left for the US. She asked how to go about obtaining the necessary proof for these matters with her application. Dosmar instructed Ruth to copy her certificate from the girls' high school she had been admitted to in Leipzig, any documentation about travel expenses, the letter notifying her of her parents' deaths, and proof of tuition paid to the University of Washington and the University of California. Ruth mailed all this documentation in February 1958, along with more questions that she had about the process and various claims. In September she received a notification that her application had been accepted for processing in Hanover.[4] Later in the fall she heard back that the URO needed proof of her and her parents' residency in Leipzig.[5] The URO received it at the beginning of 1959. In June of that year, Ruth received a check for 5,000 deutsche marks, or about $9,300 in 2018 dollars, as compensation for her loss of education.[6] However, her claim for the deaths of her parents was not approved because at the time of their deaths Ruth was, at age twenty-one, considered an adult.[7] For years Ruth and Mirjam continued to appeal this decision. In one letter to Ruth in 1962, the URO explained that since Mendel had not been deported outside of Germany, he and his descendants were not eligible for compensation that was given only to those deported beyond the country's borders.[8]

A letter that she received later, regarding her mother, simply stated with no explanation, "There are clearly no claims here."[9]

While Ruth lived overseas in the early 1960s, she missed many pieces of correspondence from the URO that never got to her until 1964. In a long letter back to the organization, she answered point by point many pending questions from the URO and expressed her frustration with the process: "Frankly, I am at a complete loss to understand either what further documentary proof is expected of me, [or] the decisions reached concerning my various claims."[10] She corrected the mistakes in the previous correspondence: she had never been on a *Kindertransport* to England nor received financial help from a Jewish organization in Switzerland.[11] She concluded this letter:

> As to the other losses, it is obvious, having left as a child of 15, I do not know the intricate details of my parents' financial affairs. I do know however, that at one time there was a fair income on the side of my father in the fur trade and on the part of my mother for managing the restaurant for the "Oesterreichisches Vaterlandsheim." There has also been considerable property (furniture, silver, household goods, etc.) as well as a complete dowry for me. Apparently all this was confiscated at the time of my parents' deportation if not before.[12]

In 1964 Ruth was notified that she was eligible for another 5,000 deutsche marks due to her loss of education, although it is unclear if she ever received the funds.[13] The correspondence between Ruth and the URO seems to have ended in 1965. This money surely helped Ruth financially, but it is doubtful that it ever brought her any sense of closure or justice concerning the gaping loss of her parents and her trauma as a refugee.

Chapter 25

In the spring of 1958, Ruth took Librarianship 220B, a course that required her to write a substantial bibliography. Writing bibliographies was a significant part of a librarian's job at the time, especially for those who worked at university libraries. Not simply a list of books, these bibliographies were guides—organized by source format and often including substantial overviews—that addressed the scholarship on specific topics. They sometimes included summaries or short critiques of each item. They were often collaboratively written and published by library-related organizations. In the information era before the internet and online union catalogs like WorldCat, bibliographies and other reference works were the first stop for anyone performing serious research on a topic. It was a task that librarians with subject expertise and language skills took on with great seriousness; they were not simply offering unbiased lists of sources, but also critiquing them and guiding researchers to the best and most appropriate publications for their specific research purposes.

Ruth chose German Jews in the United States, and, more specifically, those who had immigrated since 1933, as the topic of her bibliography. Considering her own experience as a German Jew in the US and her concurrent restitution claim, she took advantage of this assignment to pursue a personal research interest. Her bibliography was intended to provide a survey of materials available for a future sociological study of the group, and she pointed out that no definitive work had yet been written on the topic. She defined this group of recent immigrants to include those who, like her, were born in Germany and not considered citizens of that country but were classified as German according to the US. She pointed out that this group did not have its own Library of Congress subject heading, foreshadowing the work she would take up twenty years later.

Ruth selected what she considered the best material, mostly in English, from the following genres and formats: general reference works, general newspapers, Jewish periodicals, scholarly journals, publications by special agencies, fiction books, monographs, dissertations, biographies, and autobiographies. She scoured the catalogs at the University of California Library and the Hillel Foundation Library at Berkeley for sources.[1] She also contacted the American Jewish Historical Society, the United Hebrew Immigrant Aid Society Service (HIAS), the American Jewish Committee, and the Leo Baeck Institute. In total, the bibliography lists 292 sources, with a short comment or explanation by Ruth for each one. Along with other bibliographies written for this class over the years, it is still held in the Berkeley library. "A Selective Guide to Source Materials on German Jews in the U.S. from 1933 to the Present Time" reveals how Ruth channeled her past trauma and yearned to make sense of it through systematic, dogged research. She earned an A in Librarianship 220B.[2]

In the 1950s the faculty of Berkeley's School of Librarianship decided to take an active stance concerning McCarthyism in general and, more specifically, censorship in California's schools and public libraries. The witch hunt to root out Communists from both the federal government and Hollywood had also spread to librarianship, as many local libraries were accused of providing Communist books to the public. Professor Fred Mosher was the head of the California Library Association's (CLA) Intellectual Freedom Committee when a woman named Anne Smart alerted the state legislature to what she believed to be Communist materials in the Marin County school libraries. A bill was proposed to ban subversive materials in school libraries, but the CLA successfully lobbied against its passage. After this incident, the CLA decided to fund a study of censorship in California libraries but backed off the project when alternative funding was secured from the Fund for the Republic. Because this organization had supported other efforts against McCarthyism, CLA members feared more backlash. Despite opposition from the board of regents, the School of Librarianship stepped up to sponsor the study with funding from the Fund for the Republic. [3]

Marjorie Fiske, a professor in the Sociology Department, was tasked with managing the study. Along with a team of research assistants, she interviewed librarians across California about book challenges, pressure from the community and library boards, and their practices of book selection. The study uncovered the fact that while book challenges by the members of the community were relatively rare across the state, librarians were cautious about selecting books considered controversial or subversive, and when they did purchase these books for the library, they often kept them behind the reference desk or in offices. California librarians had been spooked by McCarthyism and cases of censorship in the news and, to protect themselves, had exercised what Fiske termed "preventative censorship." [4]

On July 10–12, 1958, the School of Librarianship hosted a symposium titled "The Climate of Book Selection: Social Influences on School and Public Libraries." Scholars outside the field of librarianship presented papers on censorship, and Fred Mosher gave an overview of the recent book challenges in California. Marjorie Fiske concluded by giving a summary of the findings of her report, which was to be published the next year. Librarians from across the country attended, weighing in on discussions after each paper. Mosher later explained his overall reasoning for advocating for both the study and the symposium: "I think that the idea was that library schools particularly, and library school students, ought to be made thoroughly aware of the problems of intellectual freedom and approved methods of combatting censorship of books, and also they should push to get policies so they would have backing from their board whenever a censorship incident occurred."[5]

In Ruth's collection at the University of Washington, there is a ticket stub for the symposium. She probably sat in the audience, mulling over how the blatant censorship she had lived under as a teenager was alive and well in California, just in a more subtle and polite form. Ruth may have also been aware of the widespread segregation of public libraries in the South and no doubt knew that the state of America's libraries was not what it ideally could be. She would graduate from the library school just a few weeks later and had already applied for several jobs. She hoped that whatever job she landed would finally give her the chance to live up to the ideals that she had been cultivating, not just in library school but also throughout her whole life. She was now fully prepared to claim a calling and a professional title that would give her a new lease on life: librarian.

Part VII:

Ruthie's Little Empire

OKINAWA AND VIETNAM, 1959–1970

Chapter 26

When asked about how she ended up with her first job as a librarian, Ruth liked to tell a funny story: "The head of all air force libraries in the world met me at a cocktail party. And the joke has been he sent me to Okinawa to sober me up. Because he fed me too many martinis, and he stuck me on an airplane and shipped me overseas."[1] She might have met Harry F. Cook, the chief of the air force libraries, at a party, but an air force librarian named Ruth Sieben-Morgen was the person who helped Ruth obtain the job in Okinawa and served as a mentor to her during her first few years as a librarian. The many letters between the two Ruths in Rappaport's collection at the US Army Heritage and Education Center reveal the arduous federal employment process and also a wisecracking friendship. The date of the infamous cocktail party remains unknown, but it most likely took place in 1958 or earlier. It is possible that it even happened before Ruth decided to become a librarian, and it could have been the reason she chose to go to library school; Ruth always looked out for advantageous connections. Sieben-Morgen put in a name request (the terminology for when an employer has a specific person in mind for a position) for Ruth probably in August 1958 when she graduated. Ruth was also pursuing other job leads, including one at Mills College.

Ruth wrote Sieben-Morgen an excited, appreciative letter when the air force contacted her and estimated she would leave for Okinawa on October 30.[2] But in December she was writing her again, more subdued this time, about her reluctance and confusion over why the process was taking so long. She was frustrated with the flip-flopping among the air force bureaucracy about their initial rejection of her application and with how she didn't know whether she was being considered for positions in Okinawa or Korea. She suspected she had received a negative reference from Perry Danton, the chair of Berkeley's library school, and indeed she was right.[3] Ruth was also concerned that her employment for the PIO in Israel and for the Zionist organizations might have been misunderstood. She claimed she had friends who had been in Israel with her then who now worked for the US federal government and that she herself had been a US civil servant a few years earlier. "So I don't really see where any of this is relevant, but under the circumstance, I cannot help wonder . . . whether somebody along the line had a strange notion?" she asked.[4] Understandably she had not mentioned anything about her employment with Max Lowenthal in this application or in her previous one for her job at the Oakland Army Base in 1952, when she had to undergo a loyalty review. Even though the Loyalty Review Board was abolished in 1953, Ruth still had to undergo a background check by the FBI in order to obtain federal employment.[5] Her earlier work as a Zionist and in Israel would continue to be suspect.

Regardless of all the confusion, Ruth accepted the Okinawa job in early January 1959.[6] She had been telling friends and family about the job since the fall. Many of them wrote and congratulated her and wished her well on her new adventure, as they announced their own news of births and children growing up. She most likely had joked that her odds of finding a husband were greater in Okinawa than in Berkeley; her friend Ilya wrote to her, "Your mathematics might be all right, but it very seldom helps to travel 3000 miles to get a male."[7] At age thirty-five in 1959, Ruth's chances of finding a husband were diminishing, but she would not give up yet, or at least not give up joking about her travails as a single woman.

Ruth's first job at the Naha Air Base was as a field librarian at the federal employee general schedule 7 (GS-7) level earning $4,980 per year.

She had been considered for a GS-9 appointment, appropriate for an employee with a graduate degree, but had been deemed a GS-7 due to her lack of experience working in a library. The GS system had been instituted in 1949 to regulate federal salaries and make them comparable to the private sector. The system also helped ensure that civil-service employees with similar experience and education were being paid fairly. She may have been disappointed by this ranking and salary, but it is likely that she did not have to pay housing costs in Okinawa. Working under a librarian named Mary Jane Lin, she got ample experience in all aspects of librarianship. She described this position in a later job application:

> Serving military personnel and their dependents with a collection of 24,000 volumes. In charge of four site libraries with holdings of 6740 volumes. Classifying, cataloging, weeding; reference work; readers' advisory; publicity; book reviews. Training of indigenous and/or military personnel. Selection and acquisition of books, phonograph records and magazines. Assistant to Chief Librarian.[8]

She seems to have enjoyed the work and cutting her teeth as a real librarian. But she chafed at the rules about working a regular schedule, unpaid overtime, comp-time hours, and travel itineraries. Mary Jane Lin and Ruth butted heads about her constant late arrivals in the mornings, and both seem to have written at least a few letters to Sieben-Morgen about these issues. Sieben-Morgen tried to explain the rules, which she didn't agree with either, in a letter to Ruth in September 1959, adding that all the librarians at other bases were working unpaid overtime too and that none of them earned comp time regularly. Sieben-Morgen urged her to follow the rules to make peace with Lin and, with foresight, noted, "Some day when you are supervisor, you'll see her problem. You'll have to insist on promptness from every member of your staff, and sell your standards by your own example. . . And for gosh's sakes don't give papa Danton the satisfaction: your lack of promptness was one of the things he spoke of about you, remember?" She added cryptically, "We know of course what was behind that."[9]

Ruth drafted a letter back to Sieben-Morgen to defend herself, although she might not have sent it. She insisted that other librarians had told her to track her comp time and that shifts had been unfairly dumped on her at the last minute when other librarians wanted a day off. She was angered by an incident where she had to take an Easter shift, presumably so that the other librarians who were Christians could take the day off. She pointed out the impossibility of making a firm schedule when her transportation (often by plane or helicopter) to and from the site libraries was not reliable, especially during typhoon season. A few months later she wrote to Sieben-Morgen inquiring about a job posting for a librarian at the Yakota Air Base. She mentioned that she wanted administrative experience and that her "stomach [had] very literally had its share of helicopter flights and [had] currently taken to rebelling openly in flight." Sieben-Morgen regretfully notified her that the job would be taken by the wife of a pilot.[10]

Sometime in early 1960 Sieben-Morgen came to Okinawa, presumably for an inspection visit. She wrote Ruth a letter thanking her for her hospitality and the lovely time she had: "Your party was the most elaborate ever I've been part of and I was awfully impressed too by the people who came especially your site commanders and CO [commanding officer]. That was good, Ruth, and thank you for it."[11] These strengths of Ruth's—her sociability, hospitality, and flattery of the right people above her—were strategies she had honed for a long time. While these tactics hadn't always worked for her in the past, the elaborate hierarchy and social rules of the military seemed to be a natural fit for her. Although she loathed bureaucracy and often battled those she worked closely with concerning arcane minutiae, Ruth was more than willing to play this game, not only to get ahead but also because it was a game she enjoyed.

Even though Ruth was working with other women librarians and got along well with most of the male officers at Naha, she still could not escape sexual harassment and discrimination there. In 1961 she expressed interest in applying for a GS-9 job at the Wakkanai Air Station. She wrote:

> I realize that they are looking for a man, but if they are at all interested in a woman, then the following might be of interest to them. I have just finished working on isolated sites (three of them) for two years. I'm the only Caucasian woman at any of these sites and I've lived with the troops anywhere from 3 to 18 days at a stretch on my monthly visits…My whole point here being that everyone of us is agreed that the job I now hold is really a man's job, but everybody also saying they much prefer a woman!!!!!!! Those are the little ironies of life![12]

Ruth knew that sexism was more than a little irony of life, but in 1961 it was still legal to advertise jobs for men or women only. She was not afraid to speak about these issues to her superiors and to point out that her skills and abilities as a librarian were equal to any man's. Coupled with the fact that officers' wives got priority in hiring, her disadvantage as a single woman—even in the field of librarianship, which favored them—was blatant.

In May 1962 Ruth wrote a letter to Colonel Foote, reporting sexual harassment from another colonel:

> Saturday night, after midnight, at the Naha Officers' Club, Colonel Thompson began to harass me about official library business. My attempts to change the subject and to move away from him were to no avail, and he ended his verbal attack by repeatedly telling me:

"You are a fool... The only reason Sgt. Eberwein likes working in your library is that he expects to get a piece of tail from you, and if he doesn't get it soon he's going to quit... I haven't gotten mine yet either, ... Why don't you just quit and get the hell out of here so I can close that damned library..."

This was not the first time I was subjected to verbal abuse by Col. Thompson, but it is the worst to date.[13]

Thompson was just one of many men who harassed Ruth throughout her long career, but the letter shows that Ruth would not just accept it as part of the job, if she ever did when she was younger. She was not afraid to report him, even if there would be no action (and in this case, there likely wasn't). Documenting and reporting sexual harassment in 1962—two years ahead of the passage of the Civil Rights Act, which gave new protections to women in the workplace, and thirteen years before the term "sexual harassment" was even coined—Ruth refused to be quiet about the injustices she regularly suffered, and she didn't care if speaking out gave her a reputation as a difficult woman.

In 1961 Lin wrote an evaluation for Ruth, describing her weaknesses as a professional librarian:

Miss Rappaport has had difficulty adjusting to library routines—making work schedules, keeping hours posted, etc., and has had difficulty in meeting given suspense dates [deadlines]. Her working relationship with the library staff and base personnel has not always been successful, though she is well liked by personnel at the sites she serves. The ability to do good, or even outstanding, library work is present, but Miss Rappaport must learn to conform to the military library program and its demands, and to show more mature judgment in handling library problems and personnel.[14]

Ruth surely was aware of her faults, and if she tried to reform her professional ways at this time, it was temporary. Throughout her career Ruth usually ran late, always had a messy desk, and struggled to diplomatically manage her employees. On the other hand, she would continue to follow the most important tenet of librarianship: the patron always comes first. Ruth would go the extra mile to find a needed book or source and no doubt charmed officers and patrons with her wizard-like knowledge of call numbers, subject headings, and publications.

Major Sara P. Moesker (known as Pat) was a captain in the air force in Okinawa while her husband was stationed in Korea. She was assigned a bedroom next door and a shared bathroom with Ruth, and the two became fast friends. Moesker worked with top-secret material and radio communications but spent a lot of free time in the library. She remembered the endless hijinks involving Ruth, who nearly backed up a truck off a pier and teetered dangerously on a ladder to hang decorations around the library in Okinawa. She was amazed by Ruth's ability with languages, her gift of remembering everyone, and her skills as a captivating conversationalist at cocktail parties. The two women would remain good friends for the rest of their lives.[15]

In 1961 Ruth was cited in a report for making the most library site visits and writing the best reports in the Pacific Air Force (PACAF) command.[16] She had attended many of the PACAF library conferences and networked her way across Southeast Asia. She was restless and hungry for more responsibility, more power, and a chance to make a significant impact in the lives of people who also sought books and information the way she did. In the fall of 1962, the navy's Headquarters Support Activity Saigon (HSAS) advertised a job for a librarian because the navy didn't have one there, nor did any branch of the military. There was no library to speak of, and Saigon was becoming a hotspot. This was the opportunity Ruth had been waiting for.

Chapter 27

Ruth traveled to Saigon from Okinawa in November 1962 for the HSAS job interview and to see if she liked the city.[1] The loosely defined mission for this one-year position was, first, to establish a library in Saigon to serve all branches of the military (not just the navy) and second, and if she wished to continue after that, to expand the system to perhaps six to eight annex libraries at new military bases around the country. As she wrote about this job opportunity in the summer of 1963 in a mass letter to friends and family, "It was presented as a challenge, and oy, how I'm beginning to hate that word . . . However, like a hooked fish I bit."[2]

She explained to them the situation she had walked into:

> The program is still being envisioned, but if, when and how it shall be implemented is still a mystery. So far, I've worked harder than on any other job and much less to show for it all. The difficulties, both internal and exter-nal[,] seem at times insurmountable, and the gaps between the envisioned and the existing program would be funny if [they] weren't so sad. In place of a main library, a service-center depot and branches, I'm in three little rooms, 1100 sqft., in a hotel, with almost 5,000 books of which only about 800 are properly cataloged and classified and one local national employee who hardly knows any English.[3]

With few supplies and a shoestring budget, Ruth started organizing the books available by color-coding their spines, requesting donations from other military libraries around the world, and ordering magazine subscriptions and new books from catalogs. She moved the library from an administrative office to a space in a bachelor officers' quarters (BOQ) in a former hotel, using an old bar counter as the circulation desk. At this time, Ruth implemented her field delivery kit program to men stationed in remote areas, an idea that had been conceived by librarians in World War II. She selected eight magazines and eighty paperbacks per month to be delivered to these advisory teams. In addition, men could request any book by mail, and an interlibrary loan program was established with other military libraries in the Pacific. "The man in the rice paddies had something to READ," Ruth concluded triumphantly in a report many years later.[4]

She soon grew frustrated with officers who asked her to find specific books for them in the library without bothering to learn how to use the card catalog. Creating large mock catalog cards out of poster board, Ruth held classes she called "coffee hours" for library patrons. Commenting on this method ten years later to her friend Gabe Horchler, who was building libraries in Africa, she wrote, "I found this even worked with full colonels who'd avoided looking up their own information for a lifetime as well as with the first and second graders! Only they got lollipops and candy instead of coffee!"[5]

When the books quickly outgrew the space in the hotel, she requested to move the library into the former US dispensary, previously a villa with a separate building in the back and a swimming pool. It would have enough space for the main library, the growing field distribution center (book kits), and the library service center (processing and cataloging books for the main library and branches). The move was completed in February 1964. Across the street just a week later, the movie theater for Americans was bombed. It damaged the new library, which was used as a temporary staging area for the wounded and dead.

This would not be the only time United States Information Agency and military libraries were damaged or targeted directly by the Viet Cong. A few Vietnamese employees were convinced the library was haunted and refused to work again until they were promised they could quit without penalty if they saw a ghost.[6]

After repairs the Saigon Library became a popular hangout for newly arrived soldiers and officers. As one of the only air-conditioned buildings operated by the military, it became a peaceful refuge and provided some relief from the boredom many enlisted men experienced on deployments. Besides offering recreational reading, the library also provided nonfiction and technical books needed to perform official duties. By 1965 dependents of military officers could not stay in Vietnam due to the growing dangers of war. This meant that the libraries lost some of their English-speaking staff, the wives of officers.[7]

The library system had expanded to eleven branches, and Ruth traveled by helicopter to supervise the delivery of new books, supplies, and furniture when new branches opened. By the spring of 1966, the library field distribution center was sending a hundred thousand paperback books and seventy-five thousand magazines to eight hundred addresses each month. Ruth developed a service to provide reel-to-reel tapes of spoken-word recordings of poetry and plays, as well as jazz and classical music, which were widely duplicated by troops, who took them to the field, despite copyright laws. Troops also used blank tapes to record messages to send home to their families.[8] After the draft started, the most popular books were classics, read by former college students and those enrolled in correspondence courses.[9] Ruth relished providing a wide-ranging collection of both serious and popular titles and binged on book ordering through the night while chain-smoking, right before major budget deadlines.[10]

In 1961 the *Army Library Operational Guide* stated officially that army libraries did not censor. This same guide for librarians, probably similar to the guidelines the navy followed, also contradictorily advised,

"Avoid subversive, biased, propagandist, sensational, and inflammatory books."[11] Ruth ordered thousands of subscriptions of *Playboy* each year for the magazine kits and the libraries. *Playboy* had been available at military post exchanges (known as PXs), but offering them as reading material was another thing entirely. But if anyone complained, there is no evidence of it today. Regarding an incident that occurred when she first started offering the magazine at the libraries in 1964, Ruth explained to a friend (the ellipses are Ruth's):

> The other day my CO called up and wanted to know how many *Playboys* we were getting... thinking maybe a chaplain was behind this query[,] I started to hem & haw... and Kuntze says, "Ruthie, what's the matter...you always know what you're doing...why the stall...." And I swallow and say, "Hm, well, just why do you want to know.....?" and he says...."Well, with all that money we're spending on *Esquire*....and *Playboy* is so much better....." and I says "Well, well, there's a hundred copies coming on the plane from Oki[nawa]," and he's just as pleased as punch but thinks that maybe we need 150 copies! Honestly, sometimes he's just not quite for real [...] and it's we all love Ruthie week for the time being.[12]

Ruth seems to have fit into the social scene of American expats in Vietnam very well. She had always loved to socialize, especially at cocktail parties, and to debate and discuss politics and literature. She particularly enjoyed hanging out with reporters (as she had formerly been one herself) and other well-educated civilians and officers at the Cercle Sportif Country Club, where she was a regular swimmer. Taking the lead from the French, who had colonized Vietnam for decades, the Americans there now lived in villas and employed Vietnamese staff to run their households. Ruth lived in a hotel with other civilians and was one of just a few single American women there at the time.

She didn't get along with everyone in her professional circle, however. Ruth's immediate superiors in the navy scoffed at how seriously she took her mission, calling it "Ruthie's Little Empire" and writing on her travel authorizations that her mode of transportation to the American Library Association's annual conference was by "broomstick," which she found amusing.[13] She battled them for more funding and became friendly with a supportive navy captain further up the chain of command—her "CO," as she called him, Archie Kuntze, otherwise known as the "American mayor of Saigon." Tasked with importing supplies to Vietnam for the entire military, Captain Kuntze flouted regulations by living with his Chinese girlfriend Jannie Suen, who worked at the Chinese embassy.

In his book, *To Spurn the Gods*, former navy lieutenant A. A. Allison described his arrival at the libraries to work under Ruth. He was initially both surprised and disappointed that he had been assigned the duty. He wrote:

> Indeed, Saigon did have a library. I was in charge of it, at least notionally. In truth, a remarkable forty-something American ex-patriot government librarian named Ruth Rappaport and her staff of Vietnamese ladies had been running the library for years. My job was to set up library annexes around the country and to develop a distribution system to get paperback books and magazines to the men in the field.[14]

But he soon found out that what he thought would be a boring job at the library would actually be something else entirely:

Not long after I arrived, Captain Kuntze summoned me to his office, and, after brief personal welcomes and briefer pleasantries, he told me that I would be a regular courier to deliver funds for certain "local nationals" to CIA case officers and Special Forces officers. The assignment, he said, entailed risk not only because I would be carrying substantial funds but also because the enemy would target anyone it suspected of paying agents. For this reason, I was to tell no one—he emphasized no one—about this duty. I was to do nothing or say nothing that would arouse suspicions. My travels around the country on library business would be my cover.[15]

Kuntze would pass Allison some of the thousands of dollars in different currencies from his safe; Allison would then slip it into magazines to be handed off at cafés in Saigon and while he "inspected" the branch libraries at military bases around the country. Some of the men who were paid off also supplied the libraries' furniture and equipment in order to cover up where the money came from. He suspected that the man he paid off in Hue had something to do with the bombing of the library there so that he would profit from the rebuilding and new supplies it would need.[16]

When asked if Ruth knew that Captain Kuntze was using the library system for this purpose, Allison speculated about her involvement. "I sometimes suspected that she, too, had another job. She was not supposed to know about my courier work . . . Whether I did that well enough, given Ruth's remarkable intelligence and insight, is very much open to question."[17] He observed that Ruth and Kuntze were good friends, which could have been due to their similar personalities and outlook. Whether or not she knew about or was part of Kuntze's courier network, their relationship was beneficial, if perhaps unspoken. Kuntze may have cynically encouraged her to expand the library for his own purposes, but his support for them does not preclude the possibility that he could have been just as idealistic as she was about the role of books in the Vietnam War.

The year 1966 marked a turning point in Vietnam, not only in the United States' overall strategy but within the library system as well. In the fall of 1965, it was announced that the logistics and support services the navy had operated for the whole military would be turned over to the army, although this took many months to fully implement. A. A. Allison described the spring 1966 transition:

> Turning over the libraries to the Army captain was not complicated. He had no courier responsibilities . . . He had two lieutenants and dozens of soldiers to operate the system that my petty officer, a few Vietnamese helpers, and I had operated. He assigned one of his lieutenants the magazines and paperbacks and the other the annexes. To the consternation of Ruth Rappaport and her Vietnamese ladies, the library started to look like an Army headquarters, with specialists, corporals, and privates scurrying everywhere.[18]

That same spring Allison was recovering in the hospital from an injury when he was visited by Ruth and Kuntze's second-in-command, who wanted him to write a history of the navy's HSAS division. Allison wrote about the effectiveness of the "cumshawing" that Kuntze and HSAS had employed to get things done. He wrote about his own work for the libraries but left out his courier duties. Kuntze was displeased with the report, labeled it classified, and ordered Allison to rewrite it. The captain also admitted that he was about to be court-martialed and asked Allison to contact a US senator he had interned for a few years earlier, on his behalf. Allison refused on both counts and left a week later.[19]

Captain Kuntze was court-martialed a few months later in a scandal surrounded by rumor, innuendo, and unprovable accusations. Kuntze had fallen in love with Jannie Suen, who lived openly with him and frequently used his car and military planes for her own personal needs. It turned out that Suen had connections with high-level Communists in China, but it is unclear whether she was a spy. Although Allison claimed that Kuntze made every effort to stop the tide of black-market American goods into Vietnam, it was insinuated that the captain was in fact behind it all. His lavish lifestyle was what ultimately made him a target. At his court-martial trial in San Francisco, he was found guilty of living with Suen and illegally importing Thai silk for her. Kuntze's downfall ultimately may have been a move by the army to make their takeover of logistics in Saigon easier.[20]

It may be impossible to know what really happened concerning Kuntze's court-martial, how he used the libraries, or his role with the CIA. Articles currently on the internet and those written by journalists at the time are clouded with rumors and speculation. Kuntze's court-martial records and the records of the HSAS have apparently been lost or destroyed by the navy archives.[21]

Joseph DiMona's 1972 book, *Great Court-Martial Cases*, includes a chapter on Kuntze's trial. Although he did not cite any sources, DiMona most likely had access to the trial transcripts and other materials that are lost today. He explained that the initial investigation of Kuntze centered on an unexplained $16,000 in his personal bank account and suspicious checks and loans he had given out to American men in Vietnam.[22] Most of the charges against him concerned these unexplained checks and currency transactions, which ultimately could not be traced. Many navy officers personally testified that managing logistics in Vietnam was a complex maze of United States bureaucracy and a Vietnamese free-for-all grab for resources and power. Only Archie Kuntze had been able to make sense of it—and with much success. DiMona pointed out as an aside that at Kuntze's trial:

The shadowy area of espionage was barely touched on in his testimony, but it appeared that at one point a CIA agent had approached him, and asked him to change piasters to American money. From that point on, he had habitually done this for espionage agents when they were in a jam and couldn't get money through regular channels.[23]

This confirms that Kuntze did have a CIA connection, but it barely skims the surface of what his real involvement might have entailed. After Kuntze's trial, Ruth wrote him a letter expressing support and sympathy for having to go through such an ordeal. This letter also revealed Ruth's change in attitude about her work in Vietnam. She wrote:

> I'm still in Saigon…not because I enjoy it here any longer, or because the job has any challenges left…but simply because I've been too tired and indifferent to make any decisions on where to go and what to do. I'm beginning to wonder whether in one way or another this crazy war isn't hurting all those who've gotten mixed up in it.[24]

Allison summed up what he thought Ruth's impact was as a librarian for the navy in Saigon in the early 1960s:

> In a sense, Ruth was an entrepreneur. She launched that library program from nothing. While it could [have] easily been forever a backwater special services program, through sheer will, perseverance, and hard politicking, she secured the budgets and backing to make the library into a premier project. She convinced the admirals and generals that books were weapons, that books would create a bond between us and the educated Vietnamese, that books would equip our people with the intellectual armor

they needed to pursue that kind of war, and that books and periodicals provided the critical, healthy diversion necessary for morale.[25]

Ruth understood the kind of counterinsurgency strategy the United States was undertaking in the early 1960s in Vietnam. Most of the Americans who went to Vietnam in these early years—all volunteers, whether they were civilians or military—believed that necessary resources could lead to stability and that democracy would win over the hearts and minds of the Vietnamese people. But it became increasingly clear that in order for these men—a growing number of whom had become wary of the United States' role abroad—to change their hearts and minds, they would have to learn more about Communism itself and to understand what a critical role books and the freedom of the press played in a democracy. These soldiers' free access to read whatever they wanted—even subversive material—in a war zone could only reinforce their understanding of the opportunities and freedoms afforded to citizens of the United States. If access to these ideas had to be facilitated through some kind of CIA money-laundering scheme, so be it.

Chapter 28

Allison mentioned in his book that Ruth and Kuntze's second-in-command "were an item." In a very long letter Ruth wrote in 1968 to her cousin Marvin Scott Rubinstein, a psychiatrist in San Francisco, she revealed many details about her time in Saigon and her relationship with the man that Allison referred to. Ruth started writing the letter during a week she spent in the George Washington University Hospital's psychiatric ward, where she went after suffering a mental breakdown.

The letter was dated February 2, 1968, but it was written over February 2–4. Some of the edges are cut off the thirty-page letter mimeographed onto shiny paper. It weaves in and out of time, describing the years 1965 to early 1968. Ruth began the letter by apologizing to Scott for a series of confusing phone calls. She then launched into a litany of complaints about her inattentive psychiatrist Dr. Frank, who continually missed appointments and took phone calls when he actually showed up; the teenagers on the ward who were hyped up on LSD and lashing out; the multitude of interns and medical students who inappropriately questioned her about her past; the people who left her confused about her day passes to leave the hospital and run errands; and other staff who would not stop insisting she take more than two Etrafon pills per day. Ruth finally got the attention of the powerful Dr. Yochelson, who encouraged her to stay at the Psychiatric Institute of Washington, DC, but mostly ignored her questions about various treatment options. She understandably noted, "For a place that relies on words & communication almost exclusively there seem to be more misunderstandings here than anywhere I've ever been except a conference on semantics run by Dr. Hayakawa in Tokyo one year!"[1] On page 10, she finally revealed the point of this long letter: "And somewhat reluctantly, I think I shall proceed to at least give you as adequate and honest a case record as I can. Foolish maybe . . . a little embarrassed to tell, yes, of course. I guess at least to me it was serious or I wouldn't have acted the way I did, right????"

She opened on the next page with, "This story really begins around May 1965. I was truly, completely and utterly exhausted, disillusioned, tired and fed up to the gills with Saigon." She had been ready to quit, ready to throw away the empire she was building, because she could not tolerate the officers who supervised her, their mockery of her work, and the intolerable bureaucracy that festered indifference. "Without complaint, without bitterness," she turned in her resignation. "Well, even the SSO [Special Services Officer] who wished me dead and the Admin O[fficer] who could care less were not prepared to cope with my resignation." They made her an offer: a long vacation in the US, all-expenses-paid travel to the American Library Association conference, and the option to decide afterward whether she wanted to return. She one-upped them by bargaining for her own three-bedroom villa. In addition, when she returned she would have a new supervisor as part of an annual rotation of officers assigned to Vietnam.

In DC, Ruth asked the navy librarians about her new boss. They answered, in Ruth's memory:

> He's very serious; very dedicated; a stickler for detail; almost but not quite a pedant. Yes, exceedingly interested in Special Services and the library program…a bit on the silent side; almost but not quite stuffy or pompous; very

considerate and extremely helpful if he feels you're doing your best. Gets very angry when you flub.[2]

Ruth was now almost looking forward to going back to Saigon. In her letter to Scott, she explained what happened upon her return:

> I decided to go to the lion's den and see for myself. The first thing that hit me was his asking, "may I call you Ruth?" ...stuffy? Hardly [...] temporarily I had forgotten ...no overlooked the fact that he had been at the other [end] in Washington all these months and not only read all my reports and letters but had signed many of the answers. He too was asked what he thought of our "controversial librarian" [and] told the Exec and the CO "Why—I love" her already...This after having read the broomstick bit and a few other things....[3]

Inevitably, Ruth and Hank Ferguson worked long hours together, discussed library business, and went to the same parties.[4] He escorted her home one night, but because of the curfew, they decided he would sleep over in her guest bedroom, "without managing to seduce me," as she put it. The next morning he forgot his glasses at her house, and she nervously brought them in, "thinking, oh God, is he going to be so embarrassed about it all that he will now become difficult? Was all this interest in the program for just one purpose? Is he really just another Navy Casanova?"[5] She found a friendly note on her desk: "Ruthie, forgot my glasses, will retrieve them from your office tomorrow." Everything with Hank was easy, she explained: "Eventually he not only moved into my house, but also my heart, my bedroom, my thoughts et al. There was just one problem . . . there was a Mrs. Ferguson and 5 kids!"[6]

He wasn't the first married man she had been with. She admitted in the letter that she had previously rationalized that in Vietnam things were different. The stress, the heat, and the exotic locale created a dream-like mirage where boundaries were crossed. Hank quickly moved in with her; they had planned to use two spare bedrooms as private studies in the evenings but never actually used them. Like her other affairs that had expiration dates, she knew this one would be over when Hank's term as admin officer was up the following June. But deep down Ruth knew this relationship was different: "He too acknowledged that never in all his life had he thought it possible to feel so completely at ease with another human being, to feel so free to discuss everything and anything[,] to just not worry but to say anything he felt or remembered."[7] Finally, she had found her true chaver:

> We could spend hours talking about just anything, child-hood memories and experiences, ideas, politics....and also we could just sit contentedly and quietly...sometimes we played chess... I suppose it was really the very first time since I had left Leipzig that I not only felt that another human being was truly concerned over me, but truly was. I cannot remember ever since to have been "first" with any-body...first in concern, first in just about everything except financial support...Even if it had to end, it was just a good feeling to have someone do for me, worry for me, be concerned, help me, take care of me, kind of... it was a strange & new experience to be able to stop always being the one who managed everything, finagled everything, took care of everything, to be able to get things and do things without being the sole instigator... is it surprising that I should have become so utterly dependent on this man???????[8]

Falling in love like this didn't mean the same thing for Ruth that it did for other people. Her exhaustion from always being on her own for a full thirty years is palpable in this letter. Extended family, friends, boyfriends, coworkers—they had never been able to fill the void. She wanted to explain to Scott this wasn't simply an affair. It was more.

During this same time, Archie Kuntze's world was crumbling. Around Christmas, Hank was appointed acting commanding officer while Kuntze took some time off. This threatened to thwart Ruth and Hank's upcoming romantic vacation to Bangkok, but Hank admitted to Kuntze that he had plans with Ruth, and Kuntze didn't object. Their relationship had been an open secret, but now their efforts to hide it seemed pointless. After Bangkok, a trip Ruth described as nearly magical and Hank called his "first honeymoon," everyone who knew them in Saigon knew they were a couple in the spring of 1966.

Things began to sour when Ruth planned another trip to Tokyo for the two of them and Hank had to leave early for Hawaii on orders. Ruth's creeping anxiety that his sense of duty—both to his job and to his family—would pull him away from her would turn to suspicions and resentment. Feeling sorry for his financial difficulties from supporting a wife and five children, Ruth had been paying for their trips and other luxuries. From Hawaii, Hank went to DC for a few days and returned to Saigon, announcing to Ruth, "there was nothing left at home." His children were fine, but his wife was apparently uncommunicative. On their last trip together, to Singapore, before he was to leave Vietnam for good, "he let slip the information that as soon as he returned home his wife was to be hospitalized for two operations." She went on to describe what she thought he meant: "Perhaps naively I interpreted this not as a bid for sympathy or pity but as a message . . . please don't push me."[9]

Ruth seems to have admitted in the letter her dark thoughts about his wife's possible death, but she typed a row of *x*'s over them; they were simply too appalling to admit on paper. She attempted to explain what she knew of Hank's marriage, with a caveat: "I must state [my feelings] as I felt and viewed them at the time, not as I question them in retrospect."[10] She claimed that Hank explained that he had married his wife after a brief annulled marriage during the upheaval of World War II. They didn't have much in common, because while he had "developed intellectually, educationally, socially," according to Ruth, Hank's wife had stuck to her prescribed role as "a good haus-frau." She argued, "When the breakthrough finally came, there was a wonderment at what life had to offer . . . how good it was to talk and to communicate, to express and show ones feeling."[11] Ruth had made the choice years ago to devote her life to books, ideas, and a career. She may have been in her forties and, as so many have cruelly pointed out to me, "not very attractive," but there is no doubt that Hank had fallen in love with Ruth's sharp mind and her tumultuous, adventurous life.

Of this deep connection, Ruth continued, "I may be stupid and all sorts of other things, but Scott, after all this time I still cannot and will not accept the fact that this was all fake or pretense at that time."[12] This was the crux of Ruth's mental breakdown: she simply refused to believe it had all been just in her own mind.

After Hank returned to Washington in 1966, Ruth threw herself into learning the ropes of the army, recruiting new librarians, and expanding the library system, but she spent her nights at home alone, weeping. The couple promised not to write to each other, but, of course, they did. Hank initially wrote of his plans for a divorce. He came back to Saigon months later, though, to tell her that would never happen, leaving her stunned and furious. But the letters and calls continued. She mailed him money and gifts when he mentioned he was struggling to buy Christmas presents. On another one of his trips to Saigon, she confronted him about the raw deal she was getting: when it all ended, he would have his family; she would have nothing and, for whatever reason, would never be considered wife material. Why was he dragging her through this pain, which would only leave her lonelier than before? She hated her villa now, "full of his ghost," and hated that he could "have his cake and eat it": "That way he could have a 'happy home[,]' a good middle-class existence in suburbia[,] and 'love Ruthie' way out in Saigon twice a year."[13]

After she went to the ALA conference in 1967, they took a road trip through California and went from there to DC, where they met with colleagues and visited Annapolis together. Both Ruth and Hank were miserable and did not seem to care if anyone saw them together. Back alone in Saigon as the violence grew in the fall, she resented Hank's passivity in helping her get a job with the navy in DC, where she ideally wanted to live. She started to panic when no letters arrived; panic turned to rage when the bills from the summer trip came in. She mailed receipts and photos from their trips to his wife. Knowing something dangerous was looming in Vietnam, in January 1968 she packed up her house, ordered the Saigon Library to close, and announced she was taking seventy days of leave. She got on a flight headed for DC, ready to find the truth once and for all or go down trying:

> I knew this time I'd had it...after this experience I wouldn't ever let anybody ever get close to me again. I'd gotten along alright in the past by being half a person...whether a librarian to one, a female to another, a German to some, an American to others, a Jewess to still others....but never all the little bits and pieces in front of anybody[,] and if this was the result...why bother? Exhausted, disillusioned, hopeless, alienated...that's how I boarded the plane in Honolulu while smiling [...] during that turbulence on the plane I simply knew that no matter what was to come or happen after I got there...no matter what the humiliation or consequences...I simply had to go.[14]

In a sleep-deprived haze at the Willard Hotel in downtown DC, Ruth called Hank's office. He didn't want to see her. All she wanted was an explanation of why it was over so she could move on. He met her in the lobby, refusing to go up to her room to talk. They went to a coffee shop instead. "He started in like an automaton . . . like a robot . . . in a dead monotone: You must accept reality . . . I'm a married man . . . things have changed . . . I cannot explain . . . there is nothing to explain." Back in her room she took sleeping pills and slept some but woke up disoriented. She unsuccessfully called friends and, eventually, Hank at home. She spoke with his wife before he came on the line. "Beyond this time I was in a blind, blind rage . . .when he came to the phone I asked: Hank, are you coming to see me? Answer: no. Me: I've just taken a bunch of sleeping pills . . . do you want me to take some more & die? [A]nd then I slammed down the receiver. That is the last thing I remember doing."[15]

A police report with the letter stated that a maid saw smoke in the hallway outside Ruth's room: after she fell asleep again, her cigarette had lit the bed on fire. Rushed to the hospital, she had her stomach pumped. She called Hank again from the hospital later and was floored by his request: "Wouldn't I call his wife and apologize . . . after all, we might yet all be friends and maybe he and his wife could come up and see me when I was better . . . Well Scott . . . at that point I was beginning to wonder which one of us was the sicker one."[16] She summed up the whole situation: "Maybe my behavior got so sick that he truly couldn't cope any other way than he did. Oh, I've thought up lots of answers . . . but how does one find the truth? If there is such a thing? About oneself?"[17]

She didn't know what to do next. She asked Scott, "Do I just vegetate here at $72.00 a day and passively wait for what's to come? Do I sign myself out? If I do, where do I go? Whom do I see? Just pull a switch and say 'Kiddo, you've been had . . .' and go on?"[18] In total, Ruth took nine months of medical leave.[19] If she stayed in George Washington University's psychiatric ward or another hospital for much longer after she wrote the letter to Scott, there is no record of it today. Reluctantly, in September she went back to Vietnam, where much had changed in her absence.

Chapter 29

When Ruth returned to Vietnam, the library administration offices had been moved to the army base at Long Binh. It was a huge base that had been flattened out of the jungle with napalm, killing all vegetation. Ruth now lived in an ugly trailer on the base and missed her villa and nights at the country club in Saigon. In her absence, younger librarians had stepped up to keep things running smoothly. Ruth clashed with them when she came back and let them know in no uncertain terms that she was in charge again.

Between 1965 and 1968, American troop levels in Vietnam surged from 184,000 to over 500,000 men. The army had trouble recruiting civilian women librarians, and there was no time to spend on training new men without library experience. Around 1967 Ruth ordered the staff that processed incoming troops at the Bien Hoa base to look for men with library experience in their personnel files who could work in the expanding branches and the field distribution center in Saigon. Bill Sittig, later Ruth's colleague at the Library of Congress, had just graduated from library school when he was drafted in 1967. He choked up when explaining that Ruth had probably saved his life by recruiting him. Many of the men in his original unit were later killed at the Parrot's Beak, a dangerous area on the Ho Chi Minh Trail.[1]

Francis Buckley, also a library school graduate, had been working as a librarian in Detroit when he was drafted. Although he was not referred to Ruth, he immediately went to the Saigon Library his first day in the country. He met Sittig there and asked how he got the job. Two weeks later Buckley was working at the field distribution center behind the Saigon Library.[2] Peter Young, another fresh library school graduate and future Library of Congress employee, arrived in Vietnam in 1969. After briefly working to clean training films, his first lieutenant said, "I'm going to do something that the army never does. I'm going to give you a job that meets your qualifications."[3] He gave Young a job managing a trailer library at Cu Chi for one year.

Not all drafted librarians were so lucky. Gabe Horchler, who also later worked with Ruth at the Library of Congress, was eager to work in the library system as well when he was drafted in 1968 right out of library school. Despite interviewing with Ruth, he was not allowed to take the job, because more troops were needed at the front lines. He served in combat in the Mekong delta with the Ninth Infantry Division. His friend George Gibbs, also a librarian, ended up serving as a dog handler in Vietnam.[4]

To accommodate the demands of the increased troop levels, the field distribution center behind the Saigon Library grew rapidly. These books were purchased from a separate budget for "expendable" materials, meaning that they were not cataloged like the permanent collections and were not expected to be returned. The numbers of books shipped in the permanent libraries, field station libraries, and field delivery kits were planned according to a formula based on troop levels in each unit and area. Francis Buckley supervised about fifteen Vietnamese men who unloaded at least three Conex shipping containers each month, a job that had to be done in under twenty-four hours so the containers could be returned for other uses. The books and magazines had to then be rapidly sorted and shipped out.[5] A massive amount of paperwork and correspondence was necessary to coordinate the ordering of so many books and magazine subscriptions (a contract with EBSCO, a company that managed subscriptions for libraries, in 1971 helped somewhat).[6]

The library system contracted with book leasing company McNaughton to provide a standard package of hardbound books, replenished every few months, for the permanent libraries.[7] Peter Young remembered typing up lists and summaries of these new books, which were then passed around the Cu Chi base whenever a new shipment arrived. He received a Bronze Star for this work.[8]

At the war's height in the late 1960s, the library system included thirty-eight libraries, five bookmobiles, and 280 field collections. A book budget of $4.5 million ($33.9 million in 2018 dollars) provided for about four million paperbacks and 200,000 magazine subscriptions for the field kits per year, plus another 120,000 hardbacks for the permanent libraries. From 1966 to 1969, the libraries were staffed by a total of 15–20 professional librarians, 107 full-time and 220 part-time soldier assistants, and approximately 100 Vietnamese employees.[9] The vast majority of the American employees served for one-year tours, although some civilian women—including Ella Dora Bartlett, Nell Strickland, Ramona Durbin, and Syble Adams—stayed for several years.[10] Each library was open seven days a week and late into the night, although Buckley recalled that the Vietnamese women employees at the Saigon Library often told patrons the library was closing early and then asked their supervisors if they could leave since no one was there.[11]

Moving books and magazines around Vietnam was a constant fight against nature, and each permanent library was required to have air-conditioning. Particularly during the months-long monsoon season, the staff had to go to great lengths to ensure that the books stayed clean and dry. Peter Young had to sweep clods of mud from the floor that had been tracked in by library users every day.[12] Buckley and Sittig remembered that many books donated from other military bases were stored under a tarp in the unused swimming pool behind the Saigon Library. Buckley investigated and discovered the books were water damaged and molding, then decided they should be destroyed. After loading them onto a truck and sending them to be burned at the Long Binh base, an officer in a Jeep behind the truck asked where the books were going. When told they were to be burned, the officer insisted his men could use them and diverted the truck. He was probably in for a nasty surprise when he saw them up close, but the thought of burning books and wasting funds was unthinkable.[13]

In 1967 the ALA conference was held in San Francisco (this was the one Ruth had gone to before her road trip with Hank). General Maxwell Taylor was an invited speaker. Taylor had served as the ambassador to Vietnam from 1964 to 1965 and also as the chairman of the Joint Chiefs of Staff under presidents Kennedy and Johnson. At the conference, Taylor gave a prowar speech, and antiwar librarians protested outside the hotel, while others in the audience turned their backs to him.[14] Ruth had probably met Taylor in Vietnam.[15] None of the antiwar sentiment expressed at the conference and later by antiwar librarians seemed to be concerned with librarians serving in the war—both those who were drafted and civilians who volunteered to live and work in Vietnam.

Army librarian Ann Kelsey remembered her disgust at antiwar protesters while she attended UCLA's library school in 1969. Kelsey had grown up in Riverside and was the daughter of a navy veteran and employee at the Naval Ordnance Laboratory. Although no one in the library school itself seemed to be protesting, she avoided the campus as much as possible. When the Army Special Services Program came to the library school to recruit new employees, she thought, "Well, this is perfect. I can go to Asia and I can go to Vietnam and do something for these guys that these idiots outside the window here are hanging in effigy and I can see what is going on over there. I can really see for myself."[16] The recruiters were shocked to find, as she put it, "a live one" who wanted to go to Vietnam. Most of the civilian women librarians who went were from military families and did not think twice about serving their country in a dangerous area.[17] She recalled meeting Ruth when she arrived in Vietnam. When asked why she didn't work long in the Saigon Library, she explained how Ruth had taken her to the Cercle

Sportif Country Club: "I just had this visceral feeling, you know, that this was not much different from being in Los Angeles. It just didn't seem . . . I just didn't . . . it was not why I was there. I didn't come there to party and I didn't come there to socialize in a French-colonial country club. I was just very uncomfortable with the whole atmosphere and I just didn't want to be there."[18] This new generation of civilian librarians took their service very seriously. Unlike Ruth, they followed military regulations to a T; they respected the groundwork Ruth had laid and her forceful way of getting things done, but some of them were appalled by her lack of respect for rules, regulations, and the chain of command.

While Ruth was on medical leave in 1968, Nell Strickland, another military brat and career army librarian, was temporarily appointed library director. She was stuck inside the Meyerkord Hotel with other librarians for a week and a half during the Tet Offensive, subsisting on eggs and crackers and playing Monopoly by candlelight. The library was undamaged, but Strickland noted that afterward, life in Saigon was very different. US civilians could go out only when escorted by armed military guards (curfews had been in practice years earlier).[19]

When asked if he was in any danger in Vietnam, librarian Peter Young said, "Oh, absolutely, every single minute." All librarians described incidents that frightened them, whether it was listening to incoming rockets or dodging stray bullets.[20] "I was with people who weren't, shall we say, totally in control of themselves. People would come into my trailer library and, essentially, they'd take their weapons off and would check them at the desk . . . there would be grenade launchers very seldom, they'd bring in their M-16s, machine guns . . . and their .45s."[21] Ruth also complained to one soldier's commanding officer because he kept falling asleep with a lit cigarette and burned holes into the couch.[22]

By the late 1960s marijuana use was very high among the troops, and other drugs such as heroin and painkillers were commonplace.[23] In 1971 a drug treatment center was opened at the Da Nang base (one of three to open that year), and the officers who staffed it requested a small library there.[24] The library system began to order books such as *Drugs for Young People: Their Use and Misuse* by Kenneth Leech for the permanent libraries and book kits.[25] Troops were allowed to run their own "open mess clubs," essentially bars (many of them with strippers) where they could serve alcohol and food and probably illegal drugs. Meredith H. Lair explained the lackadaisical attitude toward these quasi-official establishments in her book *Armed with Abundance: Consumerism & Soldiering in the Vietnam War*: "Open messes often emerged from the ether; all that was required was a spare room, some start-up cash, and a commander's permission, though the prevalence of unauthorized open messes suggests this last requirement was unnecessary."[26] In addition, Lair continued, soldiers funded these clubs from their own pay, and the proceeds were supposed to be returned to Special Services to fund programming (what percentage of the money was actually returned is unknown). It is likely that the large budget for expendable books, magazines, and supplies, which came from nonappropriated funds, was supplied by the troops' own drinking habits.

The open mess clubs competed directly with Special Services' own clubs, which were generally more wholesome. Staffed by American civilian women, these clubs offered board games, cards, Ping-Pong, pool, and trivia nights and held many parties, often holiday themed (they also had their own small libraries). Along with elaborate recreational sports facilities, designated R&R vacation resorts in-country, religious services, movie theaters, bowling alleys, and soldier-operated theatrical and musical groups, this elaborate system of activities and entertainment became what Lair terms "the total war on boredom."[27] As the Vietnam conflict became a war of occupation and soldiers came in for specific one-year tours, the wartime experience became increasingly more like a nine-to-five job, with all the Americanized leisure and recreation time to accompany it (and many troops had copious amounts of free time during their actual work hours). About 75–90 percent of troops never saw combat.[28] Like the other Special Services activities, reading was part of a plan to divert men from the inappropriate behavior rampant in the country. Besides illegal drug use and drinking, men also regularly visited prostitutes (many brothels or "spas" were operated openly on bases), stole from each other and the military, fought with each other, and worse, tortured and killed Vietnamese civilians or other US soldiers. Providing books and magazines was one way to keep men out of trouble and to pacify their restlessness and simmering anger.

At the American Library Association's conference in 1966, the Armed Forces Librarians section held a panel to address the topic of "Books as Weapons" in the Vietnam War and in the fight against Communism more broadly. The panel included three military officers and one publisher. The first panelist, Captain Edward L. Beach, spoke about the morale provided by the ship library to the navy men serving at sea. According to notes taken at the presentation now in the American Library Association Archives, Commander John J. O'Connor, a chaplain and Vietnam veteran in the Marines, argued in his presentation that:

> The nation's newspapers, magazines and books have a "depressing effect" on the morale of our troops in combat. [Commander O'Connor] said that although morale is "very high" among the armed forces in Vietnam, they are "affected and infected by the materials they read, and these materials have been considerably less than encouraging."

> The attempts by the nation's printed media to evaluate our position in Vietnam have a "depressing effect indeed on our military personnel." "They have to turn off their minds (from this material) if they are to get on with the grim business of war." [...]

Fr. O'Connor said that, "somebody has a grave obligation to orientate and acquaint these fighting men with the moral issues involved in Vietnam." He told the librarians that they could make their contribution by helping in every way possible to relieve the pressures and tensions of war and to help sustain morale.[29]

Major John Pustay of the air force spoke on the necessity of the availability of reading material on the enemy for the troops, and he recalled how important it was for American troops in World War II to read *Mein Kampf*. Today's soldiers, he said, needed to read about the politics in Africa and China. Bennet Cerf, president of Random House, was also on the panel and discussed the recent literature on Vietnam. He noted that publishers were willing to offer books both supportive and against the war but that the manuscript submissions coming into Random House were about five-to-one against the war. He concluded, "We must keep an open mind at all times." Whether he thought publishers had some obligation to influence the debate on the war is unclear from the write-up of this panel in the ALA archives. These speakers—notably, none of them librarians—seemed to avoid any discussion of what exactly was the role of the military library and librarians in an unpopular war: Did soldiers' need for information on what was slowly but surely becoming a morally ambiguous, if not blatantly unjust, war trump the military leadership's desire to control the narrative and maintain morale on the front lines? The brass was essentially asking military librarians to make a choice between their professional code and their loyalty to the military. But due to Ruth's influence, intellectual freedom would continue to be prioritized over censorship in the name of military morale.

~

The more I researched Ruth and the work of all the librarians in Vietnam, I had to know: What difference had this library empire made in the lives of the men sent to Vietnam? As Veterans Day approached, I knew I needed to ask them directly, somehow. I created a flyer about the libraries and included my contact information, made two hundred copies, and brought Greg with me to the ceremony at the Vietnam Memorial on the National Mall. Before the ceremony started, I awkwardly asked groups of veterans standing around if they remembered using the libraries in Vietnam. None of them did, but some did remember reading and provided me with some useful stories. After the ceremony, we passed out flyers to men who, as they left, were probably so full of emotion and grief that they were not fully there.

Before Veterans Day, I had contacted Ann Kelsey, who maintained an email list for those who had worked for Special Services at bases around the world. A group of these women who had been in Vietnam often went to the Vietnam Wall on Veterans Day and also met up in a suite at a nearby hotel. I found Ann near the memorial, and she laughed at my flyers, explaining, "These guys don't remember the libraries." She invited me to the hotel, and I stayed up late into the night with this group of women, some of whom remembered Ruth as a legend. All of them had vivid stories about Vietnam. Later I created an online survey for veterans and distributed it to a few blogs for Vietnam vets. Ann also sent it out on her email list.

Sixty-six men and women took the survey, and one contacted me later through the flyer. Only fourteen remember using the libraries. While not a scientific survey or broad enough to be truly accurate, it does call into question the visibility of the libraries at the time and how they seem to be forgettable to most veterans.[30] Although not as memorable or explicitly popular as activities such as celebrity USO tours and chatting with the Red Cross "Donut Dollies," the library service reached more men on an everyday basis than other Special Services and recreational activities, whether or not the troops were aware of its actual existence. However, many veterans who didn't remember using the libraries did remember receiving packages of books and magazines, most likely the field delivery kits. One respondent to the online survey and one veteran I spoke with in person assumed they were shipped directly from publishers for free as a gift to the troops. Another respondent did not believe in the existence of the magazine field kits provided by the libraries, which I had explained in a survey question. He doubted that the military libraries would pay for magazines for troops, because they contained so much antiwar coverage.[31]

Like other American public libraries, the military libraries participated in outreach in person and through advertising and public service announcements. Word of mouth was probably one of the best ways to reach new users, and the air-conditioning helped draw in troops. Some soldiers had used base libraries while in basic training in the US and inquired in Vietnam if they were available there too. Special Services newsletters were distributed to officers, and they always included instructions on how to request either field libraries, if they had a certain amount of men under their command, or the field delivery kits.[32] Other official printed publications delivered directly to troops included information about the libraries, and this information was always added to new troop orientation materials and to guides to bases and the Saigon area. Peter Young typed up lists of new books every few weeks and circulated them around the Cu Chi base, which drew in a lot of users.[33] The public service announcement delivered on the radio in the opening scene of the film *Good Morning, Vietnam!* is most likely indicative of the radio and television spots that the library provided to the American Forces Vietnam Network (AFVN). It is telling that the library public service announcement is read by Dan "the Man" Levitan (played by Richard Portnow) in a monotone voice, in contrast to the subversive hijinks that DJ Adrian Cronauer (played by Robin Williams) would later bring to the airwaves. An announcement for bookworms to visit the library or request a book from the field was the perfect example of a disembodied, bureaucratic nanny that troops could easily tune out.

Whether or not the troops ignored the existence of libraries, who actually read and had access to books brings into question class and race issues prevalent in the war. Reading is a leisure activity, one that implies a certain amount of free time, not to mention the education and class status needed to appreciate anything considered more challenging than *Playboy* and *Stars and Stripes*. Some of those who responded to my survey stated they did not know libraries existed in Vietnam. Others claimed they did not have time to read, and one implied that my inquiry about reading habits there was outrageous in itself.

These respondents were probably referring to a long-simmering rift among troops who were divided among "grunts" (officially combat troops) and "REMFs," which stood for Rear Echelon Mother Fuckers (officially combat support). The majority of troops were stationed on bases that were relatively safe and offered copious amounts of recreation. Even many of those designated as combat troops never saw actual combat.[34] To some veterans, admitting to reading for pleasure while in a war zone is akin to admitting to laziness, shirking responsibility, or cowardice. To them, only nerds or men afraid of combat would have the time to read anything for pleasure. Gabe Horchler remembered that reading was actively discouraged at Fort Bragg, where he went to boot camp, even though there was a library there: "It used to drive some of the drill sergeants crazy that I had all these books. They thought it was so bizarre."[35] Some officers tried to censor what the men under their command were reading. Janice Carney, a transgender woman formerly known as John, remembers in her oral history that she was a voracious reader. "We used to have access to the *Rolling Stone*," she said of her time at Camp Eagle in 1970, "which my commanding officer called a communist newspaper and took it from my desk and tried to tell me that I couldn't read communist trash like that in his office." She still managed to get copies of it and noted, "I used to like reading it in front of him."[36] She did not indicate whether the issues of *Rolling Stone* were from a book kit delivery from the library or whether she had bought them herself at the post exchange.

Underneath this divide concerning bravery and masculinity was another rift concerning class. Those who were college educated were more likely to obtain jobs, particularly desk jobs, at major bases and had more access to libraries, despite Ruth's effort to extend books to all the troops in Vietnam. Project 100,000, implemented by Secretary of Defense Robert McNamara in 1966, was a plan to lower the intelligence and health requirements for men drafted into the army. Members of this group, known as "McNamara's Morons," were marked in their personnel files and were tracked throughout their service and beyond. Conceived as a Great Society program, it was meant to lift men out of poverty, to essentially "salvage their manhood," which McNamara argued was the only way to win the war on Communism.[37] Many of the men in this program were illiterate, and special training programs were developed to improve their reading skills and to prepare them for low-skill jobs. While many deplored this program as a racist and classist effort to get more poor and minority men into combat, a recent study by Tom Sticht (who helped design Project 100,000's original testing and training materials) revealed that many participants were indeed helped by their military service. Compared to their counterparts who did not serve, they were more likely to be employed, to have higher incomes, and to have attended college after their service.[38] Whether they took advantage of the library system in Vietnam—or whether it helped them in any way—is unknown. The military offered GED and college courses at all large bases. Men who were enrolled in these courses certainly used the libraries while they studied. It is likely that the military leadership who implemented Project 100,000 believed that access to libraries could aid these men, and it could be one reason why they supported Ruth's push to rapidly expand the system.

Even though libraries were a symbol of middle-class leisure, they were an open space that cut across the rigid hierarchy of the military. Officers may have been the most likely to check out books, but it is unclear if they read them there. Officers could relax in their own air-conditioned clubs, but the libraries were the only cool, peaceful place for all troops to get away from the chaos.[39] Ann Kelsey said that the men who came in often were studying for their GED exam or other courses.[40] Despite the assumption that only well-educated "REMFs" used the library, it appears that disadvantaged men made good use of it too.

Some men, whether or not they cared about what anyone thought of their manliness or morale, read voraciously during the Vietnam War. Quite a few veterans in the survey said they weren't choosy and would read whatever they could get their hands on, as books were rare where they were stationed. Some remembered how they carried books with them everywhere, despite the popular notion conveyed at the beginning of the movie *Platoon* that books were a waste and too heavy to carry on combat missions. One veteran that I talked to at the Vietnam Wall said that the men in his unit would rip up a paperback by chapters and pass them out so that a book could be read in a chain—a book group of sorts among the unit, as they no doubt discussed it with one another. A veteran named Marc who participated in the survey recalled, "I was reading all the time. As was a good friend later KIA [killed in action]. He was an English teacher. I recall he kept a copy of Shakespeare tucked under his helmet band."[41]

Keyes Beech of the *Los Angeles Times* claimed in 1969 that "Today's GI is so much better educated and so much more sophisticated than his World War II counterpart that the difference is reflected in the quality of the books he reads." In the interview with Ruth, she revealed that in a survey the army librarians had conducted, 38 percent of the books men were reading were fiction and 27.7 percent of officers and 35.4 percent of enlisted men read for pleasure. She noted that men in Vietnam were especially interested in philosophy, religion, and the social sciences. "Men in a war zone take everything more seriously," she said.[42] Of the more than sixty men and women who responded to my survey, forty-seven said that they did read for pleasure, although the respondents were probably more likely to be readers in general, as many of them stated when asked why they read in Vietnam. Some of those who did not know of the existence of the libraries during their tours then regretted it and stated it would have been very helpful to them had they been aware of them.

'Ihree book lists from Vietnam survive in the army library system's records at the National Archives.[43] One is titled "Book Catalog, Paperbound Field Unit, 1971." This was the shipment sent out to stock the smaller field libraries, which were usually just a room or corner of an office or service club. The list contains about 1,650 titles—a mix of nonfiction (with Dewey numbers) and fiction—and includes a surprisingly broad range of subjects and themes. Another, undated list, titled "Paperbound Collection: Part A," includes 1,567 nonfiction titles— perhaps used for the permanent libraries—arranged by Dewey number (the third list is from Key Book Service and is likely the same as this one but unorganized). These three lists, along with this group of records' other scattered and partial lists of books and magazines ordered for the field kits, offer a fascinating, albeit limited, glimpse into what was available for troops to read.

The 1971 book catalog includes a lot of American fiction—some nineteenth-century classic novels—and a large amount of midcentury fiction, particularly books by authors that appealed to men: Kingsley Amis, Isaac Asimov, Ray Bradbury, John Cheever, John Dos Passos, Ian Fleming, Dashiell Hammett, James Michener, Vladimir Nabokov, John O'Hara, J. D. Salinger, John Updike, and Leon Uris. Science fiction, westerns, and mysteries were also offered in large numbers in both the field delivery kits and the field collections. Nonfiction books include helpful basic titles in languages, science, photography, travel, and various self-help topics. Also included in the catalog were comic-strip compilations such as *Peanuts* and *Andy Capp*, which would have provided some fun reading for both well-educated men and those who were nearly illiterate.

Impressive for the era was the depth and breadth of the lists' titles in the areas of African American literature, history, and culture. When the civil rights movement peaked during the Vietnam War, African American troops were eager for news about this topic (many African American magazines were ordered as well). *The Autobiography of Malcolm X* and *Why We Can't Wait* by Dr. Martin Luther King Jr. were standards in the paperback deliveries and were widely read by both African Americans and whites in the US. Despite the racial tension evident across the military during the war, librarians provided many copies of Stokely Carmichael's *Black Power*, Eldridge Cleaver's *Soul on Ice*, and new books that promoted the ideologies of the Black Power, Black Panther Party, and Black Is Beautiful movements, as well as many other classic titles by African American writers like James Baldwin.

A gaping hole in these lists concerns books related to women's issues or the feminist movement. By 1971 books such as Betty Friedan's *The Feminine Mystique*, Germaine Greer's *The Female Eunuch*, and Simone de Beauvoir's *The Second Sex* were very popular. It seems curious that none of these books appear on the field collections list. Perhaps they were available at the permanent libraries, but it is surprising that Ruth and other librarians who selected books did not include them. Perhaps they thought that men wouldn't read them or that they would get complaints. Classic novels by women writers such as Jane Austen, Edith Wharton, Willa Cather, and Virginia Woolf are also noticeably absent. Even though the libraries were serving a primarily male clientele, women were actively serving in many roles across Vietnam and certainly some of them, and some men as well, would have enjoyed reading such titles.

Veterans who answered my survey listed novels they remembered reading, such as *A Fine and Private Place* by Peter S. Beagle, *The Godfather* by Mario Puzo, *Portnoy's Complaint* by Philip Roth, and

In Cold Blood by Truman Capote. An anonymous veteran wrote that he read only John Steinbeck's books while in Vietnam and often read them while he was high—in order to get out of his head, as he put it. *Playboy* became so popular in the field kits in the late 1960s that at one point they were stored in the empty swimming pool behind the Saigon Library when there was no space to store them inside.[44] In the end the magazine may have been the most memorable aspect of the library system to the average Vietnam veteran, although most didn't realize it came from the library at all. Librarian Ann Kelsey, who worked at the library at the Cam Ranh Bay Air Base in 1970, explained, "You hear somebody who says, 'I never saw a library in Vietnam,' or, 'I never saw any books.' But they'll usually say, 'But these *Playboy* [magazines] kept coming around.' They remember the *Playboys.*"[45] The troops read the high-quality fiction and essays in *Playboy* and may have discovered new authors to explore.

Perhaps the most personally important fiction books to these troops were war novels and those that addressed colonialism. Many of these classics, such as *The Red Badge of Courage, Heart of Darkness, For Whom the Bell Tolls,* and *Mother Night,* appear in the book catalog. An anonymous veteran read *Catch-22* by Joseph Heller. Randy, an army veteran, recalled reading Anton Myrer's *Once an Eagle,* a paperback he still owns.[46] This influential novel about an ambitious army officer during World War II remains one of the most popular books read by members of the military and serves as a warning against the military industrial complex.[47] Marc read *All Quiet on the Western Front*: "I read out of boredom and likely out of fear of the unknown. Reading brought comfort. On the other hand reading Remarque in combat was an odd thing to do."[48]

Besides reading about military history in general, troops in Vietnam were also very eager to read about their own war. Stephen Fee, who served in the army from 1968 to 1970, stated in the survey, "I checked out a book titled *The Battle of Dau Tiang*[49] by S. L. A. Marshall while

I was there. The book was about the battles that took place in 1966. I knew the places and the units that were described in the book. It was eerie reading about combat while I was in combat in the same places but 3 years later."

While searching the internet for anything about the libraries in Vietnam, I came across a blog comment on a post about the death of North Vietnamese General Vo Nguyen Giap. This man wrote:

> Oddly enough I developed my admiration for General Giap during my time as a rear area soldier in the Vietnamese War.
>
> The woman who set up the Army libraries in Vietnam agreed to do it on condition that there was no censorship.
>
> I learned more about the Vietnamese leaders and their programs reading in an American Army library in-country than I learned in two years of protesting against the war.
>
> I went to a "liberal" university in a "liberal" city and I had no access to the literature about the Vietnamese efforts and policies.[50]

I assumed that "the woman who set up the Army libraries" was Ruth, even if he hadn't met her or didn't even know her name. After a few attempts, I discovered that this anonymous commenter was a man named Joe Hudson, who finally sent me an email. He had served at Qui Nhon from 1968 to 1969 and went to the library daily to search for books on Vietnam, as did many other men who were stationed there. After I explained my research on Ruth, he wrote to me:

That was without a doubt the absolutely best library that
I have ever used . . . If I asked the librarians for a book, I
got it. No ifs, ands or buts. I gave the librarians a thorough
work out on locating books. I was probably reading two to
five books a day. I was able to get translated books about
the war from French, German and Soviet Russian authors
. . . The general non-fiction books were extremely well balanced . . . I've probably dealt with over 40 libraries during
my lifetime. That library would be my ideal of a library . . .
Ms. Rappaport knew what a library and librarians should
be, in an ideal world. She was real, real damn good. That
library was the one bright spot in my eleven and a half
months in the hell we Americans created in Vietnam.[51]

As the antiwar protests heated up in the United States, there was a
concern that military censorship was blocking both the troops' and the
public's access to news about what was really happening in Vietnam.
But no books or materials were banned in the libraries, despite the
efforts of a few library employees who tried to hide magazines with
cover stories on the antiwar movement.[52] Book lists available from the
National Archives, although they were not comprehensive for the whole
library system over the full span of the war, prove that troops had ready
access—within the limits of what could physically be obtained at the
time—to the current literature on the Vietnam War and its background.
Some of the nonfiction and fiction titles available in 1971 included the
following:

- *Vietnam: The Roots of Conflict* by Chester A. Bain
- *Vietnam: A Political History* by Joseph Buttinger
- *Southeast Asia Today and Tomorrow* by Richard Butwell
- *Limited War and American Defense Policy* by Seymour
  Deitchman

- *Hell in a Very Small Place* by Bernard B. Fall
- *Southeast Asia in U.S. Policy* by Russell Fifield and Paul A. Varg
- *The Rise of Red China* by Robert Goldston
- *Dimensions of Conflict in Southeast Asia* by Bernard K. Gordon
- *One Very Hot Day* by David Halberstam
- *The Struggle for Indochina* by Ellen J. Hammer
- *Vietnam: Between Two Truces* by Jean Lacouture
- *Dateline: Vietnam* by Jim G. Lucas
- *Background to Vietnam* by Bernhard Newman
- *Vietnam in the Mud* by James H. Pickerell
- *The Vietnam Reader* by Marcus Raskin
- US House and Senate Vietnam hearing transcripts

Ann Kelsey still has in her possession a bibliography on Vietnam—regularly updated and available at every military library during the war years—that was prepared by librarians.[53] Clearly the troops had access to a wide array of opinions and research on the war, including books that exposed the corruption and lies of military leaders and politicians. Despite this, there were a few explicitly antiwar omissions, notably Mark Satin's *Manual for Draft-Age Immigrants to Canada*—which was so popular in the US it was regularly stolen from libraries but obviously not helpful for troops once they were in Vietnam—and John Kerry's *The New Soldier* (it might not have been released yet in 1971 when this list was created by the library system).

~

Although they had tried to distance themselves from this mass of antiwar media and sentiment, librarians could not ignore the reality of the war once they got there. Ann Kelsey was working at the Cam Ranh Bay library in 1970 when she was ordered to close an engineering library because the unit was headed to Cambodia. She was shocked because she had just heard Nixon on the radio announce that troops were *not* invading Cambodia. It was a turning point in her life; from then on she could never trust the American government again.[54] Other librarians similarly left Vietnam with a very bitter feeling toward the military and their government.

The massive amount of money spent in Vietnam was increasingly embarrassing and difficult to justify. By 1970 the military was trying to end the building of permanent structures and divert resources to mobile trailers.[55] Ruth continued to adapt and refine library service by installing trailer libraries at temporary bases and ordering new custom-made bookmobile trucks for the largest bases, in addition to the vans that were already used to move books around to permanent libraries. Some officers were baffled and jealous that the library system got such state-of-the-art trucks. Only two of the bookmobiles were used regularly, at Long Binh and An Khe.[56]

Floyd Zula, Ruth's assistant in 1970, was there when she quit. He described his time working for her during her last year there:

> In general we operated in crisis management mode. Ruth seemed to procrastinate on a whole array of issues until the seriousness of the matter dictated no more delay . . . My recollection is that Ruth was something of a micro-manager and that may explain why there were piles of paper everywhere. Now I remember that Ruth's actual work space on her desk was about the size of a piece of typing paper. Around that one empty space there were Alpine heaps of paper, including her in-box. And her horizontal file cabinets were equally stuffed with more paper.

I do recall a party that Ruth threw at her trailer for the troops in the Special Services office. She served a deadly punch that was laced with a variety of liquors and fruit juices which we referred to as "Rappaport Punch."

Some of the troops went into something like alcoholic bizerkness. One trooper from St. Louis became so belligerent that he intended to slug me through the window of my vehicle as I was ferrying dazed troopers back to the barracks. I quickly rolled up the window and this fellow Bill smacked the glass and broke some knuckles. He wore a cast for a time . . .

After Ruth returned to the USA, Michael Ridgeway was ordered by the then Special Services major to clean out her office. Her files, many of which contained indecipherable scribbles and all kinds of numbers, were dumped on the center of the office floor and we took turns photographing ourselves with our feet on this heap of file folders. The caption for this activity was "Ruthless."[57]

~

By 1970 Ruth was desperate to get out of Vietnam. In the form she had to fill out to officially quit, she had to name a reason. She simply wrote, "After 7 years and 9 months service in Vietnam I desire to return to CONUS [contiguous US]."[58] Even though she didn't have another job lined up, she left in October, finally quitting her mission in Vietnam, perhaps demoralized and defeated after eight years. She was tasked, like A. A. Allison had been with the HSAS, to write a history of the library system in Vietnam. She detailed the growth from just a few shelves into an enormous system, the chaos, and the budgeting and administrative issues. She commended the staff for "their know-how, experience, effort and energy; tirelessly they worked long and arduous hours to try to meet the growing demands." She concluded:

> The motto had to be [to] get the most material to the most men. Emphasis was primarily on quantity and availability, only secondarily on quality and service. After materials en masse, emphasis was placed on facilities, providing at least one place on post where a man could forget the war, if but for a little while, and sit in comfort, peace and quiet. As many a departing GI has said to many a librarian over the years, "our library, well, it was like a little bit of home..." The choice was deliberate and conscious. Under combat conditions with constant threat of destruction, even an enemy rocket in the Saigon Library in commemoration and almost as if to publicize National Library Week, 1970, certain priorities had to be observed. These were materials and more materials for the largest number of personnel.[59]

After Ruth left, the drawdown accelerated in the early 1970s, and the enormous military infrastructure in Vietnam was dismantled haphazardly. Books were either given to local Vietnamese libraries or shipped off to other base libraries.[60]

When she applied for her next job, at the Library of Congress, Ruth once again had to fill out a form that ended up in her FBI file. She listed her address from November 1970 to January 1971 while she was unemployed as "QTR 113 B, DCII House, Ford Island, Hawaii," the naval base at Pearl Harbor. I'm not sure what she did there, but I like to imagine her on the beach with a mai tai, a pack of cigarettes, and a good book.

~

The military's library system still continues to this day, although many have closed at bases in urban centers with nearby public libraries. It does not provide actual libraries in war zones anymore, perhaps because most recreational information can be found on the internet and because troops can easily order their own books online through websites such as Amazon. While I researched Ruth's work in Vietnam, Greg and his four deployments to Afghanistan were in the back of my mind. He regularly perused the books that wound up in the Morale, Welfare, and Recreation rooms (MWR) from various sources—donations from "support the troops" organizations and some left behind by other service members—and was surprised by the gems he found. In 2010 he read *Moby Dick* over the four months he was at Bagram. Even though he was required to work twelve-to-sixteen-hour days, seven days a week, he still read every night he was there. It was his only escape and the one thing that got him through.

~

Part VIII:

Some Days I Wonder What Ever Made Me Become a Cataloger

Washington, DC, 1971–1993

Chapter 30

~

A week before Obama's first inauguration, I was laid off from my first full-time job after I graduated from library school. I had been working for only nine months as a corporate archivist in the suburbs of Washington, DC, after moving there from Oregon. Although I had been unhappy in that position and was already looking for a new job, I panicked about being unemployed while living in such an expensive city. But I soon got a call about a reference librarian position in the Humanities and Social Sciences Division in the Main Reading Room at the Library of Congress. The job had seemed like a dream to me when I applied; I couldn't believe then that I had gotten an interview.

I knew I needed to understand beforehand more about the library, so I took the official tour of the Jefferson Building. Walking into the Great Hall for the first time, I was dazzled by the beauty of the building, which looked more like a gilded palace than a library. I realized that whoever designed this building didn't think of a library as just a warehouse for books; they wanted everyone who walked inside to be awed not just by the architecture but also by this building's purpose. When the tour guide took us up to the balcony overlooking the Main Reading Room, she pointed out the statues of some of the secular saints that lined the octagon-shaped room: Michelangelo, Beethoven, Herodotus, James Kent, Edward Gibbon, Plato, Shakespeare, Francis Bacon, and Homer.

Afterward I walked to Eastern Market, a focal point of the Capitol Hill neighborhood that I had heard about. I admired the old row houses on the way and noticed that on this strangely warm Saturday in February, the sidewalks were crowded with joggers and families out doing errands. I knew that if I got this job, I would want to live in this neighborhood. I sat on a bench across from the market for a while, imagining that I worked at the Library of Congress and lived on Capitol Hill. I knew that if I could make it happen somehow, my life would be perfect.

~

During her last years of working in Vietnam and her months of unemployment, Ruth had her eye on the Library of Congress. Her friends from the air force, Pat Moesker (whom she had roomed with in Okinawa) and Pat's husband, Bob, had moved to Capitol Hill in 1969 when he accepted a job at the Library of Congress in the Science and Technology Division. Her former army employee Bill Sittig had also started working there after he had come back from Saigon, as had Gabe Horchler, whom Ruth had interviewed but been unable to hire. She probably had at least a few more friends from the military who now lived in DC, and some of her cousins had also moved to the region.

Apparently, during her break after Vietnam, Ruth came to stay with Pat and Bob, or at least used their address for a few months. She started applying for cataloging jobs at the Library of Congress, hoping to utilize her expertise in sociology or German, and probably socialized with her friends and made new connections at the library. She eventually got a job at the end of August 1971 as a sociology cataloger under the supervision of Nick Hedlesky, the head of the Social Sciences Subject Cataloging Division.[1] Although the job itself wasn't prestigious, any librarian would consider it an honor and a privilege to work there. After traveling the world for thirty-three years and never staying in one place for more than a few, she was finally ready to put down roots. This palace of books and the cosmopolitan neighborhood that sprawled behind it would be the home and community—her "true chaverim"—that she had been seeking for so long.

The Library of Congress was founded in 1800 as a small library for congressmen in the Capitol. By 1975 it had grown to be the second largest library in the world, with seventeen million books, a staff of forty-five hundred, and a $116 million budget.[2] In the late nineteenth century, with title, author, and subject access, it had set the American standard for the card catalog system; in 1901 it began distributing copies of cards to other libraries, saving them time and money.[3] The post–World War II period of the Library of Congress was marked by an enormous increase in the acquisitions of collections and the development and expansions of its complicated cataloging system.[4] The library published the *Rules for Descriptive Cataloging in the United States*, a landmark guide for librarians. Cataloging in the United States had developed into three distinct branches: description (transcribing information from the front matter of a book into a catalog record), subject access (assigning linked subject headings to classify the book), and filing (assigning a call number to the book that facilitates discoverability both on the shelf and in physical relation to books on similar topics). Librarians across the country, and later the world, would look to LC to standardize its increasingly complicated rules into a universal and uniform cataloging system that would be adhered to in every library.

During World War II and its immediate aftermath, LC staff realized how crucial it was to increase the amount of international publications held by the library. Gathering recent publications from every country around the world, especially maps and newspapers, was vital so that librarians could fulfill reference requests for Congress, which was increasingly concerned with the Cold War. Besides hiring catalogers to handle the enormous volume of new acquisitions for English-language books, the library employed more catalogers and reference librarians with foreign-language expertise. Like Ruth, many of these catalogers were immigrants, and like her, some of them were refugees from countries undergoing great upheaval. Ruth's friend and coworker, Kay Elsasser, was a Romance-language cataloger for many years. She remembers this group (American-born catalogers too) as "odd ducks" that probably wouldn't have thrived in any other working environment. But LC welcomed foreigners, introverts, and anyone who had the needed expertise, regardless of personality quirks. And while arguments could be heated (especially about cataloging rules), these catalogers shared a close bond. They were able to come together at the Library of Congress to process the vast number of books coming down the pike, share their cultures with one another, and forge a truly global workplace.[5]

In the fall of 1971, Ruth started her new job on the second floor of the Annex Building, across Second Street from what was then called the Main Building.[6] The annex was the hub of cataloging and book processing. Built in the 1930s to accommodate the overflow of books, it was now overflowing itself, and funding had been approved in 1965 for another new building. Three months before Ruth began her new job, construction started across Independence Avenue for the new building, which would be named for James Madison. One of her coworkers, Thompson Yee, remembers that Ruth would show up late nearly every day, rushing into the annex to sign her time card. Ruthless supervisors would put the cards away at 8:05 sharp and mark down anyone who was late.[7]

One of Ruth's first projects was to recatalog the library's Delta Collection, which included pornography, erotica, race-track guides, and other items confiscated by the FBI, the postal service, and other federal agencies. It also included other items considered obscene or at risk of theft that were acquired through copyright deposit (LC manages copyright registration for the United States and acquires much of its collection by requiring publishers to submit two copies of all publications registered).[8] The Delta Collection was available to the public but was kept in a locked room and closely monitored. Until 1992 researchers could openly browse the general collections, but keeping these items in a locked room ensured that the library could monitor exactly who used them. According to a 1951 Library of Congress manual, the Delta Collection was stored near the Microfilm Reading Room, and researchers could view items there. The official justification for their separation from the rest of the collections was that "though not of unusual rarity or value in themselves, [the books] are nevertheless particularly liable to theft or mutilation if shelved with the general collections."[9] Furthermore, the library would not encourage researchers to use the collection and made it as embarrassing as possible to request items:

No reference service is given in connection with this Collection. Readers must obtain from the Public Catalog the author, title, and call number of any volumes they wish to see. They are allowed to have only one book at a time and are not permitted to take books out of the reading room area. Loans are made for official use only.

New books for the Collection reach the Microfilm Reading Room accompanied by two copies of the printed cards. These cards are used to maintain a classified shelf list and an author catalog for the staff's own use. No subject entries are made.

Each reader on entering the Microfilm Reading Room signs his name and address in a register maintained exclusively for readers of Delta materials, and for each book which he requests he makes out a charge slip in duplicate. Statistics are obtained from the register and the charge slips.[10]

The fact that "no subject entries [were] made" was significant. Author Melissa Adler wrote that the books were not completely cataloged to the standards that other books were but were flagged with a delta symbol on the spine.[11] A researcher could find the materials if they knew of a specific book or magazine title or author. But by denying these books subject headings, the Library of Congress would not encourage research on the topics of pornography, erotica, or gambling. Forty books that are now housed in the Rare Books Reading Room still have a note in their catalog records that reads, "Formerly in Delta Collection."

By the 1960s the library had stopped accepting items from the FBI and did not continue to collect much in this area, because the Kinsey Institute at Indiana University had started broadly collecting pornography and erotica.[12] Ruth most likely recataloged the items from the Delta Collection that were transferred to the social sciences collection. These would have included scientific books on sex in the areas of psychology and sociology or perhaps books on these topics in German. It's unclear whether Ruth did this job alone or was continuing the work someone else had started. She had no qualms about sharing what her new job entailed and in fact joked about it in letters to friends. A man named George, who was stationed in Hawaii in February 1972, wrote to her:

> You seem to have a good job and I envy you the chance to do something productive. Even though it is erotica, it's needed by somebody or it wouldn't have been written . . . Do you suppose you could absorb—along with the "expertise" in cataloging—enough of the subject matter

and the technique to put out some of your own? It might pay the rent.[13]

After a page break, he continued, "I must have been a little drunk last night when I batted out the above, but I will let it ride."[14]

Chapter 31

In August 1973 Ruth bought her first and only home. Built in 1937, it was a three-bedroom row house at 117 Third Street NE, just two blocks from the library's Annex Building. She paid $31,500 for it ($178,776 in 2018 dollars). While many residents of DC were moving out to the rapidly expanding suburbs, Ruth chose to live as close as possible to her job. This may have been because by the time she left Vietnam, she preferred not to drive, owing to her eyesight problems. Not only did she have a lazy eye, but her eyesight got worse as she aged as well. She never owned a car when she lived on Capitol Hill, and it seems to have never affected her quality of life—the neighborhood was very walkable, full of shops and corner stores and just blocks away from two stops on the city's new metro system that would open in 1976.

Just five years earlier, in April 1968, riots had broken out across the city after Dr. Martin Luther King Jr.'s assassination. The commercial strip on H Street NE, the boundary of the north side of Capitol Hill and a historic black neighborhood, was decimated. The area developed a reputation for muggings, drug dealing, and murders. Eastern Market was a known site for picking up prostitutes. The fact that so much crime was so close to the Capitol was an embarrassment to the city, and many people who worked there or came to visit refused to walk around the neighborhood after dark. But Ruth was not deterred from buying a house in a neighborhood with such a reputation. After living in two war zones, she was not fazed by a high crime rate. Her house, with a wide front porch and ample room for her books and worldly possessions, would suit her for the next thirty-seven years. She soon got to know her neighbors, many of whom were also federal employees or Capitol Hill staffers, and joined several neighborhood organizations. Many of these residents bonded over their refusal to give up on this historic, interracial neighborhood, no matter how blighted it was or its souring reputation.

In the fall of 1973, Ruth's coworker Gabe Horchler, a Vietnam veteran and a social sciences cataloger, decided to take a position as a United Nations volunteer librarian.[1] He moved to Niamey, Niger, to establish a library at the École nationale d'administration, a school for civil servants. He wrote to Ruth for advice about building a library in a developing country and jokingly asked if she wanted a new job. She responded, "The answer is definitely NO, NO, No . . . A job I have . . . What I'm looking for is a POSITION and this doesn't exactly include remote control library construction and administration!"[2] (Whether she was actually looking for a new position outside LC is unclear from this letter.) Upon Gabe's request, Ruth sprang into action, circulating his letter around the library and searching for any resource that might help him. She listed helpful cataloging manuals and guides on the construction of libraries, promising to find them and mail them to him. She answered his questions on library management in detail, reminisced about the difficulties of her work in Vietnam, and admitted what she would have done differently in hindsight. She closed with some good advice: "There is nothing, nothing, nothing that can ever substitute for personal observation and creative thinking . . . no authority in the world can tell you what you need . . . They can only help you think."[3] The four long letters that Ruth wrote to Gabe over two years at the beginning of her career at the Library of Congress, along with another letter she wrote after her retirement, are the only surviving documentation, in her own words, of what she really thought about working there.

In 1974 she wrote to Gabe that she was renting a room to an army chaplain, making minor renovations on her house, and busily attending meetings of the Bicentennial Commission. In her characteristic run-on sentences full of ellipses, Ruth described some of her frustrations with her coworkers and supervisors:

> Lately I've been letting loose at both David Remington and Ed Blume about their being totally disorganized... unsupportive of their staff; misusing their employee time, etc. etc. At least they've started to listen! No, not do anything about it, but used to be they didn't even listen.... Now, after I make my comments I get feedback which at least tells me they've understood [...] Nick's been behaving like Nick...sometimes missing his points when he could make them because he blows up at the wrong time... Powell hasn't been quite the same since I insisted on setting up Group Sex with a see ref. from "Swinging (Sex)" and gets all shook up every time the Sunday supplement refers to Kissinger or the King of Sweden as "Swingers"...[4]

The main problem of the broader Acquisitions and Bibliographic Access Directorate, which had been an endless source of conflict for decades, was the growing backlog of books that the staff simply could not keep up with. Ruth complained, "At work we have been hellishly busy . . . even with an average of 25 (and over) books per day, my backlog is building at the rate of 20 to 25 books a day! Even more on days I devote to my schedule. Oh yes . . . schedule . . ."[5] Ruth was referring to the *Library of Congress Classification* schedule, a manual published by the library for the assignment of call numbers. LCC, as it is known, is a system used by most academic libraries, and it is more in depth than the Dewey decimal system, which is commonly used by public libraries. Broad fields of knowledge are assigned a letter or two letters, with each subtopic (which could branch into many levels) assigned a number. A Cutter number, named for the librarian Charles Cutter and designed to alphabetize books primarily by last name of the author, is then added on to the class number. Subject catalogers at LC were assigned the onerous task of revising the schedules for new editions of the LCC.

Ruth's area of expertise, sociology, fell under the letters *HM*. She described to Gabe how time-consuming and tedious this job was:

> Have expanded the Soc. part and practically redone all of Soc. Psych....from 4 pages I now have 19, and from 1 through 291, numbering will probably go from one (1) to 3500 plus (of course I'm leaving plenty of room for someone else to expand!) It's been going in typical LC fashion... "no major changes."...well, yes, maybe you better move this too....OK shift that...yes, cancel that....Too bad I had to do it all so piecemeal and literally fight for every new number, but even I feel it's now beginning to take on some shape...though I'm getting a little saturated with it all...in the long run it's probably been a hell of a good review for me in the fields of social. & soc. psych.[6]

The schedule for sociology had not been revised since 1967, and the revision that Ruth was working on in 1974 would not be published until 1980. The preface for the publication, written by the chief of the Subject Cataloging Division, Mary K. D. Pietris, gave an explanation for the long delay:

> For the past ten years, the Subject Cataloging Division has wanted to issue a revised edition of Class H. However, the desire has been continually frustrated by the shortage of staff time to review the existing schedule, to propose badly-needed changes, to review and approve those proposals,

and to prepare the new edition editorially. In 1977 the decision was made to publish another edition of Class H without fail, and catalogers began to review and prepare extensive revisions . . . It was, therefore, decided to follow an unusual course of action. It was previously decided that Class H would be published in two parts: H–HJ and HM–HX. However, the first part would represent a completely revised edition, whereas the second part would be merely an unrevised cumulation, incorporating changes made since the third edition, without any necessarily time-consuming attempt to update concepts and terminology. As a result, this edition of HM–HX, an unrevised cumulation, reflects the basic outline, tone and terminology of the early twentieth century in which it was developed.[7]

Classes H through HJ cover economics, commerce, and finance, all straightforward fields of knowledge.[8] While new theories arose occasionally over the twentieth century, such as Keynesian economics, classifying them in relationship to older, established areas of the field would not have been complicated. However, HM through HX covered the following fields, listed in the synopsis of the 1980 edition:

- HM: Sociology.
- HN: Social History and Conditions. Social Problems. Social Reform.
- HQ: The Family. Marriage. Woman.
- HS: Societies: Secret, Benevolent, etc.
- HT: Communities. Classes. Races.
- HV: Social Pathology. Social and Public Welfare. Criminology.
- HX: Socialism. Communism. Anarchism.

Over the late 1960s and throughout the 1970s, debates raged among academics, professional experts, and the public about the above topics, especially concerning women, sexuality, race, and class. The civil rights and feminist movements had created entirely new academic departments and fields of study, such as Black Studies, Women's Studies, and what would later be termed queer theory. Conservatives complained that these new fields were not serious lines of academic inquiry. The debates filtered down to the field of librarianship, and catalogers had to decide how to classify this new knowledge and what exactly was the correct terminology. Pietris did not explain that this was likely another reason that the publication of the HM–HX schedule was delayed for so long. Part of the staff time to "review and approve proposals" was surely spent debating what these new fields meant and how LC would appropriately deal with them in a way that would avoid criticism or backlash from the rest of the library community, which relied heavily on these manuals.

As Ruth had noted, her colleagues were uncomfortable with openly discussing topics like "swinging" at work. She may have been one of the only catalogers in her department who, quite frankly, didn't mind these discussions or outright enjoyed the embarrassment of her more conservative colleagues. Ruth mentioned in 1974 that she was trying to expand the numbering system in the HMs from 291 to 3500, but six years later the schedule still only covered 291 numbers.[9] Today the numbers range from 1 to 1281, a large expansion but nothing close to what Ruth had originally envisioned.

She further explained to Gabe the issues with a new program called Cataloging-in-Publication. Called CIP and pronounced "sip," the new system allowed publishers to send in a form and, optionally, a galley copy of a book to LC well in advance of a new book's publication. The catalogers made a temporary, brief catalog record (this information is also printed on the back of a book's title page), which was revised later when the official copy of the book was sent to the library. Copies of the catalog card were sent out to libraries that had preordered the book, a practice that saved time and increased efficiency for libraries across the nation. Ruth explained how difficult the process was and how the target rate of books cataloged per day was impossible to achieve:

> At a meeting in which "low cataloging productivity" was the subject[,] I finally let them have it about retyping my own schedule in clean form for each meeting and asked whether they really thought I got my pay for typing! [...] [CIPs] are increasing by leaps and bounds[,] and without galleys it's becoming more and more of a crystal ball game. Bill Goslin disagrees with me…he's so anxious to sign up publishers that he's willing to settle for anything he can get from them. Personally I'd play the game differently… if the books show top-notch cataloging then the receiving librarians will press for [CIPs] and since they are the "buying public" for many publications they can or could exert the clout on both the library and the publishers to provide [CIP] info. If we go slapping any old number and heading on the books and then redo the printed cards with the corrected numbers we'll ultimately defeat the [CIP] program.[10]

Furthermore, she noted that when the upcoming presidential impeachment hearings would be broadcast live during the day, no one would get anything done. While Ruth knew that the expectations of management were absurd, she also recognized that the distractions and disgruntled feelings among staff didn't improve anything. In February 1975 Ruth wrote again to Gabe, updating him on more LC news:

> At the moment morale (as usual in subj. cat.) is fairly low…I just mind my own business and keep much busier

away from work than at work! Since the new catalogers have started I'm getting only foreign language weirdo books and porno...they get the easy stuff and some days I wonder what ever made me become a cataloger...but that too will pass???[11]

In December 1974 Librarian of Congress Quincy Mumford retired. Mumford had been one of the only men to lead LC with past experience, having served as both the director of the Cleveland Public Library and the president of the American Library Association. He faced a Congress increasingly hostile to his efforts to expand the services of the library to the public (rather than focusing on serving Congress) and reluctant to supply it more funding. But Mumford had led the charge to fund the Madison Building construction and had increased the library's yearly funding from $9.4 million to $96.7 million over his twenty years in office.[12] The uncertainty of who would be nominated to replace Mumford surely was a cause for concern among the staff.

Ruth knew that Gabe Horchler was interested in coming back to LC sometime after November 1975, when his job in Niger would end. She kept an eye out for any position that might interest him and notified him of upcoming retirements. She sent him a vacancy posting that was essentially the same one he had before at LC. Ruth explained to him the confusing application process and how she had talked to a woman who worked in the Placement and Classification Office. She was a friend of one of Ruth's employees in Vietnam, and Ruth told her who Gabe was and that he wanted to return to LC. When Ruth revealed what she had done to Ed Blume, her supervisor, Blume was very annoyed by her meddling. She explained to Gabe:

The trouble is, everyone is so afraid of equal opportunity employment that everyone is playing games and it takes a lot of guess work to figure out what people are really telling you… Personally I don't see how they can possibly come up with a more qualified applicant since for all practical purposes you've had experience on the very job they are advertising. However, I'd follow the rules of the game and play it their silly way.[13]

Ruth was referring to the recent turmoil at LC concerning job discrimination. Although libraries may appear to be democratic institutions rooted in equality and opportunity, there is an ugly history of discrimination at many of them. Several investigations and court cases emerged in the 1970s and '80s that exposed the fact that the world's largest library had been systematically discriminating against women and minorities for decades.

Chapter 32

President Nixon had resigned five months before Mumford's retirement, and the outrage and chaos of those events still lingered in Washington. The following spring, President Ford nominated Daniel J. Boorstin to be the next Librarian of Congress. At that time, he was the head historian of the Smithsonian's National Museum of History and Technology (today the National Museum of American History). Previously he had been a history professor at the University of Chicago and had recently published a Pulitzer Prize–winning book, *The Americans: The Democratic Experience*. Boorstin was an avowed conservative, who had named his fellow student Communists at Harvard during the McCarthy trials and admitted that he had briefly joined the party.[1] As the Library of Congress turned another page in its history, many librarians, especially those with a more politically liberal bent, were wary of this man nominated for the most powerful position in the field of librarianship. They wondered what would happen to this increasingly complex and troubled library if he was confirmed.

At Boorstin's confirmation hearings during the summer of 1975, Robert Wedgeworth, the president of the American Library Association, stated, "After consulting the record of his achievements, after speaking with friends and colleagues of Dr. Boorstin, the officers and members of the American Library Association have concluded that there is no relationship between his career and the ability required of the Librarian of Congress at this time in history."[2] Wedgeworth explained the many different programs and projects of the library, some of them highly technical, and how experience as a library administrator was vital to move the Library of Congress forward. He made an apt analogy by pointing out how unreasonable it would be to appoint an attorney general with no experience in law.

It was not just outside librarians who were worried about Boorstin taking the helm of the library. LC employees, and especially minorities, vocalized their concern at the hearing. Joslyn Williams, the executive director of Council 26 (the Capital Area Council of Federal Employees, number 26, the American Federation of State, County, and Municipal Employees, AFL-CIO) and a former LC employee, submitted a damning statement for the record about LC's past practice of discrimination and his doubts about Boorstin. He described the recent investigation and report by the American Library Association on patterns of discrimination at the library and argued that Boorstin's past statements against affirmative action indicated he would not do much of anything to fix the problem.[3] Despite these firm protests, Boorstin was confirmed by the Senate, with the understanding that he would not use the position to write more books, although he would continue to publish a few more while he was the Librarian of Congress. There is no doubt that many LC employees, including Ruth, were disappointed with his confirmation.

On June 23, 1971, just a few months before Ruth started her job, twenty-eight black employees of the Library of Congress were suspended for staging a sit-in along with about a hundred total black employees in the Main Reading Room. They had decided to protest the low pay and the discrimination in promotions they had faced for years. Most of the twenty-eight staff members who were suspended were deck attendants, who primarily pulled, delivered, and reshelved books for researchers.[4] This job, which could be physically demanding, offered very low pay and few chances to move into another position at the library. Nearly everyone who had the job was black, as they are at the time of the writing of this book. Two months before the protest, a group called the Black Employees of the Library of Congress (BELC) had led a "tour of racial discrimination" for the news media and the staffers of black members of Congress.[5] According to an ALA report, 38 percent of the library's employees were black, but they held 76 percent of the GS 1–4 jobs, which were the lowest paying. They held only 13.9 percent of the GS 9–11 jobs and none of the highest paying GS 16–18 positions.[6] Considering that the population of the District of Columbia at this time was 70 percent black, the discrimination was obvious.[7] And it was not just employees who had long faced bias at the Library of Congress; the library buildings had segregated spaces, likely bathrooms, for black employees and researchers until the mid-twentieth century.[8]

BELC was led by a Library of Congress employee named Howard Cook. He had started out as a deck attendant and had been denied several opportunities to move up the ranks at the library. He explained many years later, "We saw what was happening here, where Blacks were qualified for promotions but were denied. Instead, we had to train these Whites, who later became our superiors."[9] Along with another black employee, David Andrews, the two founded BELC but soon came to realize that discussions and protests were not resulting in any significant progress. In 1975 they filed a class-action lawsuit against the Library of Congress with the Equal Employment Opportunity Commission (EEOC). Cook retired in 1989, when the case was still unresolved but had moved through several layers of the court system. The Supreme Court refused to hear the case that year. A lawyer named Avis Buchanan took it on, probably because her mother was one of the plaintiffs.[10]

In 1993 the Subcommittee on Libraries and Memorials of the Committee on House Administration in the House of Representatives held the hearing *Library of Congress Personnel Policies and Procedures* to understand exactly what was going on at the library and why this lawsuit was taking so long to resolve.[11] After James Billington, the new librarian of Congress, spoke along with several library administrators,

Delegate Eleanor Holmes Norton, who represents DC in Congress, made a statement. Norton had been a leader of the civil rights movement and as a lawyer had represented a group of women who sued *Newsweek* for discrimination; she had also later served as chairwoman of the EEOC. She said:

> What is disturbing here is the long-term nature of the suit against the Library, pending 17 years, and the Library's apparent failure to move forward with significantly improved results in the face of that lawsuit. Had the Library moved more aggressively during the long period of a lawsuit that is not yet over, it might have mitigated potential liability, improved its hiring practices, and raised the morale of its employees.[12]

Finally, in 1995, a US district-court judge ruled in favor of the plaintiffs for an $8.5 million settlement, the largest ever against a federal agency for discrimination.[13] But the case did not end discrimination at the library. As of 2016 at least fifty others had sued the library for discrimination.[14] Staff have also sued because library administrators have prevented some organizations, particularly those founded to support black employees through the legal process, from being deemed "official" LC staff organizations. That meant that employees who wanted information or help on a discrimination case could not spend any official staff time seeking assistance, at least not from those organizations.

Kathy Sawyer, a *Washington Post* reporter, summed up the library's appalling record of job discrimination in 1979:

> The history of employee-management relations at the Library is written in stacks and stacks of court documents and a trail of yellowing newspaper articles about protest groups formed and sit-ins or marches at the Library.

As an extension of Congress, which has exempted itself from its own laws, the Library's employment practices lie beyond the reach of the official equal employment opportunity enforcers who monitor other private and public employers.

Thus, while the Library has filled its ornate archives with every word written about the civil rights struggles of the 1960s, some employees and critics have charged, the white men who ran the institution failed to respond to that spirit internally.[15]

Unfortunately, Sawyer's points are in many ways still true today, not only at the Library of Congress but also at other libraries across the country.

African Americans were not the only group that faced discrimination at LC. Women were in the majority at LC, as they were at every library across the country. But while many women librarians had somewhat comfortable salaries, most of them were single, especially before the 1980s. These women were continually passed over for raises and management positions, with the reasoning that men librarians had families to support on one salary.

Barbara Ringer was not a librarian, but she had started working in the library's Copyright Office as a lawyer in 1949. She steadily moved up the ranks from an examiner position to a section head, then assistant chief. After serving as chief of the Examining Division, she was appointed assistant register of copyrights.[16] During the June 1971 sit-in at the Main Reading Room, Ringer had publicly sided with black men and women who claimed they had faced discrimination. When Ringer applied for the position of register of copyrights (the director of the division) she was the only person who initially applied. George Cary, the deputy register, got the job. Ringer sued the Library of Congress for discrimination and quickly won her case. The court ruled that she had been deliberately passed over because she was a woman and because she had spoken out in defense of black employees at the library. In 1972 she was appointed register of copyrights.[17]

Ruth, too, had faced an extraordinary amount of sexism, sexual harassment, and ethnic discrimination in her lifetime, of course, from her outrage at the *Protektia* in Israel in 1948 to being stuck in secretarial positions for so long in her twenties and thirties. The cloud of anti-Semitism always hung around her as well. I have no idea if she felt empathy for those who sued the Library of Congress for discrimination, but she probably saw the situation from many sides. Whereas she had taken a job with a lower pay grade and fewer responsibilities at the Library of Congress—probably because she felt she needed a break after Vietnam—she itched to return to a job that would fully engage her expertise and abilities.

The discontent of minority and women employees seemed to spread among all LC employees in the early 1970s. In 1976 the library's professional employees, most of them librarians, decided to band together and start their own union, the Library of Congress Professional Guild, which became Local 2910 of AFSCME.[18] The guild had originated among catalogers fed up with the way administrators were tracking the number of books they cataloged. While libraries had always tracked statistics concerning number of patrons who visited the library per day or reference questions answered per day, there was something about the way LC administrators tracked the catalogers' work that felt very factorylike and almost corporate. The catalogers tried to explain that books were not a uniform widget to be processed; some were very simple and quick to catalog, while others presented problems that took considerable time to solve. Every time catalogers agreed on a new official rule, along came a new book to break it. Promotions and demotions based on such a simplistic rubric could not be a true reflection of an individual's cataloging productivity.

In June 1977 the guild's new newsletter, the *Local News*, reported that members had been forbidden from circulating union flyers inside the library. They had been forced to stand outside to distribute their information to passing employees. Library administrators went so far as to stop *all* LC organizations from distributing flyers desk to desk.[19] In October a hearing examiner ruled that LC's practice of banning the distribution of union literature in the workplace was unconstitutional. LC administrators compromised by providing individual mail slots for every employee near his or her work area.[20]

Guild members got creative about spreading their message and convincing other bargaining-unit members to join. They created new logos, wrote songs and chants for rallies, drew cartoons, and wrote poems and humorous stories for the guild's entertaining newsletter. Many stories were blatantly satirical; "Gil D. Steward" regularly interviewed his friend, "Max von Obmann-Dusel, who hangs out in various libraries." One interview, structured as a satirical Socratic dialogue, addressed LC's stance on the distribution of union literature and exposed the hypocrisy of banning it, in violation of the First Amendment.[21] Whoever wrote the interview seemed to be alluding to Nazi or Communist censorship; regardless of the political persuasion, it is notable that the author chose a fake German name.

Once the guild was firmly established, Ruth enthusiastically joined and soon became an officer. In the fall of 1976, Ruth, along with a small group from LC, was elected to be a delegate to Council 26, a regional group of locals.[22] She held this position several times, and in 1980 she was chosen as the guild's executive board member to the council. Part of this position would have been to serve as a liaison between the local union at the library and Council 26; she attended regular meetings of both organizations and wrote articles reporting on Council 26 news for the guild's newsletter. In the summer 1980 issue, Ruth probably wrote the article about Council 26's sponsorship of a Vietnamese family. With a matching grant, the guild had raised $2,000 toward helping the

Hung family emigrate from Saigon to Washington. The article directed those interested in more information to contact Gabe Horchler or Ruth Rappaport.[23] Ruth served as executive board member to Council 26 until June 1982, when she was elected a trustee of the guild, a position she likely held until 1983, when she was promoted to a management position at LC.

The guild's progress over the next few decades in securing more rights and benefits for its workers was remarkable. The administration compromised with staff on how to accurately track work accomplished. The practice of snatching away time sheets right after 8:00 a.m., which had been so troublesome for Ruth, was abolished. Credit hours and flextime, which allowed staff to arrive between 6:30 and 9:30 a.m., was instated at the library as well as across most of the federal government. Employees also won the option to work nine- or ten-hour days, with a corresponding Monday or Friday off. With the rise in personal computers, library employees who qualified could work from home one day a week. Staff members could donate their unused annual leave to another staff member undergoing a health problem or a family emergency. The guild also helped start a new day-care center, a few blocks away from the library, for library employees with children. And while the library's practice of racial discrimination would continue, workers could be assured that at least they could file a grievance with the guild or another one of the library's unions. Inch by inch, Library of Congress staff members have battled administrators to try to improve the workplace experience, not only for themselves but also for those fortunate enough to follow in their footsteps.

Chapter 33

When she started her position as a cataloger in 1971, Ruth was probably aware of Barbara Ringer's lawsuit, and she had observed that her women colleagues were not being promoted, despite their organizational skills and deep knowledge of library science. After Nick Hedlesky's retirement, Myrl Powell took over as section head of Social Sciences II for a few years until he was promoted to Assistant Chief of Subject Cataloging.[1] In the spring of 1983, Ruth temporarily replaced him. She returned to her old rank for one month and then was permanently promoted at the end of June, to the rank of GS-13 as head of the section. Ruth was probably the most qualified person for the job and may have had the most seniority in her department by this time. She had worked at LC for twelve years as a subject cataloger, had past supervisory experience, and was fluent in German. Her knowledge of cataloging rules and practices was also impressive.[2]

Ruth was now a supervisor again, but her new role may have made her coworkers uneasy. She might have started out optimistically in this position, convinced that she could reform the section (or possibly the wider Subject Cataloging Division) with her organizational methods and her ideas for greater efficiency. But Ruth ran into the same problems that she had faced as a supervisor in Vietnam: the same old bureaucracy and the same old issues with her subordinates. She would also be caught in the middle of one of the most controversial aspects of librarianship in the 1980s.

A vital task of every subject cataloger at LC is to submit proposed subject heading changes to LC's system of subject heading authorities, which are used in libraries throughout the world. Known as Library of Congress subject headings (LCSH), the system uses a controlled vocabulary, meaning that every word or phrase (there are now about 420,000 subject terms in the system[3]) must be approved as an "official" term. For instance, when searching for the word "cars" in LCSH, you will be redirected to the term "automobiles," which is an approved heading. Theoretically, every book on cars in a library will be listed under the subject heading "Automobiles." These headings can be strung together to be more specific. For example, a book on the history of Ford Motor Company could be given a heading "Automobiles—History—United States." Each subject heading has its own catalog record called an authority record, which lists when it was created, other terms that are similar but are not the authorized heading, and the rules that govern its use as a subject heading. When a subject cataloger comes across a book that contributes new knowledge, he or she must consider whether a new term should be authorized or if a rule change to an older heading is necessary. Until 1992, when the Subject Authority Cooperative Program (SACO) was founded as part of the Program for Cooperative Cataloging (PCC), only LC catalogers could propose changes to this system. Afterward any librarian who worked at a library that was an institutional member of PCC and who was trained in LCSH could nominate changes to the committee at LC.[4]

Ruth and the other subject catalogers in the Social Sciences II Section proposed many subject heading changes over the years. Until 1980 very few headings changed in LCSH, due to the manpower necessary to update thousands of catalog cards and to refile them.[5] The records of who submitted which proposed changes were not retained by LC. But the staff of the Policy and Standards Division (which is responsible for maintaining the LCSH system) found a memo that Ruth wrote in 1985 about the possibility of changing the heading "Crime and criminals" to "Criminology." She wrote about the complex problems that were endemic to all major changes:

> We have been holding off establishing the Subject Heading "Criminology" because the changes would be too voluminous, i.e. 750 corrections out of a 2,800 file under Crime and Criminals. The longer we wait to establish Criminology the larger and more unwieldy the file under "Crime and Criminals" becomes..... therefore, [supposing] we establish "Criminology" with a note, saying prior to 1985 books on this subject were entered under "Crime and criminals." This would still leave room, if and when the time comes that corrections could be done by computer programs, or if there were a period of fewer books coming in and personnel available to make changes they could always be done and the split file notation taken out of the database.
>
> At the same time, if a database user finds "criminology" turning up only books published during or after 1985[,] there would be enough of a question mark to check what went on, i.e. consult the [subject heading] authority file and learn that this is a new heading, etc. etc. Seems to me that's one of the major benefits of Subj. Hdgs. online will give users.[6]

This memo reveals not only the conundrum of making widespread changes to headings but also how new computer technology would change both the workload for catalogers and the ease of making changes. Starting in 1980, LC began a massive project to convert the main card catalog to an electronic system. This project is still not complete, and staff had to undergo extensive training sessions in the basics of personal computers and how to use them for cataloging and other library applications. Many staff members were resistant to adopting technology too quickly and understood the fallacy of spending an enormous amount of manpower creating an entirely new system that might become obsolete before it was completed. Today LC still has catalog cards backlogged to 1898 that have not been fully integrated into the online catalog.[7] But one advantage of converting the catalog was that, finally, batch corrections to vast amounts of records were possible.

By the 1980s LC was under a huge amount of pressure from outside librarians to reform LCSH. Catalogers who worked at other libraries had no say in the terms they were forced to use to describe books. They no doubt fielded questions from their users about why, for example, a term such as "Cookery" was used for cookbooks. They saw daily the difficulties their users faced in finding books and were probably at a loss to explain the complexities and minutiae of LCSH to people who simply wanted to find books quickly. One of these fed-up librarians was Sanford "Sandy" Berman, a cataloger at the Hennepin County Library in Minneapolis. In 1971 he published his first book, *Prejudices and Antipathies: A Tract on the LC Subject Headings Concerning People.* His book's chapter titles seemingly covered most of the topics that the Social Sciences II Subject Cataloging Section was responsible for:

- I. Races, nationalities, faiths, and ethnic groups
- II. Chauvinism, the "Bwana Syndrome," and the Third World
- III. Politics, peace, labor, law enforcement, etc.
- IV. Man/Woman/Sex
- V. Children, youth, "idiots," and the "underground"

In his introduction he began by admitting the usefulness and irreplaceability of LCSH but then launched into the heart of the crusade he would take on for the next forty years:

> In the realm of headings that deal with people and cultures—in short, with humanity—the LC list can only "satisfy" parochial, jingoistic Europeans and North Americans, white-hued, at least nominally Christian (and preferably Protestant) in faith, comfortably situated in the middle- and higher-income brackets, largely domiciled in suburbia, fundamentally loyal to the Established Order, and heavily imbued with the transcendent, incomparable glory of Western civilization. Further, it reflects a host of untenable—indeed, obsolete and arrogant—assumptions with respect to young people and women. And exudes something less than sympathy or even fairness toward organized labor and the sexually unorthodox or "avant-garde." . . . Just because, in short, we were "brought up that way" is no valid reason for perpetuating, either in our crania or our catalogues, the humanity-degrading, intellect-constricting rubbish that litters the LC list.[8]

Berman alluded to the fact that, despite LC's insistence that they were just following "common practice" of how terms were used in books and other scholarly works, this controlled vocabulary was not created in a vacuum. The librarians who approved LCSH terms had their own biases and prejudices, whether or not they realized it. Berman was careful to note that the point of his book was "not to riot, if you please—only to remedy long-standing mistakes and to gain for the profession a genuine, earned respect among people who read and think."[9]

When Berman's book came out, it received mixed reviews in library-related publications. But there is no doubt that it got librarians, and especially catalogers, talking about their work and questioning it in a new way.[10] When Ruth started her job as a subject cataloger in 1971, the same year *Prejudices and Antipathies* was published, she and her coworkers read and discussed the book. Some probably didn't think that LCSH needed any major changes as it was, and at least some others might have felt powerless to change a system in which they were firmly embedded. But those with a more radical bent, such as Ruth, might have seen her position as a way of fighting the system from within. There is no existing correspondence between Ruth and Sandy Berman in her collections of papers or his at the American Library Association Archives. Perhaps the two never even spoke to each other at conferences. But Ruth's coworkers agreed that she was firmly on Berman's side. She submitted many heading changes, including some that seemed irrational to other people at LC. Thompson Yee remembered an incident in which Ruth passionately advocated for a new subject heading, "State-sponsored terrorism." She fought tooth and nail for it, but the committee decided it wasn't needed.[11]

Berman's main target at LC was Mary K. D. Pietris, who was the head of the Subject Cataloging Division from 1978 until 1992 and one of Ruth's supervisors. Berman, armed with citations from books for evidence, regularly wrote letters to the library—addressing them to Pietris and the Subject Cataloging Division—to request changes to subject headings. Pietris diligently wrote back to Berman about why a term could or could not be changed.[12] In 1977, with support from the Library of Congress, the ALA Subject Analysis Committee established the Racism and Sexism in Subject Analysis Subcommittee, which was charged with writing a report with recommendations.[13] The subcommittee reported that an "important and guiding document" was Joan K. Marshall's *On Equal Terms: A Thesaurus for Nonsexist Indexing and Cataloging*—a book similar to Berman's—which had been published in 1977. The subcommittee first met in 1978 at the ALA conference, and Ruth wrote a summary of it in the *Library of Congress Information Bulletin*'s lengthy appendix of reports from the conference. She described its four current projects: an evaluation of subject heading terms applied to groups of concern to the Equal Employment Opportunity Commission, a revision of subject headings related to Native Americans, the compilation of research on African American–related headings, and a bibliography of research on terminology related to women.[14]

Berman and Pietris published an exchange of their letters in the March 1981 issue of the cataloging publication *Technicalities*. Pietris was no doubt exasperated with Berman's obsessive campaign, but she was able to keep a sense of humor about the situation and always tried to adhere to the policies and procedures in place at LC.

In 1987 Daniel Boorstin retired as librarian of Congress and President Reagan nominated Princeton University's celebrated Russian and Cold War historian, Dr. James Billington. Once again librarians were agitated that another academic was being nominated to lead the nation's largest library and library policy nationwide. Just a year and a half after Billington was confirmed as librarian of Congress, Sandy Berman wrote this outraged letter to him:

> You must be kidding! (But I'm afraid you're not.) Anyway, I lately learned that you've proposed the elimination of all subject and other tracings (i.e., access points) from LC bibliographic records as a cost-cutting, speed-enhancing measure. Rumor has it that YOU never search catalogs by anything but author or title . . . so why trouble with subject headings and various "added entries." . . . In short, what WE consumers need out here on the front lines is better, more fulsome and functional cataloging from LC, not less . . . If better, more adequate cataloging will cost more, then please tell us. Tell that to the library community and ask for our help in getting LC the greater resources in money, equipment, and personnel that it needs. I've personally

been known as a severe LC critic. But I'm at base a friendly critic. And would be among the first to sign a petition for more appropriations for LC. Or write my Congressional representatives to increase your funding. I'm completely willing and ready to do that. All I await is your admission that things need to be improved. And that you want the extra resources to start improving.[15]

Clearly Billington's proposed plan to eliminate subject headings never got off the ground (whether Billington seriously considered this or it was all a misunderstanding is unclear). But perhaps something in Berman's letter or in feedback from other librarians struck a nerve. The next February, Billington submitted to Congress a budget request that was 22 percent higher than the previous year's, the largest increase since World War II. He noted bluntly:

The Library has been allowed to fall behind. It has simply not been able to keep up with inflation in book prices, with the requirement to absorb sequestrations, and with the need to absorb all or most of recent mandated annual pay raises. An essentially declining annual appropriation has begun to erode the Library's ability to serve the nation. The Library now employs 475 fewer employees on Federal appropriations than in 1984. This alarming erosion should not be allowed to continue.[16]

Although the final appropriations bill included less funding than Billington had asked for, an extra $5.2 million was provided for hiring catalogers to tackle the library's "arrearage," its backlog of uncataloged books.[17]

A few years later, in 1992, the Program for Cooperative Cataloging was established.[18] This network allowed major research libraries to join in the process of submitting headings for approval to the Policy and Standards Division at LC. Catalogers at member libraries were trained to recognize when a new heading was needed and how to submit a new heading for consideration. Berman spoke at a cataloging forum at the Library of Congress in February 1993, a month after Ruth retired.[19] By then his influence was widely felt at the library. Slowly but surely, changes had been made to LCSH in the direction of inclusivity. An article published by University of Memphis librarian Stephen Knowlton in 2005 revealed that out of the 225 headings that Berman listed in *Prejudices and Antipathies*, 63 percent had been modified to his suggestions or something close to it.[20] For instance, "Eskimo" was changed to "Inuit," and "Group sex," the heading that Ruth established in 1974 and mentioned in her letter to Gabe Horchler, was slightly modified. Its record now reads:

```
LC control no.:      sh 85057499
LCCN Permalink:      https://lccn.loc.gov/sh85057499
HEADING:             Group sex
000                  00475cz a2200205n 450
001                  4708870
005                  20120326094948.0
008                  860211i| anannbabn |b ana
010                  __ |a sh 85057499
035                  __ |a (DLC)sh 85057499
035                  __ |a (DLC)55555
040                  __ |a DLC |c DLC |d DLC
150                  __ |a Group sex
450                  __ |a Orgies
450                  __ |a Swinging (Sexual behavior)
450                  __ |a Troilism
550                  __ |w g |a Sex
550                  __ |w g |a Sex customs
906                  __ |t 8748 |u fk03 |v 0
953                  __ |a xx00 |b fh05
```

The term "Jewish question" is still an established heading, although now there are no books cataloged with this heading.

Several of the librarians who worked under Ruth remembered that she was not an ideal boss. Even coworkers who considered her a

friend found her to be infuriating at times. She could be highly critical, micromanaging her staff and then turning around and blaming
them for not being more independent in their work. She had long,
drawn-out fights with staff members but then acted like nothing had
happened. Like in Vietnam, she had a notoriously messy desk. Kay
Elsasser described an incident when Ruth was completely enraged
that one of her supervisors wanted her to clean her desk. Ruth's chain-
smoking habit was well known around the library. When she first
started in 1971, anyone could smoke anywhere, but over time new
rules were instated about smoking only in designated lounges and
then, eventually, only outside. Ruth often tried to convince colleagues
to chat with her in the smoking lounges, probably to both gossip and
have serious discussions on her own turf. She also wanted to conduct
annual reviews with her subordinates there, which made some of them
uncomfortable.[21]

In October 1992 Ruth wrote a long letter to the parents of David
Rudman, a former Library of Congress employee who had recently
passed away. She had supervised David, and the two had become close.
While the purpose of the letter was to provide Rudman's parents with
more insight into his work as a librarian, Ruth went off on several tan-
gents that revealed the office politics of LC and her surreptitious and
fairly immature methods of dealing with them. Ruth detailed the early
years of her mentorship of David:

> Perhaps the first common bond we found was the discov-
> ery that neither of us suffered fools gladly and this led to
> various conversations of how to deal with certain higher
> up staff members and their "dumb" decisions, instruc-
> tions, etc. I think our earliest discussions, perhaps more
> aptly called "chats," revolved around cataloging issues and
> different points of analyzing books and how to sway the

fools and getting the right thing done without offending the fools.[22]

Ruth also wrote about how much she admired the way that David dealt with conflict, particularly when disagreeing with her about book analysis or how cataloging rules should be applied when a confusing situation arose. These tiffs were common among the Subject Cataloging Division, and as a supervisor Ruth had to navigate these conflicts regularly. In describing his approach, she also inadvertently revealed how other colleagues vexed her:

> I soon discovered if we had any differences of opinion on book analysis, David always offered valid reasons for disagreeing and if he felt his reasons were more cogent than mine, he would defend his opinion to the bitter end. But it was never because it was his opinion, it was because he had thought it through or researched it to the best of his ability and was convinced that the reasoning was correct. However, when given the right kind of reasons he could easily be convinced and would gracefully give in. He never argued just for the sake of argument or just to be contrary; he never argued just to win and on the rare occasions when we could not find a compromise or solution he was always willing to defer to higher authority and defer to higher judgment, usually gracefully and in good humor. This was the intellectual aspect of the work. On the procedural and technical aspects of the work he was a joy to deal with. He was the quickest study I ever had. He listened attentively, remembered accurately, and even if he didn't like certain ways of doing things, my telling him I didn't like it either, but until we could develop and sell a better way of doing

things we better keep mum and do what had to be done he could be as docile and obliging as a little lamb.[23]

Of course, not all the librarians that Ruth supervised were "little lambs." Catherine Hiebert Kerst described to me how difficult it was to work for Ruth and how she pitied other LC employees who had worked with her. Cathy struggled to please her but left LC to earn her PhD in American studies. She later returned to work at LC as a folklife specialist at the American Folklife Center. Years later, after Ruth retired, Catherine ran into her on the street nearby the library, and the two had a nice conversation. Ruth wrote her a card immediately after:

It was really wonderful to be able to speak with you really spontaneously and to find that you seem to have become the kind of person that I always felt you could be—should be—whatever? While I know that employee-supervisor relations necessarily have limits, constraints & at times tensions, I always felt we had more common [interests] than differences, but somehow I felt I could never reach you—obviously part of it may have been my fault[,] & shared interest do not necessarily make for "liking." . . . At any rate I felt you have become much more relaxed, much more mature & balanced & sure of yourself & it really makes me feel good…please believe me that I'm happy to see that you've made such strides & have become "a REAL mensch."[24]

Ruth obviously had regrets about how she had treated her former employees. Her over-the-top flattery in this letter was also typical of how Ruth sometimes manipulated friends and acquaintances she had formerly mistreated.

In 1992 the Library of Congress started a reorganization plan. This involved splitting up and reorganizing the cataloging departments. One goal of the reorganization was to move away from a top-down, hierarchical management to one that was more team based. Contractors were brought in to manage the process, which irritated many staff members. Ruth chafed at these changes and didn't seem to understand what her new employees wanted. They tried to tell her that she didn't have to treat them like children. Kersti Blumenthal worked under Ruth when Ruth became the head of a new section that cataloged German and Scandinavian materials. She remembered that Ruth probably felt "clobbered" by the whole process and her new team.[25]

A search in the Library of Congress's staff-only catalog—known as Voyager—for Ruth's cataloger codes (she had at least three) will bring up a list of almost 8,000 books that she worked on. About 2,400 of them are nonfiction books in German. Over 5,100 are sociology-related books in English. Every time Ruth created a new catalog record or modified it in some way, she entered her code into the record, letting other catalogers know she had done something to it. These catalog records live on not just at the Library of Congress but also in libraries across the nation. After Ruth's twenty-one and a half years at the library, throughout all the endless work and frustration, her catalog records had ended up in libraries just like the ones she had walked into in Zurich, Seattle, Israel, Berkeley, and Vietnam. Over the past forty-five years, readers and researchers from all walks of life have unexpectedly stumbled across these books by searching library catalogs or browsing the stacks, thanks to Ruth's steady handiwork as a cataloger. By the end of 1992, Ruth was ready to finally retire. She was almost seventy years old and had worked as a librarian and federal employee for thirty-three years, most of them at LC. Ruth retired on January 3, 1993.[26]

During Ruth's tenure at the Library of Congress, the staff created an exhibit titled *Nazi Book Burning and the American Response*. Professor Guy Stern spoke on the topic at the opening, and a small exhibit catalog was published. As the *Library of Congress Information Bulletin* reported, the exhibit included examples of condemned books, photographs, contemporary newspaper accounts, editorial cartoons, posters, and manuscripts. It was installed in the first-floor lobby of the Madison Building, which Ruth walked through at least twice a day. She might have attended the opening or viewed the exhibit later on her own. She would have remembered the book burning she saw as a ten-year-old girl in Leipzig, and it may have brought back horrible flashbacks. She rarely talked with coworkers about her earlier life, and many of them never knew what she had gone through in Germany and why she felt so strongly about the minutiae of their daily work. But when the exhibit ran during that April in 1988, twice a day Ruth was reminded of why she chose this profession, why she cataloged books, and why she wanted everyone, everywhere, to read whatever the hell they wanted.

~

I didn't get that first job I applied for at the Library of Congress. But soon after that interview, I got a job with ProQuest, a library database company that funded this split position in the International Standard Serial Number Center at LC. I cut my teeth there learning how to catalog brand new magazines and journals, and later I worked for five years at the American Folklife Center on an oral history project about the civil rights movement. I can look back now and say that working there was probably the most exhilarating professional experience I will ever have but, at times, also the most frustrating. I immersed myself in the arcane rules of cataloging and creating finding aids for the fascinating collections I worked on. I loved learning about the library's history and went to any free lecture or concert I could. When we finally got the oral histories cataloged and streaming online, my job transitioned to working on a related exhibit and promoting the collection to scholars and teachers. I met people across the library who were as excited as I was to work there and others from outside the library who told me how amazing the whole experience must be.

When my job was nearing its end, I applied for a Senate archivist position with a vague description. I quickly got a call from the office of Senator Barbara Mikulski of Maryland, one of my heroes, who had recently announced her retirement as the longest-serving woman senator and longest-serving woman in Congress. I took the job knowing I was ready for a new challenge, even though I understood that preparing her thousands of boxes of records for transfer to Johns Hopkins University by the time she retired would be backbreaking, frantic work. The resources of the Senate were vast, and it was remarkable to ask and quickly receive whatever I needed to do my job. But I also missed my LC coworkers and our camaraderie.

While I worked in the Senate, damning Government Accountability Office reports were published, revealing LC's inadequate technology funding and inept policies. Articles in the *New York Times* and *Washington Post* reported on Dr. Billington's irascibility and the fact that he communicated with staff while he was at home only through his fax machine.[27] He announced that he would retire at the end of 2015 but abruptly left in September. The next spring, I was amused by the national news stories on the LC Policy and Standards Division's decision to change the subject heading "Illegal immigrants" to "Noncitizens" and "Unauthorized immigration."

I had heard a rumor years earlier that President Obama wanted to appoint Dr. Carla Hayden, an old friend of his from Chicago, to be the next librarian of Congress. As far as I was concerned, it would have been difficult to find a better candidate. She had worked as a children's librarian in Chicago, earned her PhD in library science, taught as a professor, served as the president of the American Library Association, and transformed the Enoch Pratt Free Library of Baltimore into a modern, urban library system. The library had recently received attention because one of its branches had refused to close during the 2015 riots, even though it was physically located at the heart of them. Besides her stellar qualifications and the fact that she was an actual librarian, Hayden is a woman and she is black, two firsts that were deeply symbolic to many LC employees. The demographics of the person at the helm of the library wouldn't necessarily mean that the history of the library's discrimination would change overnight. But it would certainly send a strong message to all staff members that someone who looked like and had a similar background to many of them could make it to the top.

Just as I had hoped, President Obama nominated Hayden, and Senator Mikulski accompanied her to the hearing and introduced her. At the swearing-in ceremony, where the senator gave a rousing speech about Hayden's work in Baltimore, I watched from the back of the Great Hall. Even though I had a fantastic view, I wished I was watching from the balcony with other LC staff members who had won a ticket lottery to witness the swearing in.

I wrote this section of the book on Saturdays in the Main Reading Room, which bustled with activity despite the frequent reports that libraries are unnecessary in this digital era. With a new leader at the helm, librarians and researchers around the world are waiting and watching to see if the Library of Congress can finally catch up technologically and return to being the leader of libraries worldwide. Time will tell, but for now I'm betting on it.

∼

Part IX:

Come Sit Awhile

Chapter 34

~

As a librarian and reader, I can't resist a good library book sale. The Federation of Friends of the DC Public Library chapters at both the Southeast Neighborhood Library and Northeast Neighborhood Library on Capitol Hill host used book sales every few months. When I started writing about Ruth, my browsing and buying at these sales and bookstores swerved toward any topic, no matter how tangential, related to her life and the historical period she lived through. At one of these sales at the Northeast Neighborhood Library, I approached the cashier with a huge stack of books on Nazi Germany, Judaism, and the Vietnam War. He seemed amused by my purchases: "You must really like history," he said. He eventually got it out of me that I was writing a book and asked what it was about. I explained it was about a woman named Ruth Rappaport, who had lived in this neighborhood for many years. His eyes lit up and he said, "Ruth! Oh, I knew Ruth." Over many years Tom Fenske had run into her at meetings of the Friends of the Northeast Library and the Stanton Park Neighborhood Association. Time and again I was reminded that it seemed like everyone in this neighborhood had known Ruth and that everyone had a story about her.

~

After Ruth retired, she found it easy to stay in touch with her coworkers and friends from the Library of Congress. Because she lived just two blocks away, they could easily stop by her house, and she ran into them while walking near the library. She recalled that they came by to "pick her brains" and ask her advice related to work, especially about how to supervise difficult employees.[1] She had tried to start an official Library of Congress group for retirees to meet and stay in touch, but library administrators shot down the idea.[2]

Ruth had joined many organizations as soon as she moved to Washington, but one issue in particular became important to her as she aged: preserving historic buildings and the Capitol Hill neighborhood. In 1976 she had joined DC's commission to celebrate the American bicentennial, and she had also helped preserve the Sewall-Belmont House (now the Belmont-Paul Women's Equality National Monument), a historic building and museum—across the street from the Capitol—dedicated to the history of the women's suffrage movement. Also in the 1970s she protested the renovation of Union Station, an ill-thought plan that gutted the station to build a visitors' center in time for the American bicentennial and that moved the Amtrak station to an ugly nearby building. The renovation was so unpopular that it was redone in the 1980s, bringing back its function as a train station and adding many new shops and restaurants. Ruth joined the Capitol Hill Restoration Society, an organization founded in 1955 that successfully worked toward the goal of getting the neighborhood designated a historic district and placed onto the National Register of Historic Places.

Raymond Gamble was a deacon and custodian at the Faith Tabernacle Church, just a few doors down from Ruth's house. Ruth approached him about hiring him to mow her lawn. He agreed and the two became friends. Ruth often enlisted his help in her disputes with neighbors about following the rules set by the DC Historic Preservation Review Board, which governed what homeowners in historic districts could do concerning renovating the exterior of their homes and landscaping. Ruth often spotted violations of these codes, and she badgered Raymond to help her report them to the authorities.[3] She earned a reputation as a busybody, nosing her way into neighborhood squabbles and eager to enforce preservation rules that, to some new neighbors, were a bureaucratic headache.

She also joined causes that impacted her quality of life, particularly as a carless resident of Capitol Hill. Ruth was appointed to the advisory commission on Eastern Market, the historic food market and flea market at Seventh and C Street SE that was easily walkable from her house. She also joined an effort to change the laws regarding how DC cabs charged customers. The move would switch cars from a zone-to-zone system to time-and-distance meters that were used in other major cities.[4] The meters were more beneficial, financially, to customers who used cabs to travel short distances, much like Ruth did. Even though she supported public transportation and walkability, she was irritated when bus routes were diverted around the Capitol in 2004 by new security checkpoints built around the complex. Several bus lines now went by her house on Third Street, which was not a thoroughfare that could easily handle bus traffic. Her complaints about the pollution and noise were quoted in the *Washington Post*, and soon enough the routes were changed.[5] She could get back to reading and visiting on her front porch in peace, one of her favorite activities in retirement. One neighbor later praised the efforts of Ruth and another woman in the neighborhood, Margot Kelley, and noted that they were an incredible team known for getting things done to help their community.[6]

Sig Cohen started a group for Jews on Capitol Hill because there was no synagogue in the neighborhood. He invited his Jewish friends to a seder and encouraged them to invite other Jews who lived nearby. This group later officially organized as the Hill Havurah. Ruth heard about it and started coming in its early days, sometime after the year 2000. By then she was already in somewhat poor health and needed assistance getting to the group's meetings and events. Ruth "was a presence," Cohen said. "You could feel her presence . . . and was fascinating to talk with . . . She embodied the word 'chutzpah.'" Laurie Solnik, another leader of the group, met Ruth through the Hill Havurah. She said Ruth was very wary of institutional Judaism and warned them not to become too big or to become a synagogue (the organization is led by lay members). She remembered that Ruth said she had no use for established synagogues or the patriarchy of the rabbinate.[7]

Ruth summed up her involvement in the Capitol Hill community in an email to Cohen:

> Surely even you will admit that by comparison, serving on the DC Bicentennial Assembly, helping to keep Sewall-Belmont House as a historic structure, being active on the Eastern Market in its various incarnations, Stanton Park Neighborhood Assoc., CH Restoration Society, AFSCME Local 2910 and AFSCME Council 26, Havurah and CHV [Capitol Hill Village] are pretty tame and lame activities! I wonder if to some extent my DC activities benefited me more by keeping me active and involved than I contributed to their success. Oh I guess I did some good.....I think my fight against the "hole in the ground" at Union Station was commendable. I think my efforts at residential parking enforcement have proven worthwhile, and lastly, but NOT LEAST, it looks like I'm on the winning side of the cab zone-vs-meter controversy. I spent a lot of time these past few months lobbying city council members for meters.... had interesting conversations and emails with Ward 6

member, and Jim Graham, and Carol Schwarz.....years ago, when she ran for mayor, I started the "Democrats for Carol" movement.

I guess to some extent staying involved helps me as much or more than I help the causes I'm involved with.[8]

Although Ruth seemed to be firmly rooted in Washington once she got her job at LC and bought a home, she still traveled regularly and sated her wanderlust with at least a few overseas trips. In 1983 she took two separate trips to Spain and the British Isles, and in 1984 she traveled to China. She wrote a long, travelogue-style letter to friends, detailing China's customs, clothing, food, and historic sites.[9] At some point before the reunification of Germany in 1990, one of Ruth's friends convinced her to take a trip back to the country of her childhood, despite her deep misgivings.

Her friend Alice was working as a teacher in Frankfurt at a school for American children. Ruth decided it would be a decent place to visit, because she could do many day trips by train from there. As she put it, "There's nothing to do in Frankfurt except have coffee at a coffeehouse . . . And that takes care of Frankfurt." She took boat trips up and down the Rhine River, and visited smaller towns such as Otzberg. She and Alice rented a car and drove along the Danube River to Vienna and Budapest. But due to the fact that Leipzig was still under Communist control in East Germany, Ruth was unable to go back to her childhood home.

She explained her feelings about visiting Germany: "I went back with a horrendous amount of reluctance. I didn't think I was ever going to go back . . . I went back under, really, duress by a friend."[10] Since Alice didn't speak German, Ruth made their travel plans and conversed with

Germans in restaurants and hotels. Although it was very subtle, Ruth noticed something distinct in how these Germans treated her:

> And the Germans are very polite. And when we sat and I would order the meal in German, and inevitably they wouldn't say, "who are you, or where are you from or what is your background?" What I was getting was, "for an American you are speaking excellent German." Now this is a whole bunch of bullshit, because I do not speak excellent German. I speak a teenage German. I speak a slang German. Well, not really, just semi-slang. And it was the German way of trying to find who, what I am, without being too inquisitive.[11]

These were probably Germans who, like her, had been children during World War II. They had grown up with the heavy burden of the Holocaust. And while they may have wanted to ask Ruth directly if she was Jewish, where she was from, or what she had gone through, they knew they couldn't cross this boundary. As Ruth put it, "They were too polite to do too much fishing, but they knew there was a story. And so without being too obviously curious, they accepted the story."

Ruth was asked if she had any desire to go back to Leipzig in the future, perhaps a rhetorical question because it was obvious she was near the end of her life. She bluntly answered, "Not really. It's all so far—I mean, I've outgrown Leipzig."[12]

In the spring of 1996, Ruth traveled to Israel for two months, her first time back in the country since 1949.[13] On this trip, she went to Yad Vashem, the World Holocaust Remembrance Center. It was no doubt a moving experience for her, as she later explained that she felt more of a connection to this museum and memorial site than she did to the

United States Holocaust Memorial Museum, which opened in 1993 (it is unclear when exactly she first visited the USHMM).[14] She visited her sister Mirjam, who now lived in Beersheba. The two sisters had last seen each other in 1981, when Mirjam came to DC for a visit; now Ruth noticed that, at eighty-six, Mirjam was losing her short-term memory. She wrote in a statement concerning Mirjam's mental fitness at this point in her life, "In fact, Mirjam had said to me she would rather kill herself than leave her apartment to live in an old age home if the time came that she could not live alone anymore."[15] In 1997 Ruth wrote a letter to her cousin Rosel, expressing her sympathy that Rosel had recently moved into a retirement home. She acknowledged, "I realize that is something I will need to give some thought to also[,] some time in the not too distant future, though at the moment I'm avoiding giving it serious thought."[16] Like Mirjam, Ruth thought of herself as fiercely independent, and as she approached old age herself, she began to take steps to ensure she could remain in her own home.

Chapter 35

In 1987, when Ruth was sixty-four years old, she became the chair of LC's Employee Health Assistance Joint Advisory Committee. In this capacity, she started an eldercare discussion group for LC employees. In 1988 Ruth received an award from Dr. Billington for her efforts to bring in guest speakers and gather information for the group.[1] The discussions focused on caregivers who were helping elderly parents or relatives, and Ruth learned about which services were available and kept these in mind as she aged. She relied on a network of friends and neighbors who checked in on her and helped with errands and chores. Ruth hired Peter Bartis's partner and future husband, Ben, to take care of her yard and do odd jobs around the house. In 2006 a group of Capitol Hill residents started the organization Capitol Hill Village, modeled on Beacon Hill Village, which helped seniors stay in their own homes, a concept known as "aging-in-place." Members paid an annual fee to access services such as social events and senior clubs and to get help with errands and chores from volunteers.[2] Ruth was one of the group's first members.

As Ruth aged, she seemed to embody the stereotypes about older single women, especially librarians. Although she had long found cats a nuisance, she adopted two of them, Sparky and, later, Murphy. Ruth initially fostered Sparky, a Maine coon cat that had belonged to a friend who couldn't keep him because he didn't get along with another pet. Although Ruth was reluctant to take him, eventually she adopted and became very fond of him.³ After Sparky passed away, Ruth adopted Murphy. A friend who helped her with the process noted that Ruth felt guilty for initially overlooking Murphy because he was an older cat. She dreaded people overlooking her for the same reason.⁴ Ruth may have seemed like a "crazy cat lady," but Sparky and Murphy gave her the companionship she needed as she aged and continued to live alone.

Since at least her early adulthood, Ruth had issues with messiness and an inability to throw things away, and it seemed to get worse as she got older. Everyone who came to her house noted the piles of stuff everywhere; it got so bad after she retired that visitors noted it was difficult to walk through some rooms of the house. She stockpiled food and kept an overflow of canned goods in her first-floor bathroom and in the basement. She asked friends and neighbors if they could drive her to Costco, where she bought enormous quantities of food. She enjoyed cooking and invited friends to come over and eat with her. Peter recalled one incident, regarding her pressure cooker, that for him seemed to embody Ruth's inability to throw anything away:

> Ruth loved cooking with her pressure cooker. She had a pressure cooker that must have been forty-five years old. This thing was pockmarked, the shine was off of it. Just had to see it.

> One day she called me up and said, "I need your help. I can't take the cover off my pressure cooker."

> I said, "Oh Ruth, not now." You know she always had some chore for me. I said, "Don't use it."

> She said, "I already used it. I can't open it." So I get over there with my tools. Now, I have a lot of tools. And I tried everything to get this pressure cooker open. I yanked on

it, I used hammers, I used vise grips. I couldn't get it open. And inside was corned beef, potatoes, carrots, cabbage.

So I said, "Ruth, I can't do this, throw it out." The next day I called up, said, "What did you do with it?" There's a silence. She said, "I sent it back." I said, "Oh, you opened it?" She said, "No, I just put it in a plastic bag and sent it back." And I said, "Ruth you're going to get arrested for doing this! You can't do this, you can't do this."

And for a couple days I'm just astonished at her for doing this. About a week later, I get a phone call. "Would you help me bring this package in?" So I opened up the package and I looked inside. There was a brand new, shiny, state-of-the-art pressure cooker. This was after a week I spent telling her she can't do this. I had to think about it a minute, you know. Why did she do this, was she cheap? No, it was justice. She was going to stick it to the man, and she did. And she didn't get arrested.[5]

Gail Kohn, the director of Capitol Hill Village, explained Ruth's reasoning for why she had so much stuff and had trouble parting with it: "We like to call it collecting, rather than hoarding. I always loved her excuse for why it was that she collected things: She was a librarian. 'The truth is that you could never throw anything out when you're a librarian.'"[6] Ruth could use librarianship as an excuse for her hoarding, but she explained in a letter how overwhelming it was for her to go through her things and organize them:

I not only have boxes and boxes of books, professional journals, professional papers, and knickknacks that got shipped from overseas to Washington in 1971, but it seems I never threw out anything since moving into this house, so the stuff that went from California to Asia and then to DC is still in the basement and all over the house, but when I retired, all the files from my office, 23 years' worth of stuff[,] got moved into my house. Unfortunately I cannot just throw it out without looking at it... there is some stuff that is useful for certain archives... So in some way I am glad that the stuff I have hung onto for all these years turns out to be of value to somebody, it is a horrible chore to do all this, especially since personal stuff has crept into many of these boxes, stuff like personal letters that one does not want to get into official archives. But the worst of all this cleaning up is that in looking at the stuff one literally relives one's life and gets sidetracked thinking not only of the activities but all the people involved and sometimes it gets nostalgic and sometimes it gets depressing but always it gets very tedious.[7]

At some point Ruth did go through all her papers, perhaps with assistance from a friend or volunteer. Every letter that made it into her collection at the USHMM archives was numbered, in pen. When I first noticed this numbering system, I asked Peter if he had written them on the letters when he found them. He hadn't, and an archivist would never write with pen on any document. It appears that Ruth (or a helper) had numbered them, and the personal letters she feared getting into the archives were probably destroyed. In all three of her archival collections available to the public, although there are many letters to and from her friends and some relatives, there are virtually no letters to or from her parents, her sisters, or any of the men she dated. During this process of attempting to organize her papers, she also began to give away books and other possessions.

Ruth increasingly had trouble with walking and getting out of her house, but she stayed connected with friends and relatives. She had learned to use a computer at work in the 1980s and at some point had bought one to use at home for typing letters. In her eighties she started learning to use the internet at home. As someone who loved information, she no doubt was thrilled to be able to look up facts and read news so easily. She loved emailing friends near and far, and she even joined Facebook. Her neighbors, even though they knew they might end up doing some kind of favor or errand for her, enjoyed stopping by her house and listening to the stories she told. They recognized the value she added to the neighborhood and supported her effort to stay in her home. In an email to neighbor Petula Dvorak, Ruth wrote, "I don't think there is anything I hate more than 'age segregation.' I don't think I could survive in either assisted living or a retirement home, or whatever you call it. I enjoy the little kids from next door coming over to visit my cat . . . I enjoy sitting on the front porch and giving out loads of Halloween candy."[8]

Halloween seems to have been a favorite holiday of Ruth's. Peter once suggested to her that she don a lab coat for a costume as "Dr. Ruth." Ruth no doubt was a fan of the famous sex therapist, radio-show host, and author. But it is unclear if she knew that Ruth Westheimer had also fled Germany as a child, spent a year in Switzerland, and lived in Israel.

Ruth's neighbors always made sure that she had somewhere to go on holidays. Petula Dvorak recounted a funny Thanksgiving story. Her family had invited Ruth for dinner, however:

> An hour into our meal, we rang her bell. No answer. We banged on the door. We called. No answer. We feared something happened to her and dialed 911. The paramedics came, they kicked in the door and searched the house as our turkey and stuffing got cold. As they were stomping

A Well-Read Woman

through the house, a car pulled up and Ruth, in a silk blouse, lipstick and fresh hairdo, got out of the car, the red lights of the firetruck glinting off her jewelry and cane.

"What is going on here?" she asked. We explained.

"Well, I had other invitations to dinner. I was planning on making it to yours, eventually," she said.[9]

In her eighties Ruth's health began to deteriorate. Although she had quit smoking soon after she retired, she developed problems with breathing and a persistent cough that was diagnosed as lung cancer in 2010.[10] She was admitted to the intensive-care unit at George Washington University Hospital and was eventually discharged, although she pleaded with her doctor to let her stay, because she loved the good service there. After returning home, a hospital bed was set up in her living room, where she could visit with friends who knew that the end for her was growing close. Peter and Ben visited her nearly every day. She chose Peter to be the executor of her will, because, as he put it, "she knew I would go through *everything*." Ben remembered the day a friend took a photo of the three of them on her porch. In Ruth's lap was a present that someone had given her: a large, stuffed Clifford, of the famous children's book. He made Ruth laugh in that moment. "There was a lot of joy between the three of us," he said.[11]

One friend explained Ruth's feelings during this time: "I spent many, many, many very happy hours with her over the last several months. And she was the most engaging, interesting woman that I think I've ever met. She was bright until the end, her mind was lucid, she was cared for, she was comforted . . . She was mad that she was dying and sick, although she knew it, and I think she was at peace."[12] On October 14 Gail Schwartz came to Ruth's house to interview her for the USHMM's oral history collection. Schwartz was a longtime volunteer, who had interviewed about three hundred Holocaust survivors for the museum since 1989.[13] For almost two hours Ruth told what she remembered about her childhood in Germany, her escape to Switzerland, and her young adulthood in Seattle and Israel. This would be the last time that Ruth recounted her life in such detail.

In her capacity as a lay leader of the Hill Havurah, Laurie Solnik helped Ruth make some end-of-life decisions, and later Solnik described their conversations. Ruth had a recurring dream about her own grave, with a rosebush above it, on a hillside. She considered many options but finally settled on donating her body to GWU's medical school.[14]

Ruth passed away at home on November 17, 2010. Her neighbor Petula described that day:

> We were on our way over with "The Very Hungry Caterpillar" on Wednesday, but she died about an hour before we got there, in her bed. She had been reading "First Aid for Cats" and "Cooking With Eggs." [...]
>
> Ruth Rappaport left her front porch and was wheeled away from her Capitol Hill rowhouse on the mortician's gurney while those car horns complained. The gurney cachunked into the wagon, the doors slammed shut.
>
> It was a triumph for Ruth, leaving her home this way. And I've got to think she would've laughed to know she slowed down traffic on her beloved street for a little while. That was how she had wanted it—to die in her own home, instead of joining the millions of elderly who wind up in assisted living facilities or nursing homes.[15]

Ruth's memorial service was held a few weeks later at the Corner Store, an event space on Capitol Hill. Laurie Solnik led the Jewish service and opened it by playing a segment of Ruth's oral history. She spoke about Ruth's extraordinary life and the reverence that everyone in the room had for her. In the Jewish tradition, Ruth's relatives tore a garment. Others read Bible verses, including "Woman of Valor" from the book of Proverbs. Then friends and family members told their most memorable stories about Ruth, often provoking both laughter and tears from her mourners.

Peter began the long process of clearing out Ruth's house and carrying out her will. She left most of her estate to her nephew Guy and left funds to Capitol Hill Village, the Hill Havurah, Capitol Hill Group Ministry, and the Stanton Park Neighborhood Association. The Hill Havurah named their Torah Fund after Ruth, and the Capitol Hill Group Ministry established the Ruth Rappaport Wisdom Award, which recognizes one individual each year for their commitment to the Capitol Hill neighborhood. Peter came up with the idea for a memorial bench for Ruth, which, in 2012, was installed under a tree at the Congressional Cemetery. Its inscription is simply, "Come sit awhile."

Epilogue

While writing this book, I often visited Ruth's bench at the Congressional Cemetery, and I brought flowers on her birthday and death date. In the Jewish tradition, I placed a stone on the bench next to the others that are always there. She might find it amusing that her bench is near the gravesite of J. Edgar Hoover, the man who unsuccessfully tried to prevent her employment as a typist at the Oakland Army Base (Hoover also lived in a row house just a few blocks from Ruth's home). The cemetery has other well-known residents, including John Philip Sousa and many early US congressmen and Supreme Court justices. The more recently departed have gotten creative with their unique and often humorous headstones. The cemetery is open to dog walkers (by membership) and hosts events such as "Yoga Mortis," the "Tombs and Tomes Book Club," and concerts in the chapel. A little free library now stands outside the chapel, just a few steps up the path from Ruth's bench. When the foliage gets too thick or invasive around the perimeter fence, the cemetery brings a herd of goats to "mow" it down for a few days. No doubt, Ruth would love that she has joined this colorful, eternal community.

Since I first learned of Ruth, she has been constantly on my mind, and in a sense she's always been with me. Reminders of her are everywhere, and not just her old belongings in my house. There are signposts Ruth left behind all over Capitol Hill: the Corner Store, the Northeast Neighborhood Library, Stanton Park, and, of course, her house on Third

Street, which I liked to pass by on my way to and from work. Once, while walking down a stairwell at the Library of Congress in the Jefferson Building, I spotted a cigarette butt. It had probably traveled in on someone's shoe from outside, but I couldn't help imagining Ruth smoking in that stairwell when such vices were not banned at the library.

During the time that I worked on this book, a few people asked me if I thought Ruth was a librarian hero. I don't quite know how to answer that question. She was not the president of the American Library Association, and she never headed a major library or library system. She was never famous. But the people who met her or worked with her could not forget her. Her efforts to build a library system in Vietnam were heroic, and her diligence in cataloging social science books for over twenty years was a tedious, herculean feat. Although Ruth never used the word "radical" to describe herself, I knew since I first heard about her that she was one. The more I researched her life, the more it became apparent. It is the most fitting word to describe how she approached her job, her mission, and her life's work, even if she never called attention to her beliefs or her politics. Radicals may not necessarily be lauded in history; because they can be impatient, difficult, outspoken, and infuriating, their lives don't always make for simple, heroic narratives. But radicals are the ones in the trenches, doing the grunt work and pushing the boulders uphill, despite the resistance from above.

I've thought about my grandfather Jack, a World War II veteran who liberated Rome (and captured my Italian grandmother, he used to joke) and then became the director of the Muskogee and Lubbock public libraries. I remember from my childhood his rants about battling the city council for more funding, although I barely understood what he was talking about. I've thought about my aunt Silvia, a cataloger for NASA's audiovisual collections, who has long served as a Democratic Party foot soldier in Houston and has chosen to spend her time, now that she is retired, teaching English to refugees. For years I've had long, rambling phone conversations with my mother, Alice, about her efforts to stop the Oregon State Legislature from defunding and closing the Oregon State Library, her employer. In her retirement years, she has a part-time job at the reference desk at the Salem Public Library and volunteers at my nieces' school library in Oregon City. As she fully admits, "I just can't quit."

Document by document, book by book, and patron by patron, we are nudging along a nearly invisible revolution. We may be slowed, but we won't stop. We may be threatened, but we won't quit.

Near the end of the interview, Gail Schwartz asked Ruth her opinions on current politics. Ruth had thought that President Obama would not be reelected in 2012, a prediction that turned out to be wrong. Gail also asked her if she thought another Holocaust could happen. Ruth bluntly responded:

> Yes. Unfortunately, yes. Again, it's less apt to happen now—we have more competition. There are other groups who also have problems. The competing minorities. But anti-Semitism is not dead. Sorry about that, but anyone who thinks it can't happen here, I have news for you. It can happen anywhere, anytime. But I would not bet there would not be another. Yep.[1]

Of course, genocides have happened again in several places around the world. Until the presidential election of 2016, however, I wasn't sure if I completely agreed with Ruth about the possibility of it happening here. Soon after, while many of us were still in shock over the results, librarians sprang into action. They called attention to libraries' unique role during this time of increased racism, xenophobia, political violence, fake news, alternative facts, and post-truth. While we forge ahead through dark times, we can look to Ruth as an example for how to survive under new-wave fascism. The tenets of librarianship can guide us through assaults on the freedom to read and the right to accurate information.

It seems that Ruth saw herself as someone who was not necessarily always ambitious but just made the best of her situation. She summarized: "Looking back, I never did initiate that much—I just never let an opportunity slip. I was kind of Johnny-on-the-spot. And it was always sort of, what if it goes wrong? Well, so what. I just didn't worry about results too much."[2] In her stories in all their myriad forms, she seemed to be revealing her own maxims:

1. Read ferociously.
2. Read everyone who is forbidden.
3. Jump off the train if you don't like its direction.
4. Wonder who will read your diary.
5. Hope that no one reads your diary.
6. Meet what comes.
7. Your life is a battle, your peace a victory.
8. Don't tolerate mediocrity.
9. Life must be faced with a certain amount of realism.
10. Contribute your time, effort, and ability to stave off the course of madness.
11. Throw elaborate parties with punch named after yourself.
12. Fight bureaucracy with sheer will, perseverance, and hard politicking.
13. Get the most material to the most people.
14. There is nothing, nothing, nothing that can ever substitute for personal observation and creative thinking.
15. Sway the fools, and get the right thing done without offending the fools.
16. Call it collecting, not hoarding.
17. The stuff you hang on to for all these years will turn out to be of value to somebody.
18. Be future oriented.
19. Take the time to sit awhile.

I've thought a lot about what Ruth would think about all this: a book about her life, written by another librarian after she died. Surely she would be pleased that she had crafted her life stories so well that a younger person, me, would be mesmerized by their epic nature. She might be horrified, on the other hand, that an obsessive researcher would diligently uncover every scrap of paper left behind that had anything on it even tangentially related to her. I'd like to think that even though Ruth was a masterful storyteller who sometimes told white lies, there were also times in her life when she told uncomfortable truths that no one wants to hear, even today. I hope she would be happy to know that her epic life is now immortalized in its own book. And I hope that this book will find a place on a shelf next to others that have changed so many lives. That includes yours.

Acknowledgments

Although most nonfiction books have one author listed on the cover, we know that we didn't do it alone. Writing this book was a group effort, and I am honored to have gotten to know so many generous people along the way that I never would have met otherwise.

I'd like to thank the librarians and archivists who assisted me with uncovering hundreds of sources related to the life of Ruth Rappaport. I would especially like to thank those at the United States Holocaust Memorial Museum, the US Army Heritage and Education Center, the University of Washington, the University of California, Berkeley, the University of Minnesota, the Center for Jewish History, the Zurich Central Library, the Swiss Federal Archives, the Leipzig City Archives, the Saxony State Archives, the National Archives and Records Administration, and the Library of Congress. I know how hard you work, how underpaid you are, and that the work you do is often invisible. I hope that Ruth has inspired you to keep going. This book is for you.

A big thanks goes to my agent, Priya Doraswamy, and my editor, Erin Calligan Mooney, who took a chance on both me and Ruth. While I was at a Biographers International Organization conference, Greg Krauss saw on my name tag that I was from DC and asked if I'd like to join a biography writing group. Month after month for three years, our ragtag group met up—over a plethora of snacks and drinks—to circulate chapter drafts, share research tips, and discuss politics. Greg, Jennifer Cockburn, Avis Bohlen, Ray Palmer, Tom Benjey, and Carolyn Carr provided the pseudo-deadlines and feedback I needed to push forward and actually put words down on paper.

My feeble attempts to learn German didn't get me very far. Through a team of interpreters and translators, both paid and volunteer, Ruth's letters and diary slowly emerged from a complete puzzle into a brilliantly written, hilarious, and heartbreaking chronicle of her teenage and young adult life. Thanks to Gudrun Durmon, Maria Mueller, Johanna Rodda, Elke Müller, and Katherine Schober of SK Translations for bringing those crucial documents to life. Thank you to the Hadassah-Brandeis Institute for awarding me a grant to fund the translation of Ruth's diaries. Another big thanks goes to Colin Torres and Lisa Monhoff for finishing research for me at NYU and Berkeley.

I am indebted to Ruth's family, friends, and coworkers, who were willing to share their memories, both good and bad, of her with me. Over coffee at the LC cafeteria or over email and the phone from thousands of miles away, they trusted me with not only their stories but also photos and letters from Ruth that they had the foresight not to toss into the garbage. I hope I've captured the Ruth that they remember and have surprised them with the Ruth they never knew. Thanks to Guy Rosner, Mark Rubinstein, Gladys Rubinstein, Michael Rubinstein, Hillel Cohn, Sig Cohen, Laurie Solnik, Nell Strickland, Bill Sittig, A. A. Allison, Peter Young, Ann Kelsey, Arlene Luster, Nolan Dehner, Floyd Zula, Darro Wiley, Kay Elsasser, Thompson Yee, Mary K. D. Pietris, Kersti Blumenthal, Shirley Loo, Catherine Hiebert Kerst, Gabe Horchler, Raymond Gamble, and Ben Zuras. I'd like to also thank the Vietnam veterans who took my survey on what they read there and those who personally shared their experiences with me.

I am lucky to have been raised in a family that loves reading and writing. From the beginning, my parents and brothers have both encouraged me to write this book and been bored to tears at times by my nonstop talk of Ruth. Thanks to my father, Bill Stewart, who always told me I should write more; my stepmother, Lorie Stewart, who helped with translations of Ruth's diaries and edited drafts; and my stepfather, Richard LaViolette, who will talk anyone's ear off about this book. My aunt Beverly Rude and cousin Anne Boyd Rioux helped with research and edited my drafts. My brothers Nick and Austin and their families always make me laugh and remind me to not take myself too seriously. Two of my oldest friends, Samantha Parkes and Karissa Haugeberg, have been cheerleaders throughout the process and gave me top-notch feedback. My boyfriend, Greg Marsh, patiently corrected my grammar in every draft for six long years. Alice LaViolette is not just my mom, but also my first librarian hero. Through endless late-night phone calls, research trips, and daily emails, she has been my de facto research assistant, and most importantly, she taught me how to be a better librarian.

Everyone that I worked with at LC supported and encouraged my efforts to write this book. My six years working at the ISSN Center and American Folklife Center were a wild ride through the joys of cataloging and the chaos of pulling off, by the seat of our pants, remarkable public programs. Both at LC and many other institutions, I have worked under mentors who have guided and shaped me into a better historian and archivist while also showing me how to think on my feet and get things done. They include Leslie Schwalm, Kären Mason, Janet Weaver, Linda Geisler, Esther Simpson, Kevin Gardner, Guha Shankar, Todd Harvey, David Taylor, Steve Winnick, Jennifer Cutting, Cathy Kerst, Ann Hoog, Judith Gray, Nikki Saylor, Betsy Peterson, Senator Barbara Mikulski, and Susan Irwin. Thanks especially to my library pals LaShawn Blake, Rick Fitzgerald, Erik Bergstrom, Marcia Segal, Valda Morris, Jon Gold, Bert Lyons, Megan Harris, Maya Lerman, Eric Wolfson, Julia Kim, Melissa Lindberg, and Ashley-Dior Thomas for encouraging me to write this book, and the friendship you've given me with a whole lot of beer, pizza, and baseball games.

Acknowledgments

When I had finally finished a draft of this book, Peter Bartis told me he had been diagnosed with lung cancer. He would receive experimental treatments, and I was convinced he would make it through. Six months afterward I was happy to tell him I had found a publisher, but just a few weeks later, on December 25, 2017, he passed away. I am still filled with grief that Peter did not live to see the publication of this book, but I know that his generosity and kindness will be remembered by everyone who met him. His simple act of inviting me to an estate sale changed my life. After all, he knew exactly what treasures awaited.

Bibliography

ARCHIVAL COLLECTIONS

Armed Forces Librarian Section Subject Files. Records Relating to the
Executive Director. Record Group 29/2/6. Special Collections.
American Library Association Archives, University of Illinois,
Urbana-Champaign, Illinois.

General Records of Special Services Division, 1967–1973. Department
of Defense, Department of the Army, US Army Pacific. US Army
Vietnam / Military Assistance Command Vietnam Support
Command. Adjutant General Section. Record Group 472.
National Archives Identifier 5718061. National Archives, College
Park, Maryland.

Herzl Conservative Congregation Records, 1906–1937. Special
Collections. Collection Number 2884. University of Washington
Libraries, Seattle, Washington.

Landeshilanstalt Altscherbitz Mental Hospital Records 20047. File
03814. Saxony State Archives, Leipzig, Germany.

Leipzig Polizeipräsidium Leipzig –S- Nr. 3207. Saxony State Archives,
Leipzig, Germany.

Max Lowenthal Papers. University Archives, University of Minnesota, Minneapolis, Minnesota.

Mendel Rappaport Records. International Tracing Service. OBE-RIW/1526. United States Holocaust Memorial Museum (USHMM), Washington, DC.

Records of Hadassah. Center for Jewish History, New York, New York.

Records of the Schweizer Hilfswerk für Emigrantenkinder J2.55#1. Swiss Federal Archives, Bern, Switzerland.

Ruth Rappaport and Max Lowenthal Files. FBI Records. Winchester, Virginia.

Ruth Rappaport Collection. Collection Number 2012.431.1. United States Holocaust Memorial Museum (USHMM), Washington, DC.

Ruth Rappaport Collection. US Army Heritage and Education Center (USAHEC), Carlisle Barracks, Pennsylvania.

Ruth Rappaport Official Personnel Folders. National Archives and Records Administration (NARA), Valmeyer, Illinois.

Ruth Rappaport Papers, 1946–1957. Special Collections. Collection Number 5797. University of Washington Libraries, Seattle, Washington.

BOOKS AND DISSERTATIONS

Ackerman, Kenneth D. *Trotsky in New York, 1917: A Radical on the Eve of Revolution.* Berkeley: Counterpoint, 2016.

Adler, Melissa. *Cruising the Library: Perversities in the Organization of Knowledge.* New York City: Fordham University Press, 2017.

———. "For SEXUAL PERVERSION See PARAPHILIAS: Disciplining Sexual Deviance at the Library of Congress." PhD diss., University of Wisconsin, 2012.

Allison, A. A. *To Spurn the Gods: A Viet Nam Memoir.* Bloomington, IN. Booktango, 2012.

Army Library Program. *Army Library Operational Guide.* Washington, DC: Army Library Program, 1961.

Barbian, Jan-Pieter. *The Politics of Literature in Nazi Germany: Books in the Media Dictatorship.* New York City: Bloomsbury, 2013.

Berman, Sanford. *Prejudices and Antipathies: A Tract on the LC Subject Headings Concerning People.* Metuchen, NJ: Scarecrow Press, 1971.

[Bluwstein], Ra'hel. *Flowers of Perhaps: A Bilingual Edition of Selected Poems.* Translated by Robert Friend. With Shimon Sandbank. New Milford, CT: Toby Press, 2008.

Bosworth, Patricia. *Anything Your Little Heart Desires: An American Family Story.* New York City: Touchstone, 1997.

Cone, Molly, Howard Droker, and Jacqueline Williams. *Family of Strangers: Building a Jewish Community in Washington State.* Seattle: Washington State Jewish Historical Society, 2003.

Cristán, Ana L. "SACO and Subject Gateways." In *Authority Control in Organizing and Accessing Information*, edited by Arlene G. Taylor and Barbara B. Tillett. New York City: Routledge, 2005.

DiMona, Joseph. *Great Court-Martial Cases*. New York City: Grosset and Dunlap, 1972.

Eshelman, William R. *No Silence! A Library Life*. Lanham, MD: Scarecrow Press, 1997.

Hogan, Michael J. *A Cross of Iron: Harry S. Truman and the Origins of the National Security States, 1945–1954*. New York City: Cambridge University Press, 2000.

Hubbard, Douglass H., Jr. *Special Agent, Vietnam: A Naval Intelligence Memoir*. Washington, DC: Potomac Books, 2006.

Jewish Publication Society of America. "Statistics of Jews." In *The American Jewish Year Book* 4 (1941). Edited by Harry Schneiderman. Philadelphia: Jewish Publication Society of America.

Knopf, Sabine. *Der Leipziger Gutenbergweg: Geschichte und Topographie einer Buchstadt* [The Leipzig Gutenberg path: history and topography of a book city]. Beucha, Germany: Sax-Verlag, 2001.

Lair, Meredith H. *Armed with Abundance: Consumerism & Soldiering in the Vietnam War*. Chapel Hill: University of North Carolina Press, 2011.

Marshall, John Douglas. *Place of Learning, Place of Dreams: A History of the Seattle Public Library*. Seattle: University of Washington Press, 2004.

Mersky, Roy M. and Michael L. Richmond. "Treatment of Sexually Oriented Magazines by Libraries." In *Sex Magazines in the Library Collection: A Scholarly Study of Sex in Serials and Periodicals* 4 (1979/1980), edited by Peter Gellatly, of *A Monographic Supplement to the Serials Librarian*. New York City: Haworth Press, 1981.

Reinharz, Shulamit, and Mark A. Raider. *American Jewish Women and the Zionist Enterprise*. Waltham, MA: Brandeis University Press, 2005.

Rosenbaum, Fred. *Cosmopolitans: A Social and Cultural History of the Jews in the San Francisco Bay Area*. Berkeley: University of California Press, 2009.

Rydell, Anders. *The Book Thieves: The Nazi Looting of Europe's Libraries and the Race to Return a Literary Inheritance*. New York City: Viking, 2015.

Segal, Lore. *Other People's Houses*. New York City: New American Library, 1964.

Stielow, Frederick J. "The War and Librarianship: A Study in Political Activism." In *Activism in American Librarianship, 1962–1972*, edited by Mary Lee Bundy and Frederick J. Sticlow. New York City: Greenwood Press, 1987.

Subject Cataloging Division, Processing Services, Library of Congress. *Classification: Class H, Subclasses HM–HX, Social Sciences: Sociology*. Washington, DC: Library of Congress, 1980.

Vogel, Peter. *The Last Wave from Port Chicago*. Self-published[?], 2002.

Westheimer, Ruth. *All in a Lifetime*. New York City: Grand Central Publishing, 1987.

Whelan, Richard. *Robert Capa: A Biography*. New York City: Alfred A. Knopf, 1985.

Wiener, Jon. *Professors, Politics and Pop*. New York City: Verso Books, 1994.

Willingham, Robert Allen. *Jews in Leipzig, Germany under Nazism, Communism and Democracy: Politics and Identity in the 20th Century*. Lewiston: Edwin Mellon Press, 2011.

Worsencroft, John Christian. "Salvageable Manhood: Project 100,000 and the Gendered Politics of the Vietnam War." Master's thesis, University of Utah, 2011.

NEWSPAPERS AND NEWSLETTERS

Jewish Tribune (San Francisco)

Library of Congress Information Bulletin

Local News, A News-Symposium of the Library of Congress Professional Guild, AFSCME Local 2910

Nevada State Journal

Oakland Tribune

Seattle Times

The Transcript (Seattle, formerly the *Jewish Transcript*)

Washington Informer

Washington Post

ARTICLES

"Ale & Quail Society Active in Host of Press Club Affairs." *Gentleman of the Press* (newsletter of the Washington State Press Club), October 1951. Accessed via JackGordon.org on October 25, 2018. http://www.jackgordon.org/WashPressClub/AleQuailHistory.htm.

Burawoy, Michael, and Jonathan VanAntwerpen. *Berkeley Sociology: Past, Present and Future*, November 2001. http://burawoy.berkeley.edu/PS/Berkeley%20Sociology.pdf.

Danton, J. Periam. "The Functions of a Graduate School of Librarianship," *California Librarian* 15 (March 1954): pp. 157–60.

Deery, Phillip. "'A Blot Upon Liberty': McCarthyism, Dr. Barsky and the Joint Anti-Fascist Refugee Committee." *American Communist History* 8, no. 2 (2009): pp. 167–96. https://doi.org/10.1080/14743890903335948.

Dvorak, Petula. "Proof of Gifts That Come When Generations Mingle." *Washington Post*, November 23, 2010.

DW staff. "Leipzig Celebrates Long Literary History." *DW*, March 13, 2008. http://www.dw.de/leipzig-celebrates-long-literary-history/a-3185443.

Engelmann, Larry. "Rise and Fall of the American Mayor of Saigon." *Pushing On* (blog), April 3, 2012. http://lde421.blogspot.com /2012/04/rise-and-fall-of-american-mayor-of.html.

Fiske, Marjorie. "Book Selection and Retention in California Public and School Libraries," edited by J. Periam Danton. Papers presented at Climate of Book Selection: Social Influences on School and Public Libraries (symposium), University of California, July 10–12, 1958.

Harmelin, Wilhelm. "Jews in the Leipzig Fur Industry." *Leo Baeck Institute Year Book* 9, no. 1 (January 1964): pp. 239–66. https:// doi.org/10.1093/leobaeck/9.1.239.

Hess, Bill. "Holocaust Survivor Who Hates Cats Winds Up Living with One." *No Cats Allowed!* (blog), January 16, 2009. http:// nocatsallowed.blogspot.com/2009/01/holocaust-survivor-who -hates-cats-winds.html.

"Hilde Schocken Mann." *Seattle Times*, August 14–15, 2007. Obituary. Accessed via Legacy.com, October 25, 2018. http://www.legacy.com /obituaries/seattletimes/obituary.aspx?n=hilde-schocken-mann &pid=92601843.

Kayiran, Zeki. "In Memoriam: Dr. Mohammad Gamal Mostafa." *Orange County Branch Newsletter*, August 2011. American Society of Civil Engineers. http://www.asceoc.org/newsletter/article /in_memoriam_mostafa.

Knowlton, Stephen A. "Three Decades Since *Prejudices and Antipathies*: A Study of Changes in the Library of Congress Subject Headings," *Cataloging and Classification Quarterly* 40, no. 2 (2005).

Lowenthal, David. "Out of the Box and into the Archives." *Continuum: The Magazine of the University of Minnesota Libraries*, Fall 2008.

Mediavilla, Cindy. "The War on Books and Ideas: The California Library Association and Anti-Communist Censorship in the 1940s and 1950s," *Library Trends* 46, no. 2 (Fall 1997): pp. 331–47.

Moran, Caitlin Keefe. "In Praise of Difficult Women: The Forgotten Work of Nancy Hale." *The Toast*, September 23, 2014.

Taylor, Quintard. "Swing the Door Wide: World War II Wrought a Profound Transformation in Seattle's Black Community." *Columbia: The Magazine of Northwest History* 9, no. 2 (Summer 1995).

Thorin, Suzanne E., and Robert Wedgeworth. "The Librarians of Congress: Past and Future." American Libraries. https://americanlibrariesmagazine.org/librarians-of-congress/.

PERSONAL COLLECTIONS

Bartis, Peter

Cohen, Sig

Horchler, Gabe

Kerst, Catherine Hiebert

Rosner, Guy

Rubinstein, Mark

AUTHOR CORRESPONDENCE/INTERVIEWS

Allison, A. A.

Blumenthal, Kersti

Cohen, Sig

Cohn, Hillel

Dehner, Nolan

Elsasser, Kay

Gamble, Raymond

Hudson, Joe

Kelsey, Ann

Kerst, Catherine Hiebert

Rosner, Guy

Rubinstein, Mark

Rubinstein, Michael

Sittig, Bill

Solnik, Laurie

Strickland, Nell

Vietnam Vets Reading Survey, conducted by author, 2013–2014

Wiley, Darro

Yee, Thompson

Young, Peter

Zula, Floyd

ORAL HISTORIES AND INTERVIEWS

Carney, Janice. Interview by Laura M. Calkin. OH0426. Vietnam
  Archive, Texas Tech University, Lubbock, Texas (May 24, June
  6–8, 2005).

Danton, J. Periam. "Dean and Professor at UC Berkeley's School
  of Librarianship, 1946–1976." Interviews by Laura McCreery
  (1999) and Mary Hanel (1993). The Regents of the University of
  California, 2000.

Kelsey, Ann. Interview by Steve Maxner. Vietnam Archive, Texas Tech
  University, Lubbock, Texas (March 27, 2001).

Mosher, Fredric J. *Reference and Rare Books: Three Decades at UC
  Berkeley's School of Librarianship, 1950–1981*. Library School Oral
  History Series. The Regents of the University of California, 2000.

Peter Robert Young Collection. Veterans History Project. AFC/2001/001/66648. American Folklife Center, Library of Congress, Washington, DC.

Ruth Rappaport Oral History. 2010.374. United States Holocaust Memorial Museum (USHMM), Washington, DC.

Shechter, Hillel. Testimony about Jewish life in Leipzig during the 1930s. Shoah Research Center, Yad Vashem, 03. 9059.

Veteran Librarians. With Fran Buckley and William Sittig. Veterans History Project. American Folklife Center, Library of Congress. https://www.loc.gov/today/cyberlc/feature_wdesc.php?rec=3821.

William John Sittig Collection. Veterans History Project. AFC/2001/001/25883. American Folklife Center, Library of Congress, Washington, DC.

TELEVISION SHOWS

White, Joshua, dir. *Seinfeld*. "The Library," season 3, episode 5. Written by Larry David. Aired October 16, 1991, on NBC.

VIDEOS

Department of the Army Overseas Recruitment Center. "Special Services: Where the Action Is." Recruitment video. 1970. https://www.youtube.com/watch?v=piyqtiosYYw.

WEBSITES

Ancestry.com

"Emil Carlebach—Lebenslauf." politische Häftlinge im Gefängnis Hameln [Political prisoners in Hameln prison], *Hamelns Geschichte—abseits vom Rattenfänger* [Hameln's story: away from the pied piper]. http://www.gelderblom-hameln.de/zuchthaus /nszeit/gefaengnis/carlebach.html.

Kadosh, Sara. "Nettie Sutro-Katzenstein." In *Jewish Women: A Comprehensive Historical Encyclopedia.* Jewish Women's Archive, online edition. Accessed October 8, 2018. http://jwa.org /encyclopedia/article/sutro-katzenstein-nettie.

"Mission, Vision & Programs." Amara. Accessed October 25, 2018. https://amaraputskidsfirst.org/mission-vision-programs/.

Schoenherr, Steven. "Cold War Spies." History Department. University of San Diego. http://history.sandiego.edu/gen/20th /coldwarspies.html.

Wawrzyn, Heidemarie. "Leipzig—Introduction." Destroyed German Synagogues and Communities. http://germansynagogues.com /index.php/synagogues-and-communities?pid=59&sid=811 :leipzig-introduction.

Notes

PROLOGUE

1. Petula Dvorak, "Proof of Gifts That Come When Generations Mingle," *Washington Post*, November 23, 2010, http://www.washingtonpost.com /wp-dyn/content/article/2010/11/22/AR2010112207165.html.
2. Ruth Rappaport oral history, interview by Gail Schwartz (accession number 2010.374), Jeff and Toby Herr Oral History Archive, United States Holocaust Memorial Museum, Washington, DC, https:// collections.ushmm.org/search/catalog/irn42274 (hereafter cited as RR oral history, USHMM; additional sources from the Ruth Rappaport Collection, 2012.431.1, at the United States Holocaust Memorial Museum are hereafter cited with RRC, USHMM).
3. *Seinfeld*, "The Library," season 3, episode 5, directed by Joshua White, written by Larry David, aired October 16, 1991, on NBC.

CHAPTER 1

1. Mendel Rappaport records, International Tracing Service, OBE-RIW/1526, USHMM. This area would later be ceded to Romania and is now in the Chernivtsi Oblast of Ukraine.
2. RR oral history, USHMM.
3. Mendel Rappaport city registration form, Saxony State Archives, Leipzig, Germany.
4. Postcard from Mendel Rappaport to his parents, November 14, 1918, Guy Rosner personal collection.
5. Mendel Rappaport city registration form, Saxony State Archives; emails from Guy Rosner to author, March 9, 2017, and March 11, 2017.

6. Akten Polizeiamts der Stadt Leipzig, Joel Leib Rubinstein file, 1/79 STA Leipzig Polizeipräsidium Leipzig –S- Nr. 3207, Saxony State Archives, Leipzig, Germany.

7. Mark Rubinstein, in discussion with the author, July 5, 2013. Mark said his father, Sam (Carl's son), told him this story but later denied it.

8. Restitution documentation records, March 24, 1959, RRC, USHMM; marriage certificate for Mendel Rappaport and Chaja Rubinstein, October 4, 1922, Saxony State Archives, Leipzig, Germany.

9. Heidemarie Wawrzyn, "Leipzig—Introduction," Destroyed German Synagogues and Communities (website), accessed October 8, 2018, http://germansynagogues.com/index.php/synagogues-and-communities ?pid=59&sid=811:leipzig-introduction.

10. Robert Allen Willingham, Jews in Leipzig, Germany under Nazism, Communism and Democracy: Politics and Identity in the 20th Century (Lewiston: Edwin Mellon Press, 2011), pp. 17–21.

11. Willingham, Jews in Leipzig, p. 22.

12. "Leipzig—4 Apels Garten (Originally 6–8 Otto Schiller Strasse), Ez Chaim Synagogue," Destroyed German Synagogues and Communities (website), accessed October 8, 2018, http://germansynagogues.com /index.php/synagogues-and-communities?pid=64&sid=812:leipzig-4 -apels-garten-originally-6-8-otto-schiller-strasse-ez-chaim-synagogue.

13. Ruth Rappaport diary, January 12, 1941, Ruth Rappaport Collection (RRC), United States Holocaust Memorial Museum (USHMM) (hereafter cited, along with the date of entry, as RR diary).

14. RR oral history, USHMM.

15. RR diary, November 16, 1941.

16. Sig Cohen and Laurie Solnik, in discussion with the author, April 16, 2013.

17. Ruth Rappaport, "Curriculum Vita," written for restitution documentation records, circa 1958, RRC, USHMM.

18. RR oral history, USHMM.

19. RR oral history, USHMM.

20. Personal documents folder, RRC, USHMM.

21. RR diary, April 20, 1939.

22. RR oral history, USHMM.

23. Letter from Ruth Rappaport to "Whom It May Concern," undated, concerning Miriam Schneider's will, Peter Bartis personal collection.

24. DW staff, "Leipzig Celebrates Long Literary History," DW, March 13, 2008, http://www.dw.de/leipzig-celebrates-long-literary-history /a-3185443.

25. RR oral history, USHMM.

26. Sabine Knopf, Der Leipziger Gutenbergweg: Geschichte und Topographie einer Buchstadt [The Leipzig Gutenberg path: history and topography of a book city] (Beucha, Germany: Sax-Verlag, 2001), p. 191.
27. RR oral history, USHMM.

CHAPTER 2

1. RR oral history, USHMM. Hitler made many visits to Leipzig during his time in power; it is unclear when exactly Ruth saw him.
2. Acceptance letter, April 25, 1933, restitution documentation records, RRC, USHMM.
3. Willingham, Jews in Leipzig, pp. 38–39.
4. Ruth Rappaport, "Curriculum Vita," circa 1958, RRC, USHMM. Ruth did not explain why she had to briefly return to her elementary school after Jews were banned; perhaps it was because of overcrowding.
5. RR oral history, USHMM.
6. Hillel Shechter, testimony, Yad Vashem Archive, no. 03 9059, Yad Vashem [The World Holocaust Remembrance Center], Jerusalem, Israel, http://www.yadvashem.org/odot_pdf/Microsoft%20Word %20-%203324.pdf.
7. Willingham, Jews in Leipzig, pp. 39–40.
8. Report cards, personal documents, 1929–1938, RRC, USHMM.
9. RR diary, May 8, 1939.
10. RR diary, May 27, 1939.
11. RR oral history, USHMM.
12. Letter from Der Regierungspräsident der Entschädigungsbehörde [District Governor of the Reparations Authority] to United Restitution Organization (URO), June 12, 1963, restitution documentation records, RRC, USHMM.
13. RR diary, May 27, 1939.
14. Restitution documentation records, March 24, 1959, RRC, USHMM.
15. Willingham, Jews in Leipzig, p. 63.
16. Jan-Pieter Barbian, The Politics of Literature in Nazi Germany: Books in the Media Dictatorship (New York City: Bloomsbury, 2010), pp. 23–25.
17. Hans Jürgen Friederici, "Bücherverbote und Bücherverbannung in der Buchstadt Leipzig" [Book bans and book banishment in the book city of Leipzig], Verbrannt, verboten, verbannt. Vergessen? [Burned, forbidden, exiled. Forgotten?], Kolloquium zum 60. Jahrestag der

Bücherverbrennung von 1933 (Leipzig, Germany: Rosa-Luxemburg-Verein, 1995), p. 33.

18. "Lesung zum tag der Bücherverbrennung 1933" [Reading on the day of the book burning, 1933], May 25, 2016, https://www.sachsen-fernsehen.de/lesung-zum-tag-der-buecherverbrennung-1933-266068/.
19. RR oral history, USHMM.
20. Barbian, *The Politics of Literature in Nazi Germany*, pp. 13–14.
21. Barbian, The Politics of Literature in Nazi Germany, p. 180.
22. Barbian, The Politics of Literature in Nazi Germany, p. 13.
23. Guenter Lewy, *Harmful and Undesirable: Book Censorship in Nazi Germany* (New York City: Oxford University Press, 2016), pp. 37–38.
24. RR diary, July 8, 1939.

CHAPTER 3

1. RR oral history, USHMM.
2. RR oral history, USHMM.
3. Letter from Jakob Gross to the Rappaport family, May 1, 1938, RRC, USHMM.
4. Ruth Rappaport, "Curriculum Vita," circa 1958, RRC, USHMM.
5. Guy Rosner, in discussion with the author, July 28, 2014.
6. RR oral history, USHMM.
7. RR diary, April 30, 1939.
8. The Chaluzisch movement was a Zionist pioneer movement.
9. RR diary, May 27, 1939.
10. RR diary, May 8, 1939.
11. Leo Rubinstein, US naturalization record, 1942, Ancestry.com; 1/79 STA Leipzig Polizeipräsidium Leipzig –S- number 3207, Saxony State Archives, Leipzig, Germany; Sarah Deborah Rubinstein file, Landeshilanstalt Altscherbitz Mental Hospital records 20047, file 03814, Saxony State Archives.
12. RR diary, December 31, 1936. The Miriam mentioned here is probably a friend, not Ruth's sister Mirjam.
13. RR diary, April 20, 1939, and January 8, 1940.
14. RR diary, April 20, 1939.
15. RR diary, April 20, 1939.
16. RR diary, April 20, 1939.
17. RR diary, May 27, 1939.
18. Willingham, *Jews in Leipzig*, pp. 43–49.

19. RR oral history, USHMM.
20. RR diary, December 31, 1941.
21. RR diary, May 5, 1941.
22. RR oral history, USHMM.
23. RR oral history, USHMM.

CHAPTER 4

1. Willingham, Jews in Leipzig, pp. 88–99.
2. RR oral history, USHMM.
3. RR oral history, USHMM.
4. Willingham, Jews in Leipzig, p. 100.
5. RR oral history, USHMM.
6. RR oral history, USHMM.

CHAPTER 5

1. Ruth Rappaport, "Curriculum Vita," circa 1958, RRC, USHMM.
2. Email from Angela Ruider (of the Zurich City Archives) to author, September 9, 2014.
3. RR diary, April 25, 1939.
4. RR diary, April 25, 1939.
5. RR oral history, USHMM.
6. RR diary, May 8, 1939.
7. RR diary, May 10, 1939.
8. "Unter der Fahne der Heilsarmee" [Under the Salvation Army Flag], annual report for 1938, Switzerland National Salvation Army Headquarters, Bern, Switzerland.
9. Richard Röschard to SHEK, November 22, 1938, records of the Schweizer Hilfswerk für Emigrantenkinder [Swiss Aid Society for Immigrant Children], J2.55#1000/1246#132*, Pj-Ric, Ruth Rappaport file, Swiss Federal Archives (in citations hereafter, the Schweizer Hilfswerk für Emigrantenkinder, Swiss National Archives, Bern, Switzerland, will be referred to simply as SHEK).
10. Jewish Women: A Comprehensive Historical Encyclopedia, s.v. "Nettie Sutro-Katzenstein," by Sara Kadosh, accessed October 8, 2018, http://jwa.org/encyclopedia/article/sutro-katzenstein-nettie.
11. Ruth Westheimer, All in a Lifetime (New York City: Grand Central Publishing, 1987); "300 Kinder Aktion" file, 1938–1939, SHEK.

12. Letter from Dr. Bertha Keller to Richard Röschard, December 7, 1938, Ruth Rappaport file, records of SHEK.

CHAPTER 6

1. Lore Segal, *Other People's Houses* (New York City: New American Library, 1964).
2. Letter from Richard Röschard to Dr. Bertha Keller, December 28, 1938, Ruth Rappaport file, records of SHEK.
3. Letter from Dr. Bertha Keller to Richard Röschard, January 2, 1939, Ruth Rappaport file, records of SHEK.
4. Letter from Richard Röschard to Dr. Bertha Keller, January 6, 1939, Ruth Rappaport file, records of SHEK.
5. Some refugee children in Zurich were restricted from attending public schools, although some schools were created specifically for them at orphanages and camps. See Elsa Castendyck, "Refugee Children in Europe," Social Service Review (University of Chicago Press) 13, no. 4 (1939): p. 595.
6. Letter from Ruth Rappaport to Carl Rubinstein, February 17, 1939, personal documents, RRC, USHMM.
7. RR diary, May 4, 1939.
8. Email from Angela Ruider (of the Zurich City Archives) to author, September 9, 2014.
9. RR diary, May 4, 1939.
10. RR diary, May 8, 1939.
11. RR diary, May 8, 1939.
12. RR diary, April 25, 1939.
13. RR diary, April 25, 1939.
14. RR diary, May 1, 1939.
15. RR diary, May 8, 1939.

CHAPTER 7

1. RR diary, April 20, 1939.
2. Letter from Ruth Rappaport to Rose Rubinstein, July 15, 1939, RRC, USHMM.
3. RR diary, April 24, 1939.

4. Ruth Rappaport, autobiographical essay, Ruth Rappaport Papers, Special Collections, collection no. 5797, University of Washington Libraries, Seattle, Washington (location hereafter cited as *RRP, UW*).
5. Email from Bettina Roncelli Büchel (archivist at Zentralbibliothek Zürich [Zurich Central Library]) to author, October 8, 2014.
6. Kenneth D. Ackerman, Trotsky in New York 1917: A Radical on the Eve of Revolution (Berkeley: Counterpoint, 2016), p. 139.
7. RR diary, April 30, 1939.
8. RR diary, April 25, 1939.
9. RR oral history, USHMM.
10. RR diary, April 23, 1939.
11. RR diary, April 20, 1939.
12. RR diary, April 23, 1939.
13. RR diary, April 30, 1939.
14. RR diary, April 25, 1939.
15. RR diary, April 23, 1939.
16. RR diary, September 16, 1939.
17. Sara Kadosh, "Jewish Refugee Children in Switzerland, 1939–1950," in Remembering for the Future: The Holocaust in an Age of Genocide, ed. John K. Roth, Elisabeth Maxwell, Margot Levy, and Wendy Whitworth (New York City: Palgrave, 2001), p. 282; summons for Ruth Rappaport to appear at the Stadtpolizei [city police] Zurich, February 13, 1939, personal documents, RRC, USHMM.
18. Letter from American consulate in Zurich to Ruth Rappaport, February 13, 1939, personal documents, RRC, USHMM.
19. Letter from Romanian consulate in Zurich to Ruth Rappaport, April 14, 1939, personal documents, RRC, USHMM.
20. Letter from American consulate in Zurich to Ruth Rappaport, April 28, 1939, personal documents, RRC, USHMM.
21. Letter from Ruth Rappaport to Carl Rubinstein, May 1, 1939, personal documents, RRC, USHMM.
22. Miscellaneous letters from summer 1939, personal documents, RRC, USHMM.
23. Letter from Chaja Rappaport to Dr. Bertha Keller, September 27, 1939, Ruth Rappaport file, SHEK.
24. RR diary, outline of trip on loose sheet, undated.
25. Ruth Rappaport, "Curriculum Vita," circa 1958, RRC, USHMM.
26. RR oral history, USHMM.

CHAPTER 8

1. RR diary, December 16, 1939.
2. RR oral history, USHMM.
3. RR diary, December 16, 1939.
4. RR oral history, USHMM.
5. RR oral history, USHMM.
6. Email from Ruth Rappaport to Sig Cohen, February 7, 2008, Sig Cohen personal collection.
7. Harry Schneiderman, ed., "Statistics of Jews," in *The American Jewish Year Book* 4 (Philadelphia: Jewish Publication Society of America, 1941), p. 661, http://www.ajcarchives.org/AJC_DATA/Files/1941_1942_9_Statistics.pdf; Molly Cone, Howard Droker, and Jacqueline Williams, *Family of Strangers: Building a Jewish Community in Washington State* (Seattle: Washington State Jewish Historical Society, 2003), p. 234.
8. Seattle city directories; Mark Rubinstein, in discussion with the author, July 13, 2013.
9. Advertisement for Helena Rubinstein Salon, Seattle Times, April 8, 1934, p. 13.
10. RR oral history, USHMM.
11. Mark Rubinstein, in discussion with the author, July 13, 2013.
12. Census records, 1940.
13. Seattle city directories, 1937–38.
14. RR diary, December 16, 1939.
15. RR diary, December 16, 1939.
16. Michael Rubinstein, in discussion with the author, April 27, 2017.
17. RR diary, December 17, 1939.
18. Email from Ruth Rappaport to Sig Cohen, February 7, 2008, Sig Cohen personal collection.
19. RR diary, December 17, 1939.
20. RR diary, December 17, 1939.
21. RR diary, February 9, 1940.

CHAPTER 9

1. *Sealth* [Broadway High School yearbook], (Seattle: Broadway High School, 1941), RRP, UW; RR diary, May 28, 1940.
2. RR oral history, USHMM.
3. RR diary, May 28, 1940.

4. RR oral history, USHMM.
5. Quintard Taylor, "Swing the Door Wide: World War II Wrought a Profound Transformation in Seattle's Black Community," *Columbia: The Magazine of Northwest History* 9, no. 2 (Summer 1995), http://www.washingtonhistory.org/files/library/swing-door-wide.pdf.
6. RR diary, December 17, 1939.
7. RR diary, December 20, 1939; "Hilde Schocken Mann" (obituary), *Seattle Times*, August 14–15, 2007, http://www.legacy.com/obituaries/seattletimes/obituary.aspx?n=hilde-schocken-mann&pid=92601843.
8. RR diary, January 10, 1940; "Miss Rose Rubinstein Is Married," Seattle Daily Times, February 19, 1940, p. 8.
9. RR diary, February 19, 1940.
10. RR diary, January 19, 1940.
11. RR diary, February 15, 1940.
12. RR diary, February 6, 1940.
13. RR diary, March 4, 1940.
14. RR diary, January 10, 1941.
15. Ra'hel Bluwstein, *Flowers of Perhaps: A Bilingual Edition of Selected Poems*, trans. Robert Friend, with Shimon Sandbank (New Milford, CT: Toby Press, 2008), pp. vii–xviii.
16. John Douglas Marshall, *Place of Learning, Place of Dreams: A History of the Seattle Public Library* (Seattle: University of Washington Press, 2004), pp. 62–79.
17. RR diary, January 12, 1941.
18. Finger waves were a hairstyle popular in the 1940s.
19. RR diary, January 12, 1941.

CHAPTER 10

1. RR diary, January 1, 1941.
2. RR diary, January 1 and 25, 1951.
3. RR diary, November 25, 1940.
4. *Sealth* [Broadway High School yearbook], (Seattle: Broadway High School, 1941), RRP, UW.
5. RR diary, July 21, 1941.
6. RR diary, August 29, 1941.
7. RR diary, September 21, 1941.
8. RR diary, September 2, 1942.

9. Record 5346, Mendel and Chaja Rappaport, Jewish Transmigration Bureau Deposit Cards, 1939–1954, American Jewish Joint Distribution Committee Archives.
10. RR oral history, USHMM.
11. RR diary, December 3, 1941.
12. RR diary, December 8, 1941.
13. RR diary, December 11, 1941.
14. RR diary, February 27, 1942.
15. RR diary, February 27, 1942.
16. RR diary, May 4, 1942.
17. RR diary, May 4, 1942.
18. RR diary, January 1, 1941.
19. RR diary, March 1, 1942.
20. RR diary March 1, 1942.
21. RR diary March 1, 1942.
22. RR diary, September 2, 1942.
23. RR diary, September 23, 1942.
24. RR oral history, USHMM.
25. "Seattle Youth among Highest at Air School," *Seattle Times*, October 30, 1942.
26. RR diary, June 2, 1942.

CHAPTER 11

1. RR diary, June 19, 1942.
2. "Herzl Synagogue Greets New Rabbi; Officers Elected," The *Transcript*, September 7, 1942.
3. RR diary, August 6, 1942.
4. RR diary, August 6, 1942. Her picture appeared in the July 25, 1942, issue of the *Seattle Times*.
5. Email from Ruth Rappaport to Sig Cohen, February 7, 2008, Sig Cohen personal collection.
6. RR diary, November 16, 1941.
7. RR diary, September 2, 1942.
8. RR diary, September 14, 1942.
9. Hillel Cohn, in discussion with the author, May 27, 2013.
10. RR diary, September 23, 1942.
11. RR diary, September 23, 1942.
12. RR diary, September 23, 1942.

13. "Jewish Calendar for Soldiers and Sailors," October 4, 1942, RRC, USHMM.
14. "Jewish Girls Launch New Study Class," *Seattle Times*, November 8, 1942.
15. Ruth Rappaport résumé, July 1948, personal documents file, RRC, USHMM.
16. RR diary, September 24, 1942.
17. Letter from Ruth Rappaport to Mendel and Chaja Rappaport, October 8, 1942, RRC, USHMM.
18. Letter from Mendel and Chaja Rappaport to Ruth Rappaport, January 7, 1943, RRC, USHMM.
19. Willingham, *Jews in Leipzig*, p. 118.
20. Ellen Bertram, Menschen ohne Grabstein: Gedenkbuch für die jüdischen Opfer der nationalsozialistischen Verfolgung aus Leipzig [People with no gravestone: memorial book for the Leipzig Jewish victims of National Socialist persecution] (Leipzig: Passage-Verlag, 2011), p. 288.
21. Correspondence between Ruth Rappaport and her parents, 1938–1946, RRC, USHMM.
22. "Europe's Jews Face Extermination in '43," *The Transcript*, April 26, 1943.
23. "Junior Hadassah," *The Transcript*, May 24, 1943.
24. "Junior Hadassah Over Subscribes," *The Transcript*, July 5, 1943.
25. "Zionist Youths Plan Breakfast for Levinthal," *Seattle Times*, July 27, 1943.
26. Minutes of Junior Hadassah National Board Meeting, May 13, 1943, records of Hadassah, RG 15, box 9, Center for Jewish History.
27. Letter from Ruth Rappaport to Naomi Chertoff, October 18, 1943, RRC, USHMM.
28. Junior Hadassah convention program, 1943, RRC, USHMM.
29. Letters from Ruth Reicher to Ruth Rappaport, 1944, RRC, USHMM.
30. Letters from Zeanna Berliner to Ruth Rappaport, November 21 and 29, 1943, RRC, USHMM.
31. Letter from Ruth Rappaport to Caroline Ruelf, March 13, 1944, RRC, USHMM.
32. Ruth Rappaport résumé, July 1948, personal documents, RRC, USHMM; "Mission, Vision & Programs," Amara (website), https://amaraputskidsfirst.org/mission-vision-programs/.
33. Anne Swensson, "King County Baby Adoptions Increased 300 Pct. by War," *Seattle Times*, February 10, 1944.
34. Letter from Ruth Rappaport to Esther Elbaum, March 1945, RRC, USHMM.

35. Letter from Ruth Rappaport to Caroline Ruelf, March 13, 1944, RRC, USHMM.
36. Rappaport to Ruelf, March 13, 1944.
37. Letter from Ruth Rappaport to Ruth Reicher, March 1, 1944, RRC, USHMM.
38. Letter from Ruth Rappaport to Caroline Ruelf, March 13, 1944, RRC, USHMM.
39. Letter from Ruth Rappaport to Esther Elbaum, July 1944, RRC, USHMM.
40. Rappaport to Elbaum, July 1944.
41. Rappaport to Elbaum, July 1944.
42. Letter from Ruth Rappaport to Naomi Chertoff, September 14, 1944, RRC, USHMM. One reason for American support of Zionism was to ensure access to oil supplies in the Middle East.
43. Letter from Hans Lemm (of the American Zionist Emergency Council) to Ruth Rappaport, August 11, 1944, RRC, USHMM.
44. Letter from Ruth Rappaport to Alice Bernstein Jacobson, October 7, 1944, RRC, USHMM.
45. Letter from Alice Bernstein Jacobson to Ruth Rappaport and Marian Elyn, January 22, 1945, RRC, USHMM.
46. Letter from Ruth Rappaport to Esther Elbaum, circa March 1945, RRC, USHMM.
47. "Request That Applicant Appear with Witnesses," Immigration and Naturalization Service, February 21, 1945, RRC, USHMM.
48. RR oral history, USHMM.
49. RR oral history, USHMM.
50. RR oral history, USHMM.

CHAPTER 12

1. "Now Japan! City Works on V-E Day," *Seattle Times*, May 8, 1945, p. 1; "Victorious News Fails to Touch Off Riotous Celebrations Here," *Seattle Times*, May 8, 1945, p. 8.
2. DW staff, "Leipzig Celebrates Long Literary History," *DW*, 2008, http://www.dw.com/en/leipzig-celebrates-long-literary-history/a-3185443.
3. Letter from Alice Bernstein Jacobson to Ruth Rappaport, May 31, 1945, RRC, USHMM.
4. Report from FBI special agent in charge (SAC), Seattle, to FBI director, October 17, 1951, Ruth Rappaport FBI file.

5. Phillip Deery, "'A Blot Upon Liberty': McCarthyism, Dr. Barsky and the Joint Anti-Fascist Refugee Committee," *American Communist History* 8, no. 2 (2009), pp. 167–96.
6. Letter from Ruth Rappaport to Esther Elbaum, June 1, 1945, RRC, USHMM.
7. Letter from Esther Elbaum to Ruth Rappaport, June 5, 1945, RRC, USHMM.
8. Mendel Rappaport records, International Tracing Service, OBE-RIW/1526, USHMM.
9. Aileen Hicks Finley, "War Service Jobs Continue; Women Face Big Peace Tasks," *Seattle Times*, August 19, 1945, p. 2.
10. USS Annual Volunteer Recognition Day program, October 28, 1945, RRC, USHMM.

CHAPTER 13

1. Ruth Rappaport résumé, July 1948, personal documents, RRC, USHMM.
2. Masthead, The Transcript, March 4, 1946, p. 4.
3. Email from Ruth Rappaport to Sig Cohen, February 7, 2008, Sig Cohen personal collection.
4. Ruth Rappaport University of Washington academic transcript, RRP, UW.
5. American Society of Civil Engineers, "In Memoriam: Dr. Mohammad Gamal Mostafa," Orange County Branch newsletter, August 2011, http://www.asceoc.org/newsletter/article/in_memoriam_mostafa.
6. Letter from Ruth Rappaport to the Washington State Press Club, July 31, 1946, RRP, UW.
7. "Ale & Quail Society Active in Host of Press Club Affairs," *Gentlemen of the Press*, the newsletter of the Washington State Press Club, October 1951, http://www.jackgordon.org/WashPressClub/AleQuailHistory.htm.
8. Letter from Dudley Brown to Ruth Rappaport, August 21, 1946, RRP, UW.

CHAPTER 14

1. Letter from Ruth Rappaport to Jüdische Gemeinde zu Leipzig, July 8, 1946, Leipzig Jewish Community records (1933–1945), RG-14.035M, reel 41, USHMM.

2. Letter from Jüdische Gemeinde zu Leipzig to Ruth Rappaport, August 27, 1946, RRC, USHMM.
3. Guy Rosner, in discussion with the author, July 28, 2014.
4. Michael Rubinstein, in discussion with the author, April 27, 2017.
5. Ellen Bertram, Menschen ohne Grabstein [People with no gravestone], p. 288.
6. Document 91706849 (60000/60300/0060399/2 Inbound/0002@6.3.3.2), International Tracing Service Archives, USHMM.
7. Document 33461659 (/Image vorhanden/_R/R0095/07156@0.1), International Tracing Service Archives, USHMM.
8. Document 91706835 (/60000/60300/0060398/3 Outbound/001@6.3.3.2) International Tracing Service Archives, USHMM.
9. "Buchenwald Concentration Camp, 1937–1945," Buchenwald and Mittelbau-Dora Memorials Foundation, https://www.buchenwald.de /en/72/.
10. "Emil Carlebach—Lebenslauf," politische Häftlinge im Gefängnis Hameln [Political prisoners in Hameln prison], Hamelns Geschichte— abseits vom Rattenfänger [Hameln's story: away from the pied piper], http://www.gelderblom-hameln.de/zuchthaus/nszeit/gefaengnis /carlebach.html.
11. Anders Rydell, The Book Thieves: The Nazi Looting of Europe's Libraries and the Race to Return a Literary Inheritance (New York City: Viking, 2015), pp. 35–58.
12. Restitution documentation records, RRC, USHMM.
13. RR oral history, USHMM.

CHAPTER 15

1. RR diary, June 13, 1948.
2. RR diary, December 26, 1948. Aziz Sedky, the future prime minister of Egypt, was probably Jim's friend.
3. January to September 1947 issues of The Transcript did not survive.
4. "Carl Rubinstein," Seattle Times, March 26, 1947, p. 20.
5. "Carl Rubinstein Estate $540,000," Seattle Times, March 31, 1947, p. 2.
6. RR diary, May 28, 1928.
7. "Bronner Speaks on Palestine," Mill Valley Record, April 16, 1948, p. 10.
8. Shilchim are emissaries from Israel.
9. Email from Ruth Rappaport to Sig Cohen, February 7, 2008, Sig Cohen personal collection.

10. Fred Rosenbaum, Cosmopolitans: A Social and Cultural History of the Jews in the San Francisco Bay Area (Berkeley: University of California Press, 2009), pp. 314–17.

11. Benny Morris, 1948: The First Arab-Israeli War (New Haven, CT: Yale University Press, 2008), pp. 40–59.

12. Patricia Bosworth, *Anything Your Little Heart Desires: An American Family Story* (New York City: Touchstone, 1997), pp. 173–206.

13. Ruth Rappaport résumé, July 1948, personal documents, RRC, USHMM.

14. Doreen Bierbrier, "The American Zionist Emergency Council: An Analysis of a Pressure Group," *American Jewish Historical Quarterly* 60, no. 1 (September 1970): p. 88.

15. RR diary, June 13, 1948.

16. Letter from Esther Elbaum to Ruth Rappaport, July 18, 1947, RRC, USHMM.

17. Standard Form 57, 1960, Ruth Rappaport's Official Personnel Folders, National Archives and Records Administration (NARA), Valmeyer, Illinois (additional sources from the National Archives and Records Administration (NARA), Valmeyer, Illinois, are hereafter cited as from *NARA*).

18. RR diary, May 28, 1948.

19. Letter from Rabbi Franklin Cohn to Ruth Rappaport, September 2, 1947, RRC, USHMM. Sam Tarshis was the president of Seattle Zionist District.

20. Letter from Ruth Rappaport to Rabbi Franklin Cohn, September 9, 1947, RRC, USHMM.

CHAPTER 16

1. "ZOA Reorganizes S.F. District," *Jewish Tribune*, October 17, 1947, p. 2.

2. Letter from Rabbi Franklin Cohn to Ruth Rappaport, October 9, 1947, RRC, USHMM.

3. Letter from Ruth Rappaport to Rabbi Franklin Cohn, October 20, 1947, RRC, USHMM.

4. "Balfour Day Observance Features Jackman, Goldberg," *Jewish Tribune*, November 7, 1947, p. 1.

5. "Zionist Leaders Signalize U.N. Decision," *Jewish Tribune*, December 5, 1947, p. 2.

6. Email from Ruth Rappaport to Sig Cohen, February 7, 2008, Sig Cohen personal collection.
7. RR diary, August 10, 1948.
8. "Yehudith Simchonit—Palestine Women's Leader—to Speak," *Jewish Tribune*, November 21, 1947, p. 1.
9. Letter from Ruth Rappaport to Mrs. Allen, February 29, 1948, RRC, USHMM; letter from Ruth Rappaport to George Edelstein, December 26, 1948, RRC, USHMM.
10. RR oral history, USHMM.
11. Shulamit Reinharz and Mark A. Raider, *American Jewish Women and the Zionist Enterprise* (Waltham, MA: Brandeis University Press, 2005), p. 185.
12. Reinharz and Raider, *American Jewish Women and the Zionist Enterprise*, pp. 185–86.
13. RR diary, January 3–6, 1948.
14. RR diary, January 3–6, 1948.

CHAPTER 17

1. Letter from Ruth Rappaport to "Whom It May Concern" regarding Mirjam Schneider's will, undated, Peter Bartis personal collection.
2. Ruth Rappaport to "Whom It May Concern" regarding Mirjam Schneider's will.
3. RR diary, April 23, 1948.
4. Letter from Ruth Rappaport to W. Zev Bronner, February 3, 1948, RRC, USHMM.
5. Letter from Ruth Rappaport to May [last name unknown], May 17, 1948, RRC, USHMM.
6. Rappaport to May [last name unknown], May 17, 1948.
7. Letter from Ruth Rappaport to W. Zev Bronner, February 3, 1948, RRC, USHMM.
8. Letter from Ruth Rappaport to Victor Bloom, February 23, 1948, RRC, USHMM; draft article "Many Victims in Jerusalem Outrage," RRC, USHMM.
9. Ruth Rappaport, "Jerusalem, a Besieged City," *Jewish Tribune*, March 19, 1948, p. 5.
10. Rappaport, "Jerusalem, a Besieged City."
11. Letter from Ruth Rappaport to Victor Bloom, February 23, 1948, RRC, USHMM; letter from Ruth Rappaport to W. Zev Bronner, February 3, 1948, RRC, USHMM.

12. RR oral history, USHMM.
13. RR oral history, USHMM.
14. Letters from Ruth Rappaport, January–April 1948, RRC, USHMM.
15. Letter from Ruth Rappaport to Phyllis and Jim, March 9, 1948, RRC, USHMM.
16. RR diary, April 25, 1948.
17. RR diary, April 30, 1946.
18. Richard Whelan, *Robert Capa: A Biography* (New York City: Alfred A. Knopf, 1985), pp. 238–69.
19. Email from Ruth Rappaport to Sig Cohen, February 7, 2008, Sig Cohen personal collection.
20. RR diary, May 10, 1949; RR diary, undated, circa May 1949.
21. RR diary, May 2, 1948.
22. RR diary, May 6, 1948.
23. RR diary, May 6, 1948.
24. RR diary, May 2 and 6, 1948.
25. RR diary, May 15, 1948.
26. RR diary, May 15, 1948.
27. RR diary, May 16, 1948.
28. RR diary, May 23, 1948.
29. RR diary, May 28, 1948; RR diary May 31, 1948; RR diary June 2, 1948; RR diary June 4, 1948.
30. RR diary, May 28, 1948.
31. RR diary, May 28, 1948.
32. RR diary, June 13, 1948.
33. RR diary, May 23, 1948.
34. RR diary, June 4, 1948.
35. RR diary, June 4, 1948. Ruth also seems to have used this word—*Protektia*—to refer to nepotism.
36. RR diary, April 25, 1948.
37. RR diary, April 25, 1948.
38. RR diary, May 23, 1948.
39. RR diary, May 23, 1948.
40. RR diary, June 8, 1948.
41. RR diary, May 31, 1948.
42. RR diary, June 1, 1948.
43. RR diary, May 26, 1948.
44. RR diary, June 4, 1948.
45. RR diary, July 17, 1948.
46. RR diary, July 17, 1948.

47. Video of Ruth's memorial service, December 12, 2010, Peter Bartis personal collection.

CHAPTER 18

1. RR diary, July 17, 1948.
2. RR diary, July 17, 1948.
3. RR diary, July 17, 1948.
4. RR diary, July 23, 1948.
5. RR diary, July 23, 1948.
6. RR diary, August 8, 1948.
7. RR diary, August 16, 1948.
8. RR diary, August 19, 1948.
9. RR diary, August 19, 1948.
10. RR diary, August 26, 1948.
11. RR diary, August 26, 1948.
12. RR diary, May 10, 1949.
13. RR diary, May 10, 1949.
14. RR diary, August 29, 1948.
15. Letter from Ruth Rappaport to Rabbi Franklin Cohn, September 2, 1948, RRC, USHMM. Sochnut is the Hebrew name for the Jewish Agency.
16. Letter from Ruth Rappaport to Mila, February 11, 1949, RRC, USHMM.
17. Letter from Ruth Rappaport to Rabbi Franklin Cohn, September 2, 1948, RRC, USHMM.
18. RR diary, August 10, 1948.
19. RR diary, August 26, 1948.

CHAPTER 19

1. RR diary, November 2, 1948; personal documents from Israel, 1948, RRC, USHMM. The PIO was officially known as the Ministry of Foreign Affairs—Press and Information Division.
2. RR oral history, USHMM.
3. RR diary, November 2, 1948. The ellipses in this quote are original.
4. RR diary, November 21, 1948.
5. RR diary, undated, circa February 1949.

6. Letter from Ruth Rappaport to the Eisemanns, March 3, 1949, RRC, USHMM.

7. Letter from Ruth Rappaport to Esther Elbaum, September 5, 1949, RRC, USHMM; letter from Ruth Rappaport to Lynn Atterman, August 23, 1949, RRC, USHMM.

8. Letter from Ruth Rappaport to the Eisemanns, March 3, 1949, RRC, USHMM. Ruth may have been referring to Kenneth Bilby of the *New York Tribune* (not *Times*) and Stephen Rosenfeld of the *Washington Post* (not the *New York Post*).

9. RR diary, May 10, 1949. Ruth might be referring to Spencer Irwin, a foreign correspondent for the Cleveland Plain Dealer.

10. RR oral history, USHMM.

11. RR oral history, USHMM.

12. RR diary, November 21, 1948. This man was probably Canadian pilot George "Lee" Sinclair.

13. RR diary, March 1, 1949.

14. RR diary, undated, circa May 1949.

15. Caitlin Keefe Moran, "In Praise of Difficult Women: The Forgotten Work of Nancy Hale," *The Toast*, September 24, 2014, http://the-toast .net/2014/09/23/forgotten-work-on-nancy-hale.

16. RR diary, February 5, 1949.

17. RR diary, April 29, 1949.

18. RR diary, June 5, 1949. The "worsening conditions" she referred to may have been the start of McCarthyism and blacklisting.

19. RR diary, February 24, 1949.

20. Letter from Ruth Rappaport to Bartley Crum, October 18, 1950, RRC, USHMM.

21. Letter from Ruth Rappaport to Mila, February 11, 1949, RRC, USHMM.

22. Letter from Ruth Rappaport to Mila and family, November 7, 1949, RRC, USHMM.

23. Personal memoirs of Sam Rubinstein, undated, Mark Rubinstein personal collection.

24. Ruth Rappaport's Official Personnel Folders, NARA; RR oral history, USHMM.

Chapter 20

1. Illustration of Ruth Rappaport, Guy Rosner personal collection.

2. Investigation report, 1992, Ruth Rappaport FBI file, 121-HQ-34502.

3. Passport, personal documents, RRC, USHMM.
4. Letter from Ruth Rappaport to Chaja, December 15, 1950, RRC, USHMM. This Chaja is not Ruth's mother nor her mother's cousin Helena Rubinstein.
5. Rappaport to Chaja, December 15, 1950.
6. Rappaport to Chaja, December 15, 1950.
7. Rappaport to Chaja, December 15, 1950.
8. Letter from Ruth Rappaport to Lynn, December 15, 1950, RRC, USHMM.
9. Max Lowenthal papers, "Collection Overview," University Archives, University of Minnesota Twin Cities, https://archives.lib.umn.edu /repositories/14/resources/1715.
10. David Lowenthal, "Out of the Box and into the Archives," *Continuum: The Magazine of the University of Minnesota Libraries* 7, Fall 2008, pp. 10–12.
11. Lowenthal, "Out of the Box and into the Archives," pp. 10–12.
12. Letter to Eric from Max Lowenthal, August 7, 1950, Max Lowenthal papers, University Archives, University of Minnesota Twin Cities, box 18, folder 10.
13. Letter from Max Lowenthal to Ruben Levin, January 10, 1951, Max Lowenthal papers, University Archives, University of Minnesota Twin Cities, box 18, folder 18.
14. Max Lowenthal papers, University Archives, University of Minnesota Twin Cities, box 18, folders 9 and 20.
15. Letter from David M. Hardy (of the FBI) to author regarding FOIA request, August 26, 2013.
16. Letter from Max Lowenthal to President Harry Truman, September 1, 1950, Max Lowenthal papers, University Archives, University of Minnesota Twin Cities, box 14, folder 19.
17. Letter from Ruth Rappaport to Lynn Atterman, December 15, 1950, RRC, USHMM.

CHAPTER 21

1. Letter from Ruth Rappaport to Esther Elbaum, August 12, 1950, RRC, USHMM.
2. Ruth Rappaport to the University of California, Berkeley, Office of the Director of Admissions, August 10, 1950, RRP, UW.

3. "Timeline: Summary of Events of the Loyalty Oath Controversy, 1949–54," *The University Loyalty Oath: A 50th Anniversary Retrospective*, University of California History Digital Archives, http://www.lib.berkeley .edu/uchistory/archives_exhibits/loyaltyoath/symposium/timeline/short .html.

4. Ruth Rappaport University of California academic transcript, RRP, UW.

5. Letter and materials concerning International House to Ruth Rappaport, September 11, 1950, RRP, UW.

6. Michael Burawoy and Jonathan VanAntwerpen, "Berkeley Sociology: Past, Present and Future," November 2001, https://publicsociology .berkeley.edu/intro/berkeleysociology/berkeleysociology.pdf.

7. Steve Schoenherr, "Cold War Spies," University of San Diego (website), http://history.sandiego.edu/gen/20th/coldwarspies.html; Michael J. Hogan, *A Cross of Iron: Harry S. Truman and the Origins of the National Security States, 1945–1954* (New York City: Cambridge University Press, 1998), pp. 254–57.

8. Report from FBI special agent in charge (SAC), Seattle, to FBI director, October 17, 1951, Ruth Rappaport FBI file.

9. Deery, *American Communist History* 8: pp. 167–96; Abraham Lincoln Brigade Archives, s.v. "Edward K. Barsky," accessed October 8, 2018, http://www.alba-valb.org/volunteers/edward-k.-barsky.

10. Report from FBI special agent in charge (SAC), Seattle, to FBI director, December 6, 1951, Ruth Rappaport FBI file.

11. Report from FBI special agent in charge (SAC), Seattle, to FBI director, December 6, 1951, Ruth Rappaport FBI file.

12. Report from FBI special agent in charge (SAC), Seattle, to FBI director, December 6, 1951, Ruth Rappaport FBI file.

13. Memorandum from J. Edgar Hoover (FBI director) to assistant chief of staff, Department of the Army, January 2, 1952, Ruth Rappaport FBI file.

14. "The Hoover Legacy, 40 Years After, Part 2: His First Job and the FBI Files," News, FBI (website), June 28, 2012, https://www.fbi.gov/news /stories/copy_of_the-hoover-legacy-40-years-after.

15. "XII. Results of Investigation," San Francisco, February 2, 1952, Ruth Rappaport FBI file.

16. "Results of Investigation," Chicago, January 16, 1952, Ruth Rappaport FBI file; "Results of Investigation," Cleveland, February 6, 1952, Ruth Rappaport FBI file; "Personal History and Results of Investigation," Seattle, February 4, 1952, Ruth Rappaport FBI file; "Results of Investigation," San Francisco, February 2, 1925, Ruth Rappaport FBI file; "Results of Investigation," New York, February 12, 1952, Ruth

Rappaport FBI file; "Security Investigation Data for Nonsensitive Position," December 5, 1964, Ruth Rappaport FBI file.

CHAPTER 22

1. "Cyclist Killed, Bride Critically Injured in Flaming Crash with Auto," *Oakland Tribune*, March 11, 1952.
2. Letter from Jack M. Scollard to Ruth Rappaport, May 9, 1952, RRP, UW.
3. Letter from Ruth Rappaport to Professor Wolfram Eberhard, August 21, 1957, RRC, USHMM.
4. Dvorak, "Proof of Gifts That Come When Generations Mingle."
5. Report from FBI special agent in charge (SAC), San Francisco, to FBI director, April 2, 1954, Ruth Rappaport FBI file.
6. Bill Hess, "Holocaust Survivor Who Hates Cats Ends Up Living with One," *No Cats Allowed!* (blog), January 16, 2009, http://nocatsallowed .blogspot.com/2009/01/holocaust-survivor-who-hates-cats-winds.html.
7. "Strong Vocational Interest Test—Women," RRP, UW.
8. Ruth Rappaport's Official Personnel Folders, NARA.
9. RRP, UW.
10. "University of California in Memoriam, 1990. Wolfram Eberhard, Berkeley, Sociology," http://texts.cdlib.org/view?docId=hb5f59n9gs& query=&brand=calisphere.
11. Letter from Ruth Rappaport to Professor Wolfram Eberhard, August 21, 1957, RRC, USHMM.
12. "Autobiographical Essay," graduate school records, RRP, UW.
13. "Books Read over Last Six-Month Period," graduate school records, RRP, UW. Author has corrected spelling and other errors in authors and titles. Zweig is not an author of the book Tehilla and Other Israeli Tales.

CHAPTER 23

1. Michael K. Buckland, "Introduction," in *Dean and Professor at UC Berkeley's School of Librarianship, 1946–1976* (discussion with J. Periam Danton), interviews conducted by Laura McCreery (1999) and Mary Hanel (1993), Library School Oral History Series, the Regents of the University of California, http://content.cdlib.org/view?docId=kt4f59n6 x3&query=&brand=calisphere.

2. Michael K. Buckland, "Introduction," in *Dean and Professor at UC Berkeley's School of Librarianship, 1946–1976* (discussion with J. Periam Danton).

3. J. Periam Danton, "The Functions of a Graduate School of Librarianship," *California Librarian* 15 (March 1954): pp. 157–58.

4. J. Periam Danton, "The Functions of a Graduate School of Librarianship," pp. 158–60.

5. Fredric J. Mosher, *Reference and Rare Books: Three Decades at UC Berkeley's School of Librarianship, 1950–1981*, Library School Oral History Series, 2000, the Regents of the University of California, transcript, p. 42, https://archive.org/details/refrarebooks00moshrich.

6. William R. Eshelman, *No Silence! A Library Life* (Lanham, MD: Scarecrow Press, 1997), p. 72.

7. Mosher, Reference and Rare Books, p. 62.

8. Department of Defense employment inquiry, October 10, 1958, box 1, folder 5, Ruth Rappaport Collection, United States Army Heritage and Education Center, Carlisle Barracks, Pennsylvania (additional sources from the Ruth Rappaport Collection at the United States Army Heritage and Education Center are hereafter cited as from RRC, USAHEC).

CHAPTER 24

1. Letter from Ruth Rappaport to the United Restitution Organization (URO), November 18, 1957, RRC, USHMM.

2. Norman Bentwich, *The United Restitution Organisation, 1948–1968: The Work of Restitution and Compensation for Victims of Nazi Oppression* (London: Vallentine, Mitchell, 1968); "BEG: General Information," https://afw.lff-rlp.de/en/federal-german-compensation-law/general-information/index.html.

3. Letter from Edith Dosmar to Ruth Rappaport, November 25, 1957, RRC, USHMM.

4. Letter from Ruth Rappaport to Edith Dosmar, February 23, 1958, RRC, USHMM.

5. Letter from Walter Peters to Ruth Rappaport, November 19, 1958, RRC, USHMM.

6. Letter from Walter Peters to Ruth Rappaport, June 1, 1959, RRC, USHMM.

7. Letter from Walter Peters to Ruth Rappaport, September 21, 1960, RRC, USHMM.

8. *Partial Decision of the Reparations Authority,* December 10, 1962, RRC, USHMM.
9. Letter from URO to Ruth Rappaport, October 20, 1964.
10. Letter from Ruth Rappaport to Dr. Berger, September 20, 1964, RRC, USHMM.
11. Ruth had received financial support from SHEK in Switzerland, but it was not an explicitly Jewish organization.
12. Letter from Ruth Rappaport to Dr. Berger, September 20, 1964, RRC, USHMM.
13. Letter to Ruth Rappaport from Der Regierungspräsident der Entschädigungsbehörde [District Governor of the Reparations Authority], November 6, 1964, RRC, USHMM.

CHAPTER 25

1. Ruth Rappaport, "A Selective Guide to Source Materials on German Jews in the U.S. from 1933 to the Present Time," Librarianship 220B (university course), May 19, 1958, University of California, Berkeley Library, p. v.
2. Rappaport, "A Selective Guide to Source Materials on German Jews in the U.S. from 1933 to the Present Time."
3. Cindy Mediavilla, "The War on Books and Ideas: The California Library Association and Anti-Communist Censorship in the 1940s and 1950s," *Library Trends* 46, no. 2 (Fall 1997): pp. 338–39; Mosher, *Reference and Rare Books,* p. 104.
4. Marjorie Fiske, "Book Selection and Retention in California Public and School Libraries," edited by J. Periam Danton, papers presented at Climate of Book Selection: Social Influences on School and Public Libraries (symposium), University of California, July 10–12, 1958.
5. Mosher, *Reference and Rare Books,* p. 103.

CHAPTER 26

1. RR oral history, USHMM.
2. Letter from Ruth Rappaport to Ruth Sieben-Morgen, undated, box 1, folder 1, RRC, USAHEC.
3. Letter from Ruth Rappaport to Ruth Sieben-Morgen, December 11, 1958, box 1, folder 1, RRC, USAHEC.
4. Rappaport to Sieben-Morgen, December 11, 1958.

5. Ruth Rappaport's Official Personnel Folders, NARA.
6. Ruth Rappaport's Official Personnel Folders, NARA.
7. Letter from Ilya Belzitzman to Ruth Rappaport, November 15, 1958, RRC, USHMM.
8. Job application, December 28, 1962, Ruth Rappaport's Official Personnel Folders, NARA.
9. Letter from Ruth Sieben-Morgen to Ruth Rappaport, September 13, 1959, box 1, folder 1, RRC, USAHEC.
10. Letter from Ruth Rappaport to Ruth Sieben-Morgen, September 18, 1959, box 1, folder 1, RRC, USAHEC; letter from Ruth Sieben-Morgen to Ruth Rappaport, October 23, 1959, box 1, folder 1, RRC, USAHEC; letter from Ruth Sieben-Morgen to Ruth Rappaport, December 30, 1959, box 1, folder 1, RRC, USAHEC.
11. Letter from Ruth Sieben-Morgen to Ruth Rappaport, March 30, 1960, box 1, folder 1, RRC, USAHEC.
12. Letter from Ruth Rappaport to Des [last name unknown], January 2, 1961, box 1, folder 1, RRC, USAHEC.
13. Letter from Ruth Rappaport to Colonel E. P. Foote, May 7, 1962, box 1, folder 1, RRC, USAHEC. Colonel Thompson is a pseudonym to protect the privacy of the accused.
14. Evaluation form for Ruth Rappaport completed by Mary Jane Lin, March 1, 1961, Ruth Rappaport's Official Personnel Folders, NARA.
15. Pat Moesker, in discussion with the author, July 20, 2013.
16. Special Services, daily diary of Captain Charles C. Trexler Jr., box 1, folder 1, RRC, USAHEC.

CHAPTER 27

1. Letter regarding travel authorization, November 15, 1962, box 1, folder 1, RRC, USAHEC.
2. Letter from Ruth Rappaport, summer 1963, RRC, USHMM.
3. Letter from Ruth Rappaport to "all [her] good friends," summer 1963, RRC, USHMM.
4. Ruth Rappaport, "The USARV Library Program—In Retrospect." Obtained from Katherine Harig. Ruth probably wrote this report for her supervisors when she left her job in 1971, but it does not seem to have been saved in any official archive.
5. Letter from Ruth Rappaport to Gabe Horchler, June 1974, Gabe Horchler personal collection.

6. Rappaport, "The USARV Library Program—In Retrospect."
7. Rappaport, "The USARV Library Program—In Retrospect."
8. "Incentive Award Nomination and Approval" form for Ruth Rappaport, May 17, 1966, Ruth Rappaport's Official Personnel Folders, NARA.
9. Nell Strickland, in discussion with the author, September 7, 2013.
10. Bill Sittig, in discussion with the author, May 4, 2013.
11. *Army Library Operational Guide: Army Library Program*, [Washington], 1961, http://catalog.hathitrust.org/Record/001344736.
12. Letter from Ruth Rappaport to Cele [last name unknown], November 21, 1964, RRC, USHMM.
13. Letter from Ruth Rappaport to Marvin Scott Rubinstein, February 2, 1968, Peter Bartis personal collection.
14. A. A. Allison, *To Spurn the Gods* (Bloomington, IN: Booktango, 2012), p. 86.
15. Allison, *To Spurn the Gods*, pp. 87–88.
16. Allison, *To Spurn the Gods*, pp. 84–88.
17. Email from A. A. Allison to author, April 11, 2013.
18. Allison, *To Spurn the Gods*, p. 124.
19. Allison, *To Spurn the Gods*, pp. 126–28.
20. Larry Engelmann, "The Rise and Fall of the American Mayor of Saigon," *Pushing On* (blog), April 3, 2012, http://lde421.blogspot.com/2012/04/rise-and-fall-of-american-mayor-of.html; Peter Vogel, "Paul Masters, Captain Archie Kuntze and Madame Sun," chap. 2 in *The Last Wave from Port Chicago* ([self-pub.?], 2002), http://www.petervogel.us/chapters/LastWave_Ch2.pdf; Douglass H. Hubbard Jr., *Special Agent, Vietnam: A Naval Intelligence Memoir* (Washington, DC: Potomac Books, 2006), p. 26.
21. Letter from Michael D. Lawrence (commander, Judge Advocate General's Core, US Navy) to author concerning FOIA request for Archie Kuntze's trial records, July 9, 2013.
22. Joseph DiMona, *Great Court-Martial Cases* (New York City: Grosset and Dunlap, 1972), p. 191.
23. DiMona, *Great Court-Martial Cases*, p. 208.
24. Letter from Ruth Rappaport to Archie Kuntze, November 16, 1966, RRC, USHMM.
25. Email from A. A. Allison to author, April 11, 2013.

CHAPTER 28

1. Letter from Ruth Rappaport to Marvin Scott Rubinstein, February 2, 1968, Peter Bartis personal collection.
2. Rappaport to Rubinstein, February 2, 1968.
3. Rappaport to Rubinstein, February 2, 1968.
4. Hank Ferguson is a pseudonym.
5. Rappaport to Rubinstein, February 2, 1968.
6. Rappaport to Rubinstein, February 2, 1968.
7. Rappaport to Rubinstein, February 2, 1968.
8. Rappaport to Rubinstein, February 2, 1968.
9. Rappaport to Rubinstein, February 2, 1968.
10. Rappaport to Rubinstein, February 2, 1968.
11. Rappaport to Rubinstein, February 2, 1968.
12. Rappaport to Rubinstein, February 2, 1968.
13. Rappaport to Rubinstein, February 2, 1968.
14. Rappaport to Rubinstein, February 2, 1968.
15. Rappaport to Rubinstein, February 2, 1968.
16. Rappaport to Rubinstein, February 2, 1968.
17. Rappaport to Rubinstein, February 2, 1968.
18. Rappaport to Rubinstein, February 2, 1968.
19. Nell Strickland, in discussion with the author, September 7, 2013.

CHAPTER 29

1. Bill Sittig, in discussion with the author, May 4, 2013.
2. Fran Buckley and William Sittig, "Veteran Librarians" (webcast), November 1, 2005, Veterans History Project, American Folklife Center, Library of Congress, https://www.loc.gov/today/cyberlc/feature_wdesc.php?rec=3821.
3. Peter Robert Young oral history, Veterans History Project, American Folklife Center, AFC/2001/001/66648, Library of Congress.
4. Gabe Horchler, in discussion with the author, May 14, 2013; oral history in Gabriel Francis Horchler Collection, Veterans History Project, American Folklife Center, AFC/2001/001/27689, Library of Congress.
5. Veteran Librarians webcast.
6. Disposition form, October 5, 1971, Special Services General Records, box 2, folder "LSC- Magazines and Newspapers," Record Group 472, NARA.

7. Ann Kelsey, interview conducted by Steve Maxner, Vietnam Archive at Texas Tech University, March 27, 2001.
8. Oral history interview in Peter Young Collection (AFC/2001/001/66648), Veterans History Project, American Folklife Center, Library of Congress; email from Peter Young to author, February 11, 2018.
9. These numbers are from Ruth Rappaport's résumé on her federal job application, November 1970, Official Personnel Folders, NARA, and Ruth Rappaport, "The USARV Library Program—In Retrospect."
10. Bill Sittig, in discussion with the author, May 4, 2013; Nell Strickland, in discussion with the author, September 7, 2013.
11. Veteran Librarians webcast.
12. Email from Peter Young to author, February 11, 2018.
13. Veteran Librarians webcast.
14. Frederick J. Stielow, "The War and Librarianship: A Study in Political Activism," in *Activism in American Librarianship, 1962–1972*, edited by Mary Lee Bundy and Frederick J. Stielow (New York City: Greenwood Press, 1987).
15. In his book *To Spurn the Gods*, A. A. Allison mentions meeting General Taylor in Saigon with Archie Kuntze. Therefore, Rappaport most likely met him as well.
16. Ann Kelsey, interview conducted by Steve Maxner, Vietnam Archive at Texas Tech University, March 27, 2001.
17. Nell Strickland, in discussion with the author, September 7, 2013.
18. Ann Kelsey, interview conducted by Steve Maxner, Vietnam Archive at Texas Tech University, March 27, 2001.
19. Nell Strickland, in discussion with the author, September 7, 2013.
20. Ann Kelsey, interview conducted by Steve Maxner, Vietnam Archive at Texas Tech University, March 27, 2001.
21. Oral history interview in Peter Young Collection (AFC/2001/001/66648), Veterans History Project, American Folklife Center, Library of Congress.
22. Letter from Ruth Rappaport to Special Services officer, February 25, 1965, RRC, USAHEC.
23. Meredith H. Lair, *Armed with Abundance: Consumerism & Soldiering in the Vietnam War* (Chapel Hill, NC: University of North Carolina Press, 2011), p. 172.
24. Request for Expendable Reading Materials, July 8, 1971, National Archives, RG 472, Special Services General Records, box 2, folder "Magazine Requests and Distribution, 1967–71"; Norman M. Camp, *US Army Psychiatry in the Vietnam War: New Challenges in Extended*

Counterinsurgency Warfare (Washington, DC: Borden Institute, US Army Medical Department Center and School, 2014), pp. 349–52.

25. Book catalog, 1971, National Archives, RG 472, Special Services General Records, box 4, folder "SOP Field Collections."

26. Lair, *Armed with Abundance*, p. 136.

27. "U.S. Army Special Services: Where the Action Is" (recruitment video), 1970, https://www.youtube.com/watch?v=piyqtiosYYw; Lair, *Armed with Abundance*, pp. 134–35.

28. Lair, *Armed with Abundance*, pp. 25–26. As Lair argues, these statistics greatly differ from the common narrative from popular culture of young men dying in the jungle. It is possible that recognizing the massive amount of leisure activities available in Vietnam can reframe how we view the war, without disrespecting those who served and died in combat roles and did not participate in or benefit from these other activities.

29. Summary of program meeting on "Books as Weapons," July 12, 1996, American Library Association, Public Library Association, Armed Forces Librarian Section, American Library Association Archives, Record Group 29/2/6, box 18, folder "AFLS Board Minutes and Agenda, 1966–1967."

30. Ann Kelsey, who served as an army librarian in Vietnam, has also conducted personal research into the history of the libraries there and has regularly participated in veterans' events since the 1990s. She also concurs that most veterans do not remember the library system.

31. Vietnam Vets Reading Survey, conducted by author, 2013–2014.

32. Adjutant general and Special Services newsletters, Record Group 472, Special Services General Records, box 1, NARA.

33. Oral history interview in Peter Young Collection (AFC/2001/001/66648), Veterans History Project, American Folklife Center, Library of Congress.

34. Lair, Armed with Abundance, pp. 23–65.

35. Gabriel Francis Horchler, oral history interview, Gabriel Francis Horchler Collection, Veterans History Project, American Folklife Center, Library of Congress.

36. Janice Carney, interview conducted by Laura M. Calkin, OH0426, Vietnam Archive at Texas Tech University, May 24, June 6, 7, and 8, 2005.

37. John Christian Worsencroft, "Salvageable Manhood: Project 100,000 and the Gendered Politics of the Vietnam War," master's thesis, University of Utah, 2011, http://content.lib.utah.edu/cdm/ref/collection/etd3/id/594.

38. Tom Sticht, "'McNamara's Moron Corps': They Done Good After All!" August 9, 2012, https://www.researchgate.net/publication/327369169_McNamara's_Moron_Corps_They_Done_Good_After_All.

39. Email from Joe Hudson to author, January 28, 2014; Peter Young oral history, Veterans History Project, Library of Congress.
40. Email from Ann Kelsey to author, January 26, 2014.
41. Vietnam Vets Reading Survey, conducted by author, 2013–2014.
42. Keyes Beech, "U.S. Troops in Vietnam Quite Bookish," *Los Angeles Times*, June 19, 1969, p. B4.
43. These three complete and comprehensive lists appear in the National Archives, RG 472, Special Services General Records, box 4, folder "SOP Field Collections." Other book and magazine lists (some partial) appear in the Special Services General Records.
44. Email from Nolan Dehner to author, May 12, 2013.
45. Ann Kelsey, interview conducted by Steve Maxner, Vietnam Archive, Texas Tech University, March 27, 2001.
46. Vietnam Vets Reading Survey, conducted by author, 2013–2014.
47. Book reviews for *Once an Eagle* on Amazon.com, http://www.amazon .com/Once-Eagle-Novel-Anton-Myrer/dp/1455121355.
48. Vietnam Vets Reading Survey, conducted by author, 2013–2014.
49. The title of this book is Ambush: The Battle of Dau Tiang.
50. Comment by Anonymous [Joe Hudson] on the post, "Vo Nguyen Giap, 1911–2013," October 4, 2013, http://unsolicitedopinion .blogspot.com/2013/10/vo-nguyen-giap-1911-2013.html.
51. Emails from Joe Hudson to author, January 26 and 28, 2014.
52. Nell Strickland, in discussion with the author, September 7, 2013.
53. Email from Ann Kelsey to author, January 26, 2014.
54. Ann Kelsey, interview conducted by Steve Maxner, Vietnam Archive at Texas Tech University, March 27, 2001.
55. Requests for construction, March 17, 1970, RG 472, Special Services General Records, box 3, folder "Library Buildings Damaged w/ Plans to Rebuild," NARA.
56. Darro Wiley, in discussion with the author, February 22, 2014.
57. Email from Floyd Zula to author, May 2, 2013.
58. Ruth Rappaport's Official Personnel Folders, NARA.
59. Ruth Rappaport, "The USARV Library Program—In Retrospect."
60. Lee Dreyfus Report, March 1972, RG 472, Special Services General Records, box 1, folder "Lee Dreyfus Report," NARA.

CHAPTER 30

1. Ruth Rappaport's Official Personnel Folders, NARA.

2. John Y. Cole, *America's Greatest Library:* An Illustrated History of the Library of Congress (Washington, DC: Library of Congress, 2017), p. 158.

3. John Y. Cole, "The Library of Congress & the Library Community: Bicentennial Background," Library of Congress (website), http://www.loc.gov/loc/lcib/9908/biback.html.

4. "History of the Library of Congress," Library of Congress (website), https://www.loc.gov/about/history-of-the-library/.

5. Kay Elsasser, in discussion with the author, May 11, 2013.

6. The Annex Building was later renamed the John Adams Building, and the Main Building was renamed the Thomas Jefferson Building.

7. Thompson Yee, in discussion with the author, May 8, 2013.

8. Ruth told Peter several times about her work with the Delta Collection, although other sources indicate that it was fully recataloged by the time Ruth started her job. She may have continued the regular cataloging of pornographic and other sex-related materials. See Roy M. Mersky and Michael L. Richmond, "Treatment of Sexually Oriented Magazines by Libraries," in *Sex Magazines in the Library Collection: A Scholarly Study of Sex in Serials and Periodicals,* A Monographic Supplement to the Serials Librarian 4, 1979/1980 (New York City: Haworth Press, 1981), p. 51.

9. *Departmental & Divisional Manuals,* no. 18–18A (Library of Congress, 1951), http://babel.hathitrust.org/cgi/pt?id=ucl.b5168447;view=1up;seq=5.

10. *Departmental & Divisional Manuals,* p. 44.

11. Melissa Adler, *Cruising the Library: Perversities in the Organization of Knowledge* (New York City: Fordham University Press, 2017), p. 82.

12. Mersky and Richmond, *Sex Magazines in the Library Collection,* p. 51.

13. Letter from George to Ruth Rappaport, February 23, 1972, Peter Bartis personal collection.

14. George to Rappaport, February 23, 1972.

CHAPTER 31

1. Letter from Gabe Horchler to Ruth Rappaport, November 30, 1973, Peter Bartis personal collection.

2. Letter from Ruth Rappaport to Gabe Horchler, January 1974, Peter Bartis personal collection.

3. Rappaport to Horchler, January 1974.

4. Letter from Ruth Rappaport to Gabe Horchler, June 1974, Peter Bartis personal collection.

5. Rappaport to Horchler, June 1974.
6. Rappaport to Horchler, June 1974.
7. Subject Cataloging Division, Processing Services, Library of Congress, *Classification: Class H, Subclasses HM–HX, Social Sciences: Sociology*, 1980.
8. "Library of Congress Classification Outline: Class H," https://www.loc .gov/aba/cataloging/classification/lcco/lcco_h.pdf.
9. Rappaport to Horchler, June 1974; Subject Cataloging Division, Processing Services, Library of Congress, *Classification: Class H, Subclasses HM–HX, Social Sciences: Sociology*, 1980.
10. Rappaport to Horchler, June 1974.
11. Letter from Ruth Rappaport to Gabe Horchler, February 1975, Peter Bartis personal collection.
12. Suzanne E. Thorin and Robert Wedgeworth, "The Librarians of Congress: Past and Future," *American Libraries*, https://americanlibrariesmagazine .org/librarians-of-congress/.
13. Letter from Ruth Rappaport to Gabe Horchler, August 23, 1975, Peter Bartis personal collection.

CHAPTER 32

1. Jon Wiener, *Professors, Politics and Pop* (New York City: Verso Books, 1994), p. 55.
2. *Nomination of Daniel J. Boorstin of the District of Columbia to be Librarian of Congress: Hearings before the Committee on Rules and Administration*, United States Senate, Ninety-Fourth Congress, July 30 and 31, and September 10, 1975 (Washington: GPO, 1975), p. 138.
3. *Nomination of Daniel J. Boorstin of the District of Columbia to be Librarian of Congress*, p. 177. Williams was fired from his job as a copyright examiner when it was revealed that he had lied about having a law degree from Georgetown University. While at LC, he had become a trusted leader among black employees and held several leadership positions in the AFGE Local 1826 union and the Black Employees of the Library of Congress organization. Williams later unsuccessfully sued LC for discrimination in the case *Joslyn N. Williams v. Daniel J. Boorstin, Librarian of the Library of Congress, Appellant*, 1980.
4. "Library of Congress Suspends 28 Employees Staging Protest," *Washington Post*, June 24, 1971.
5. "Library of Congress Suspends 28 Employees Staging Protest," *Washington Post*.

6. "Peers' Challenging Library of Congress: Library Challenged by Peers," *Washington Post*, January 31, 1972.

7. "District of Columbia—Race and Hispanic Origin: 1800 to 1990," United States Census Bureau, 2002.

8. Bridget Bowman, "Diversity Concerns Linger at the Library of Congress," *Roll Call*, July 12, 2016, https://www.rollcall.com/news /diversity-concerns-linger-library-congress.

9. "Longest EEOC Class-Action Case Nears End for Black Federal Employees," *Washington Informer*, July 19, 1995.

10. "Longest EEOC Class-Action Case Nears End for Black Federal Employees," *Washington Informer*.

11. *Library of Congress Personnel Policies and Procedures, Joint Hearings before the Subcommittee on Libraries and Memorials of the Committee on House Administration*, House of Representatives, March 18 and 24, 1993.

12. *Prepared Statement of Eleanor Holmes Norton, US Delegate from the District of Columbia, Library of Congress Personnel Policies and Procedures, Joint Hearings before the Subcommittee on Libraries and Memorials of the Committee on House Administration*, House of Representatives, March 18 and 24, 1993, p. 48.

13. "Longest EEOC Class-Action Case Nears End for Black Federal Employees," *Washington Informer*.

14. Bowman, "Diversity Concerns Linger at the Library of Congress."

15. Kathy Sawyer, "Library's Bias Complaints Unsolved Despite Court Order," *Washington Post*, March 5, 1979.

16. "Barbara Ringer, 1973–1980," US Copyright Office.

17. "Library of Congress Is Found to Discriminate against Women," *Washington Post*, August 10, 1972; Barbara A. Ringer, Plaintiff, v. L. Quincy Mumford, Individually and as Librarian of Congress, et al., Defendants, Civ. A. No. 2074-72, US District Court, DC, February 28, 1973.

18. Another union at LC, the AFCSME Local 2477 for non-professional employees, had formed sometime previously according to the LC Bulletin.

19. "Leaflet, Anyone!?&%," *Local News, A News-Symposium of the Library of Congress Professional Guild, AFSCME Local 2910* 2, no. 4 (June 1977).

20. "Guild News Distribution Comes in From the Cold!" The Local News, A News-Symposium of the Library of Congress Professional Guild, AFSCME Local 2910 2, no. 8 (December 1977).

21. "Let Them Read Cake Recipes!" The Local News, A News-Symposium of the Library of Congress Professional Guild, AFSCME Local 2910 2, no. 6 (September 1977).

22. "Announcements," *Library of Congress Information Bulletin*, November 5, 1976.
23. "Council 26 Sponsors Vietnamese Family," *Local News, A News-Symposium of the Library of Congress Professional Guild, AFSCME Local 2910* 5, no. 2 (Summer 1980).

CHAPTER 33

1. Email from Thompson Yee to the author, October 26, 2018.
2. Ruth Rappaport's Official Personnel Folders, NARA.
3. "About Library of Congress Authorities," Library of Congress (website), https://authorities.loc.gov/help/contents.htm.
4. Philip Hider and Ross Harvey, Organising Knowledge in a Global Society: Principles and Practices in Libraries and Information Centres (San Diego, CA: Elsevier, 2008), p. 140.
5. Melissa Adler, "For SEXUAL PERVERSION See PARAPHILIAS: Disciplining Sexual Deviance at the Library of Congress" (PhD diss., University of Wisconsin, 2012), p. 178.
6. Memorandum from Ruth Rappaport to Regene Ross, August 29, 1985, retrieved by the LC Subject Policy Committee. This heading was later split into two separate terms, "Crime" and "Criminology."
7. "About the LC Online Catalog," Library of Congress (website), https://catalog.loc.gov/vwebv/ui/en_US/htdocs/help/.
8. Sanford Berman, *Prejudices and Antipathies: A Tract on the LC Subject Headings Concerning People* (Metuchen, NJ: Scarecrow Press, 1971), pp. ix–x.
9. Berman, *Prejudices and Antipathies*, p. xi.
10. Stephen A. Knowlton, "Three Decades Since *Prejudices and Antipathies*: A Study of Changes in the Library of Congress Subject Headings," *Cataloging and Classification Quarterly* 40, no. 2 (2005): pp. 123–45.
11. Thompson Yee, in discussion with the author, May 8, 2013.
12. These letters are available in Sandy Berman's collection of papers at the American Library Association archives.
13. "Report of the Racism and Sexism in Subject Analysis Subcommittee to the RTSD/CCS Subject Analysis Committee," midwinter 1980, ALA Archives, Association for Library Collections and Technical Services (ALCTS) collection.
14. Ruth Rappaport, "SAC Subcommittee on Racism and Subject Analysis," in "Appendix II: Continuing Reports on the Annual Conference of the

American Library Association, Chicago, IL., June 24–30, 1978," Library of Congress Information Bulletin, August 18, 1978, pp. 501–502.

15. Letter from Sandy Berman to James Billington, December 13, 1989, Sandy Berman Collection, ALA Archives.

16. "Librarian of Congress Testifies before House Committee on 1991 Budget," *Library of Congress Information Bulletin*, February 26, 1990, p. 92.

17. "Congress Comes through on LC Appropriations," *Library of Congress Information Bulletin*, November 19, 1990, p. 387.

18. Ana L. Cristán, "SACO and Subject Gateways," *Authority Control in Organizing and Accessing information*, edited by Arlene G. Taylor, Barbara B. Tillett (New York City: Routledge, 2005), p. 315.

19. "Cataloging in the 1990s: Sanford Berman's Challenge to LC," Library of Congress Information Bulletin, February 22, 1993, p. 86.

20. Knowlton, "Three Decades Since *Prejudices and Antipathies*," pp. 127–28.

21. Kay Elsasser, Kersti Blumenthal, Thompson Yee, Peter Bartis, and Catherine Hiebert Kerst, all in discussion with the author.

22. Letter from Ruth Rappaport to Mr. and Mrs. Rudman, October 17, 1992, Peter Bartis personal collection. Joseph David Rudman worked at LC two separate times, with a break to earn a PhD in Scandinavian studies. He later went to law school and worked as a law cataloger at the University of Washington Library. He died of AIDS in 1992 and has a panel on the memorial AIDS quilt.

23. Rappaport to Mr. and Mrs. Rudman, October 17, 1992.

24. Letter from Ruth Rappaport to Catherine Hiebert Kerst, September 9, 1999, Catherine Hiebert Kerst personal collection.

25. Kersti Blumenthal, in discussion with the author, May 2, 2013.

26. Ruth Rappaport's Official Personnel Folders, NARA.

27. Peggy McGlone, "America's 'National Library' Is Lacking in Leadership, Yet Another Report Finds," Washington Post, March 31, 2015; Michael D. Shear, "Library of Congress Chief Retires Under Fire," New York Times, June 10, 2015.

CHAPTER 34

1. RR oral history, USHMM.

2. Peter Bartis, in discussion with the author, undated.

3. Raymond Gamble, in discussion with the author, November 22, 2016.

4. Sue Anne Pressley Montes and Yolanda Woodlee, "D.C. Cabs Told to Switch from Zone Fares to Meters," *Washington Post*, October 18, 2007.

5. Paul Schwartzman, "Buses Cause Rumble of Unrest," *Washington Post*, September 16, 2004.
6. Unidentified neighbor who spoke at Ruth's memorial service.
7. Sig Cohen and Laurie Solnik, in discussion with the author, April 16, 2013.
8. Email from Ruth Rappaport to Sig Cohen, February 7, 2008, Sig Cohen personal collection.
9. Letter from Ruth Rappaport to "all my dears," December 1984, Peter Bartis personal collection.
10. RR oral history, USHMM.
11. RR oral history, USHMM.
12. RR oral history, USHMM.
13. Letter from Ruth Rappaport regarding Mirjam Schneider's will, undated, Peter Bartis personal collection.
14. RR oral history, USHMM.
15. Letter from Ruth Rappaport regarding Mirjam Schneider's will.
16. Letter from Ruth Rappaport to Rosel Rubinstein, April 1, 1997, Peter Bartis personal collection.

CHAPTER 35

1. Letter from James H. Billington to Ruth Rappaport, October 11, 1988, Ruth Rappaport's Official Personnel Folders, NARA.
2. "Capitol Hill Village: How We Got Started," History, Capitol Hill Village (website), accessed October 25, 2018, http://www.capitolhillvillage.org /?pg=40.
3. "Holocaust Survivor Who Hates Cats Ends Up Living With One," http://nocatsallowed.blogspot.com/2009/01/holocaust-survivor-who -hates-cats-winds.html, January 16, 2009.
4. Email by unknown author quoted by Petula Dvorak at Ruth's memorial service.
5. Peter Bartis speaking at Ruth's memorial service.
6. Dvorak, "Proof of Gifts That Come When Generations Mingle."
7. Letter from Ruth Rappaport to Rosel, April 1, 1997, Peter Bartis personal collection.
8. Dvorak, "Proof of Gifts That Come When Generations Mingle."
9. Dvorak, "Proof of Gifts That Come When Generations Mingle."
10. Peter Bartis, in discussion with the author, undated.
11. Ben Zuras, in discussion with the author, May 28, 2018.
12. Unidentified friend speaking at Ruth's memorial service.

13. Gail Schwartz, in discussion with the author, November 5, 2016.
14. Laurie Solnik speaking at Ruth's memorial service, December 12, 2010.
15. Dvorak, "Proof of Gifts That Come When Generations Mingle."

EPILOGUE

1. RR oral history, USHMM.
2. RR oral history, USHMM.

Index

About the Author

Kate Stewart is a third-generation librarian, born and raised in the Midwest. She graduated from Vassar College with a bachelor of arts in history and from the University of Iowa with master's degrees in history and library science. She has worked as a librarian and archivist for ProQuest, the Library of Congress, and the US Senate in Washington, DC. She is currently an archivist at the Arizona Historical Society in Tucson, Arizona. Learn more about Kate at www. kate-stewart.com.